JEWISH AND CHRISTIAN TEXTS IN CONTEXTS AND RELATED STUDIES

Series

Executive Editor
James H. Charlesworth

THE PSALMS OF SOLOMON

A Critical Edition of the Greek Text

JEWISH AND CHRISTIAN TEXTS IN CONTEXTS
AND RELATED STUDIES
Volume 1

EDITED BY

ROBERT B. WRIGHT

t &t clark

T & T Clark International, 80 Maiden Lane, New York, NY 10038

T & T Clark International, The Tower Building, 11 York Road, London SE1 7NX

T & T Clark International is a Continuum imprint.

1. The Psalms of Solomon : a critical edition of the Greek text / edited by Robert B. Wright.
p. cm. -- (Jewish and Christian texts in contexts and related studies ; v. 1)
Includes bibliographical references.
ISBN-13: 978-0-567-02643-9 (hardcover : alk. paper)
ISBN-10: 0-567-02643-4 (hardcover : alk. paper)
1. Psalms of Solomon. Greek--Criticism, interpretation, etc. I. Wright, Robert B. II. Title. III. Series.

BS1830.P73P73 2007
229'.912--dc22

2007014911

Printed in Great Britain by Biddles Ltd, King's Lynn, Norfolk

CONTENTS

"God Made Him Powerful in the Holy Spirit":
Psalms of Solomon 17.37

In the library of ancient books called the TANAKH, or Old Testament, three documents are attributed to Solomon: *The Song of Solomon*, *Proverbs of Solomon*, and *Ecclesiastes*. In the Old Testament Apocrypha another work was known as the work of David's son: *The Wisdom of Solomon*. In the Old Testament Pseudepigrapha three additional compositions were attributed to the wisest man in biblical history: the *Testament of Solomon*, the *Odes of Solomon*, and the *Psalms of Solomon*. Most experts claim these seven poetic or wisdom books were attributed to Solomon, as an honor and because of the claim in 1 Kings 4:32 that Solomon composed 3000 proverbs and 1005 songs. In 240 CE Origen of Alexandria, however, reported that "the Churches of God" know nothing about these thousands of Solomonic songs (*Cant. Cant. Prologus* 36).

In 1626 John Louis de la Cerda published the *edition princeps* of the *Psalms of Solomon*. In 1895 O. von Gebhardt drew attention to eight Greek manuscripts of the *Psalms of Solomon*. In 1913, the translation by G. B. Gray in R. H. Charles' classical work, *The Apocrypha and Pseudepigrapha of the Old Testament*, was based on Gebhardt's publication. These 18 psalms were discovered in Syriac manuscripts beginning in 1909. Now, almost one hundred years later, most scholars conclude that the *Psalms of Solomon* is a hymnbook composed in Hebrew, in Jerusalem, and sometime shortly before the reign of Herod the Great (40-4 BCE).

The *Psalms of Solomon* is thus a singularly important document. In contrast to many apocryphal compositions, we know its date and provenience – and it was a major composition known to many Jews living in Jerusalem in the century before the burning of the Temple by Titus in 70 CE.

I am impressed with three aspects of this hymnbook: First, It contains an eyewitness account of the Roman incursion into Jerusalem and the demise of the Roman General Pompey who brought Roman rule over Palestine: "I did not have long to wait until God showed me his arrogance. Stabbed on the sand dunes of Egypt, he was more despised than anything in the whole world . . . . His body was violently carried over the waves and there was no one to bury him, because God contemptuously despised him" [PsSol 2.26-27].

Second, the work contains a reference to the Jewish belief in resurrection and just before the time of Jesus of Nazareth: "This is the fate of sinners forever; but those who fear the Lord shall rise up to eternal life, and their life shall be in the LORD's light and it shall never end" [PsSol 3.12]

Third, the composition contains perhaps the *locus classicus* for belief in a Davidic Messiah and it antedates by a few decades the Palestinian Jesus Movement: "Look, O Lord, and raise up for them their king, a son of David, to rule over your servant Israel in the time that you know, O God. He will be a righteous king over them, taught by God, there will be no unrighteousness among them in his reign, because everyone will be holy, and their king will be the Lord Messiah" [PsSol 17.21,32]

Why is it important to draw attention to the Psalms of Solomon now? It is because a magnificent research tool for studying a hymnbook from just before the time of Jesus, and from Jerusalem, now enriches the world of scholarship. Professor Robert B. Wright of Temple University, who contributed the introduction and translation of the Psalms of Solomon to *The Old Testament Pseudepigrapha*, has completed this, the first full critical edition of this hymnbook. He has also made available in high-resolution images, the twelve Greek and four Syriac manuscripts of the Psalms of Solomon. Together the CDs contain approximately 350 color photographs of the manuscripts. Most of these manuscripts are now photographed in color for the first time. Wright's archive is probably the only collection of ancient manuscripts that are available in high-resolution color images (some of the Dead Sea Scrolls are also now available with this quality). In addition, Wright supplies about 150 supporting photographs, including the full text of de la Cerda's 1626 edition of this pseudepigraphon (the first published edition, in Greek and a Latin translation), the text of Frantz Delitzsch's unpublished "Rückübersetzung der Psaumes Salomon ins Hebräische," (from the library of the University of Leipzig, ca. 1860 ["Re-translation of the Psalms of Solomon into Hebrew"]), and the index page of *Codex Alexandrinus*, showing the entry of the Psalms of Solomon.

Professor Wright, the photographer of the Harvard University/Hebrew Union College archaeological excavations at Tell Gezer, took many of these photographs. Others were supplied by libraries or monasteries. Among the most important locations for the manuscripts themselves are the following: the British Library (London), the Bibliothèque Nationale (Paris), the Bibliotheek der Rijksuniversiteit (Leiden), the State Historical Museum (Moscow), the Österreichische National Bibliothek (Vienna), the Bibliotheca Apostolica Vaticana (Vatican), the Benaki Museum (Athens), and the Iveron Monastery (Mount Athos).

Thanks to the focused research of Professor Wright, specialists on the literature of Second Temple Judaism will be able to possess not only a critical edition but also all color photographs of this valuable pseudepigraphon called the *Psalms of Solomon*. Those not gifted in ancient Greek will be able to read and study a reliable English translation of a hymnbook used by Jews, in Jerusalem, during the time of Hillel and Jesus. A copy of the CD, for research and teaching purposes, may be obtained from Professor Wright without charge, save for a modest shipping/handling fee. See notice at the end of this book.

James H. Charlesworth
George L. Collord Professor of New Testament Language and Literature;
Director and Editor, PTS Dead Sea Scrolls Project
Princeton Theological Seminary

PREFACE

This critical edition of the Greek text of the Psalms of Solomon goes back to my graduate-school study of sacrifice in the intertestamental literature[1]. One of the writings that contained divergent attitudes concerning sacrifice and the Jerusalem cultus was the *Psalms of Solomon*. Unfortunately, no critical edition that included all the Greek manuscripts listed in Rahlfs' *Verzeichnis*[2] was available, and, of course, Baars' collation of a newly discovered fragment in 1961[3] was to be found in no edition. Although work on the present project was protracted because of twenty years of academic administration, the first phase, a provisional collated Greek text, was completed in 1974 and privately distributed.[4] That same year James H. Charlesworth invited me to contribute an introduction and translation to *The Pseudepigrapha of the Old Testament*,[5] that appeared in 1985.

A sage once said: "I have learned much from my teachers; I have learned more from my colleagues; I have learned most from my students."[6] We are all indebted to a web of mentors; here are my heartfelt acknowledgments:

- My teachers: Fred Afman, Charles Smith, John Priest, and G. Ernest Wright.
- My colleagues: Robert R. Hann formerly of Florida International University, whose important study of the manuscripts provided much of the foundation for this analysis,[7] Thomas F. McDaniel Professor Emeritus of The Eastern Baptist Theological Seminary, Vasiliki Limberis of Temple University, Joseph L. Trafton of Western Kentucky University, and Kenneth Atkinson of the University of Northern Iowa. Of course, to James H. Charlesworth of Princeton Theological Seminary, editor of this series, and patient encourager of the projects.
- My special thanks to Dr. James T. McDonough, classicist extraordinary and gentle soul, whose encouragement and keen eye helped to bring this project to completion.
- Appreciation is due also to Professor Marinus de Jonge of the Rijksuniversiteit

---

[1] R.B. Wright, "The Spiritualization of Sacrifice in the Prophets and in the Psalter," S.T.M. thesis, Hartford Seminary Foundation, 1964; "Sacrifice in the Intertestamental Literature," Ph.D. dissertation, 1966.

[2] A. Rahlfs, *Verzeichnis der griechischen Handschriften des Alten Testaments* (Göttingen: K. Gesellschaft der Wissenschaften, 1914).

[3] W. Baars, "A New Fragment of the Greek Version of the Psalms of Solomon," *VT 11* (1961), pp. 441–444.

[4] This provisional collation was later used by Joseph Trafton and included with his *The Syriac Version of the Psalms of Solomon: A Critical Evaluation* (*SBLSCS* 11; Atlanta, GA: Scholars Press/Society of Biblical Literature, 1985).

[5] R. Wright, "The Psalms of Solomon," *OTP*, II, pp. 639–670.

[6] Rabbi Ḥanina, b. Ta 'an. 7a, *The Babylonian Talmud*, Seder Moʻed.

[7] R.R. Hann, *The Manuscript History of the Psalms of Solomon* (*SBLSCS* 13; Chico, CA: Scholars Press, 1982).

of Leiden and to Professor Albert Pietersma of the University of Toronto for their exceptionally valuable suggestions.

- There is a long list of graduate students who have helped in various stages of the project: during the first collation phase, none more so than Robert Hann and Kenneth Cohen. During the medial phase: Grant Ward, Kenneth Cohen, Lewis Eron, Joel Reizburg, John Puckett, Douglas McCready, Jody Kolodzey, D. John Woodcock, Thomas Thompson, Victoria Schwartz, Luke Keefer, Sung Jong Shen, Chul Soon Lee, Rollin Blackburn, John Gommel, Joseph McGovern, Vernon Carter, Julia Beck, Kenneth Ofslager, Omar Zambrana, Jeffrey Hargis, James Hewett, Irene Riegner, Lynn Wolcott, Richard Fonda, and Alfons Teipen. Kenneth Atkinson has proposed some imaginative new reconstructions that are reflected in the section on the dating and redaction. Special appreciation to Lester Dean who both helped in the early collating of the manuscripts and did the computer programming that manipulated and formatted the text. Those involved in the creation of a new English translation include: Karen Onesti, Bong Choi, Deborah Spink, Robert Sheddinger, Kenneth Ofslager, Nancy Heisey, and Andrei Vashestov.

Those involved in the decipherment of MS 629 in the Spring of 2000 include: Dr. Robert Sheddinger of Luther College, Thomas Mathes, Dr. Matthew Mitchell, Dr. Thomas McDaniel and Dr. James McDonnough. Dr. Sheddinger also helped analyze the Syriac photos.

Acknowledgment is due to the directors of the libraries and museums, the custodians of the manuscripts. They were uniformly helpful and forthcoming when asked for access to the manuscripts, photographs of their manuscripts, and detailed descriptions of their texts:

MS 149: Univ.-Doz. Ernst Gamillscheg, Direktor, Österreichische NationalBibliothek, Vienna.

MSS 253, 655 and 659: Ambrogio M. Piazzoni, Vice Prefect of the Biblioteca Apostolica Vaticana and Fr. Paul Canart, Librarian.

MS 260: Palle Ringsted, Assistant, Det Kongelige Bibliotek, Copenhagen, Denmark.

MS 336: Archimandrite Vassilios, Monk Christoforos, Secretary; and Monk Theologos, Librarian, of the Holy Monastery of Iveron, Mt. Athos, Greece. Also thanks to Daniel Deckers, of the University of Hamburg, who provided an important image.

MS 471: Tamara Igoumnova, Deputy Director, State Historical Museum, Moscow.

MS 606: M. Christian Förstel, Conservateur de la Section grecque, Département des Manuscrits, Bibliothèque Nationale de France, Paris.

MS 629: Angela Adriana Cavarra, *Direttore* of the Biblioteca Casanatense, Rome.

MS 769: Rita Tsakona, Librarian of the Benaki Museum, Athens.

MS 3004: Dr. A. Th. Bouwman, Keeper of Western Manuscripts, Universiteitsbibliotheek, Leiden, the Netherlands.

Syriac MS 10h1 and MS S: Ms. Sarah Mitchell, The British Library, London. Specific and grateful appreciation to Professor Sebastian Brock of Oxford University for his insightful analysis of the situation with Syriac MS "S" held by the British Library.

Syriac MS 16h1: Dr. Dorothy Clayton, Head of Publications, The John Rylands
    University Library, Manchester, England.
Syriac MS 14k1: D. J. Hall, Deputy Librarian, Cambridge University, England.
Syriac MS 16g7: Selly Oak Colleges, University of Birmingham, England. Ms. Meline
    E. Nielsen, Deputy Director

Special appreciation is extended to the *Center for the Preservation of Ancient
Religious Texts*, at Brigham Young University, Provo, Utah. Their photographic team
traveled from Naples to Rome in the Winter of 1999-2000 to re-photograph MS 629
using their "Multi-Spectral Imaging" to reveal its obscured text. Jan Wilson is the
Associate Director of CPART and Steven Booras is the Operations Manager.

The OdysseaUBS Greek font used by license to create this work is © 1994-2004
Payne Loving Trust. All rights reserved. By copyright law this font may not be copied
for others or modified. LaserGreek II, the product that includes this font and input tools
is available from Linguist's software, Inc., PO Box 580, Edmonds, WA 98020-0580
USA, tel (425) 775-1130, www.linguistsoftware.com. The Syriac font I adapted from
one generously supplied by Stephen A. Kaufman of Hebrew Union College, Cincinnati
(the Syriac font is now also available from Linguist's Software). The camera-ready
copy was formatted with WordPerfect X3 for Windows XP on a Sony VAIO 505, 300-
MMX computer and printed on an HP PhotoSmart 7350.

The project was assisted by Study Leave grants from Temple University in 1977 and
in 1992, by two *Grants-in-Aid of Research* awards in 1978 and in 1999, a Summer
Research Grant in 1999, Travel Grants from the Religion Department, and by generous
support from the College of Liberal Arts for computer equipment and staff. The
Princeton Theological Seminary Library supported the preparation of the CD-ROM of
350 color images of all fifteen Greek and Syriac manuscripts of the PssSol. A copy of
the CD, for personal research and use in the classroom, is available free from the
author for a nominal fee for shipping.

Robert B. Wright, Professor of Hebrew Bible, Emeritus
Department of Religion, Temple University,
Philadelphia, Pennsylvania,
April, 2007

INTRODUCTION

The Psalms of Solomon (PssSol), the most important early psalm book outside the canonical psalter, reflects the turmoil of events in the last pre-Christian century, gives an apparently eyewitness account of the first invasions of the Romans into Jerusalem, gives a specific reference to the doctrine of the resurrection of the dead just before the beginning of the Christian and Rabbinic periods, and provides the most detailed expectation of the Jewish Messiah before the New Testament.

HISTORICAL BACKGROUND

Historically, the eighteen Psalms of Solomon represent the response of a group of pious Jews to the invasion and capture of Jerusalem by the Roman army under Pompey in the year 63 BCE and the siege of Jerusalem by Herod the Great and the Roman general Sosius in 37 BCE. Psalms 1, 2, 8, and 17 are a vivid, apparently eyewitness, reflections on these events. The remainder of the psalms is more like the canonical Psalter and the Qumrân Hymn Scroll (1Q Hodayot) as these Psalms confront a variety of more conventional topics common to the psalm genre: evil and good, sin and salvation, threat and rescue. PsSol 17, in addition, is an extended messianic hymn describing the anticipated victory and reign of the expected redeeming king, the anointed Son of David. This *Lord Messiah,* as he is called, is to lead the pious in a rebellion against the occupying forces, in the expulsion of foreign influences, and in the displacement of the corrupt administrations of state and temple. He is to establish an independent and holy Jewish theocratic state to which foreign nations would be subordinate.

DATE AND HISTORICAL REFERENCES

The earliest direct historical evidence we have of the Psalms of Solomon is from the fifth century C.E. when the "Psalms of Solomon, 18" were included in the catalog of the Codex Alexandrinus. In that list they follow the Septuagint, the New Testament, and the Clementine Epistles. Their position at the very end of the list, after a count of the total books in the MS, does not tell us if they were regarded as part of a canonical enumeration, or merely the contents of that MS. They stand, in the words of Rendel Harris, "in the very penumbra of canonicity."[8] The leaves at the end of the codex that would have contained the text of the Psalms of Solomon, unfortunately, are missing.

---

[8] J.R. Harris, *The Odes and Psalms of Solomon: Now First Published from the Syriac Version*, (Cambridge [England], Cambridge University Press: 1909, p. 4 (second edition, 1911).

[9] The British Library, ADD Royal MS 1 DV, folio 4; available in: *Facsimile of the Codex Alexandrinus*, 4 vols, ed. E. M. Thompson I, folio 4 (London: British Museum, 1879–1883). The index is discussed in Th. Zahn, *Geschichte des neutestamentlichen Kanons*, vol. 2 (Erlangen: A. Deichert, 1890), pp. 288-289. J. R. Harris suggested, based on his study of stichometry, that the Codex Sinaiticus also may once have contained the PssSol, on the six missing leaves between the Epistle of Barnabas and

The Psalms of Solomon are listed in the *Synopsis Sanctae Scripturae* of Pseudo-Athanasius that dates from the early sixth century. They are included with the Odes of Solomon as "antilegomena" of the Old Testament, following Maccabees and an unknown Ptolemaic history, and preceding Susanna.[10] They are cataloged among what we call *pseudepigrapha* in the sixth-century list of "Sixty Books [of Scripture]" at the end of Anastasius Sinaita's *Quaestiones et Responsiones*. They follow the canonical and deuterocanonical books, set between the Assumption of Moses and the Apocalypse of Elijah.[11]

The PssSol appear with the Odes of Solomon in the ninth-century stichometry that is attributed to Nicephorus, Patriarch of Constantinople, where they are found between Sirach and Esther.[12] The PssSol are included among the apocrypha in a tenth-century

---

the Shepherd of Hermas (presented in a paper delivered to the Johns Hopkins University Philological Association on January 7, 1884, as reported in "Notes on the Sinaitic and Vatican Codices," in the *Johns Hopkins University Circular 29* (March 1884), p. 54; a transcript of the full lecture is no longer extant). See also C. Graux, "Nouvelles Recherches sur la Stichométrie," *Revue de Philologie, de Littérature et d'Histoire anciennes* ,NS (Paris: F. Klincksiek, 1878) II, pp. 97–143 (117). A.-M. Denis, "Les Psaumes de Salomon," in *Introduction aux Pseudépigraphes grecs d'Ancien Testament*, pp. 60–69, *SVTP*, vol. I (Leiden: Brill, 1970), p. 62) also suggested that the PssSol may have appeared in the Codex Sinaiticus. See also J. Viteau, *Les Psaumes de Salomon: Introduction, texte Grec et traduction, avec les principales variantes de la version Syriaque par François Martin*, Documents pour l'étude de la Bible (Paris: Letouzey et Ané, 1911), pp. 186–191.

[10] Athanasius, *Synopsis Sanctae Scripturae*, J.-P. Migne, *PG* (Paris: Migne, 1857–1966), Vol 28, Col 432. See Zahn, *Geschichte* II, p. 317.

[11] Called "ἀπόκρυφα" in the list, *Indiculus librorum canonicorum et apocryphorum, quem Anastasii Niceni Quaestionibus subiectum in publica Oxoniensis Academiae bibliotheca invenimus, ubi* διδαχαὶ τῶν ἀποστόλων *et* διδασκαλία Κλήμεντος *ut distincta opera recensentur et in scriptorum apocryphorum censu pariter reponuntur*, in Jean–Baptiste Cotelier, *S. Patrum, qui temporibus apostolicis floruerunt* (Antwerp: Clericus, 1700; 2nd ed., Amsterdam: Wetstenios, 1724), I, p. 196. See Zahn, *Geschichte*, II .289–293; Viteau, *Psaumes de Salomon*, p. 186.

[12] Nicephorus, "Chronographis,"in *S. Nicephori, Patriarchæ Constantinopolitani Breuiarium Historicum* (Paris: S. Chappelet, 1616) pp. 286–414. See C. de Boor, "Nicephori Archiepiscopi Constantinopolitani Opuscula Historica" in *Bibliotheca Teubneriana* (Leipzig: Teubner, 1880), p. 134, and B.F. Westcott, *A General Survey of the History of the Canon of the New Testament*, Appendix D, "Catalogs of the Books of the Bible," No. XIX, 56 (Cambridge, MA: Macmillan, 1889), and Zahn, *Geschichte*, II, p. 299. Gray says, incorrectly, that the PssSol lie between "Eccles. and Esther" (elsewhere "Eccles." is his abbreviation for Qoheleth). G.B. Gray, "The Psalms of Solomon," *APOT* II, pp. 625–652 (627), (ed. R.A. Charles; Oxford: Clarendon Press, 1912). Some have contended that the list attributed to Nicephorus is, in fact, much earlier, perhaps originating in Syria about 500 C.E. and that the Athanasian list is an Alexandrine abridgement (K.A. Credner, *Zur Geschichte des*

manuscript of the Coislin library.[13] The 13th century Arminian Canon list identified with Mechitar of Ayrivank[14] lists the PssSol with the "Books that the Jews have in Secret."

That these notices refer to the Psalms of Solomon as we know them may be claimed with some degree of certainty.[15]

If the passages in PsSol 11 shared with First Baruch 5 suggest a dependence of First Baruch upon our psalms, this would indicate that the PssSol were available by the late first century C.E.[16]

Kanons, pp. 120, 144 (Halle: Waiserhauses, 1847). See also E. Schürer, *Neutestamentliche Geschichte*, III, p. 123 (Leipzig: Hinrichs, 1898–1901). Denis (*Introduction*, p. xii) suggests, convincingly, that all these lists come from a common ancestor that he dates between 400 and 450 C.E. There are also later canon lists that include the PssSol in Armenian (Melchithar of Aïrivank, 1290) and in six Slavic lists (14–16th centuries). See Zahn, *Geschichte*, II, p. 202; Viteau, *Psaumes de Salomon*, pp. 176–191; W. Lüdtke, "Beiträge zu slavischen Apokryphen," pp. 218-235, *ZAW* 31 (1911).

[13] J.–B. Cotelier, *S. Patrum*, I, p. 196.

[14] M.E. Stone, "Armenian Canon Lists III–The lists of Mechitar of Ayrivank (c. 1285 C.E.)" *HTR* 63 (1976), pp. 289-300.

[15] There are a number of other possible references to the PssSol cited in the literature, but all of them are accompanied by varying degrees of doubt as to their applicability to the PssSol. In the fifty-ninth canon of the Council of Laodicea (c. 360 C. E.) the directive, "ὅτι οὐ δεῖ ἰδιωτικοὺς ψαλμοὺς λέγεσθαι ἐν τῇ ἐκκλησίᾳ, οὐδὲ ἀκανόνιστα βιβλία, ἀλλὰ μόνα τὰ κανονικὰ τῆς παλαιᾶς καὶ καινῆς διαθήκης," may be against church use of the PssSol (See Zahn, *Geschichte*, II, p. 202; Viteau, *Psaumes de Salomon*, pp. 176–191). Theodorus Balsamon and Joahnes Zonaras Christian writiers of the twelfth century, and the fifteenth century writer Mathieu Blastaris, believed that the Council of Laodicea had forbidden the public reading of the PssSol: *Canones synodi Laodicenea* (J. Migne, *PG*, Vol 144, col 1144; Vol 137, Col 1420); W. Beverage, *Synodicum sive Pandectae Canonum* (Oxford: 1672, I, p. 480). Likewise, there may be a similar mandate in Ambrose, *Praef. in Lib. Psalmorum*, where he writes: "Salomo ipse David filius licet innumera cantica cecinisse dicatur, unum tamen quod ecclesia receperit canticorum canticum dereliquit." But, neither of these is unambiguously referring to our Psalms. There were numerous non-canonical psalters in circulation during these early centuries (See Zahn, *Geschichte*, II, pp. 122-123, 140). To the extent that these *Psalms* have been paired with the *Odes of Solomon* in some early canon lists and texts, as is shown by the Syriac MSS, the PssSol may also have been alluded to in the *Pistis Sophia* in c. 250 C.E., *Pistis Sophia*, C.Schmidt, tr. V. MacDermot, (Leiden: E. J. Brill, 1978). Also, see Lactantius in the fourth century: H. Ross, *Lactantius, Divinae institutiones*, Humanitas Christiana. Lateinische Reihe (Munich: Kösel, 1963).

[16] Gray (*APOT*, 628) and Ryle and James (H.E. Ryle and M.R. James, ΨΑΛΜΟΙ ΣΟΛΟΜΟΝΤΟΣ: *The Psalms of the Pharisees, Commonly Called the Psalms of*

Thus, the direct external evidence for the date of the PssSol takes us back to the fifth century C.E. Depending upon the date of First Baruch, our psalms' relation to that writing gives testimony of the existence of the PssSol in Greek as early as the last third of the first century C.E.

On internal evidence, the descriptions of the foreign conqueror are concrete to a degree paralleled only in Daniel and offer the best evidence we have for dating the Psalms of Solomon. The identifications of the conqueror with Antiochus IV–Epiphanes, Pompey, Herod the Great, and Titus have each had supporters. Nevertheless, most scholars have concluded that the allusions, when taken together, best match the descriptions in Josephus[17] of the Roman general Pompey, who invaded

---

Solomon (Cambridge (England): University Press, 1891), pp. lxxii–lxxvii, 100–103 considered Baruch to be dependent upon the PssSol. However, P.E.E. Geiger, *Der Psalter Salomo's, herausgegeben und erklärt* (Augsburg: J. Wolff, 1871), p. 137, and later Viteau (*Psaumes de Salomon*, p. 161) rejected the dependence of Baruch on PssSol. More recently, W. Pesch ("Die Abhängigkeit des 11. salomonischen Psalms vom letzten Kapitel des Buches Baruch," ZAW 67 (1955), pp. 251–263, argued that E. Geiger and Viteau had the correct order of derivation: that the PssSol are, indeed, dependent upon Baruch. See also C.C. Torrey, The Apocryphal Literature: *a Brief Introduction* (New Haven: Yale University Press, 1945), p. 62; and D.G. Burke, *The Poetry of Baruch: A Reconstruction and Analysis of the Original Hebrew Text of Baruch 3:9–5:9*, SBLSCS 10 (1982). These later arguments depend upon an earlier dating of Baruch, most often to the Maccabean period, or between the 4th and 2nd centuries BCE See also C.A. Moore, "Toward the Dating of the Book of Baruch, *CBQ* xxxvi (3: 1974), pp. 312–320, and A.K. Mukenge, *L'unité du livre deBaruch,Etudes bibliques;nouv. Sér.*, no38 (Paris: J. Gabalda, 1998), 431.

[17] Josephus, Flavius. *Antiquities*; *The Jewish War*, II. Loeb Classical Library. Tr: H. St. J. Thackeray (Cambridge, MA: Harvard University Press, 1927, 1928). *Antiquities* 14.4.1–4 *Wars* 1.7.1–6; and also Cassius Dio Cocceianus, *Dio's Roman History* (London: W. Heinemann, 1914-1927). Franz Karl Movers ("Apokryphen-Literatur," in *Kirchen-Lexikon, oder Encyklopädie der katholischen Theologie und ihrer Hilfswissenschaften,* ed. H. J. Wetzer and B. Welte , I, p. 340 (Freiburg im Breisgau: Herder, 1847–1882) was the first modern commentator (1847) to date the PssSol to the first century BCE. He placed the composition at the time of Pompey, however, he believed the text had been revised later to include the events at the time of Herod the Great. See also J. Langen, *Das Judenthum in Palästina zur Zeit Christi*, p. 64 (Freiburg im Breisgau, Herder, 1866); A. Hilgenfeld, "Prologomena; Psalmi Salomonis" *Messias Judaeorum, libris eorum paulo ante et paulo post Christum natum conscriptis illustratus,* XI–XVIII (Leipzig: Reisland, 1869), E. Schürer, *Neutestamentliche Geschichte*, p. 141, A. Hausrath, *Die Zeit Jesu*, I, p. 158 (Heidelberg: Bassermann, 1873), A. Caquot, "Les Hasmonéens, les Romains et Hérode: observations sur *Ps Sal* 17" in *Hellenica et Judaica*, ed. A. Caquot, M. Hadas-Lebel, and J. Riaud, pp. 213–218,(213), (Leuven–Paris: Éditions Peeters, 1986), Ryle and James, *The Psalms of the Pharisees*, p. xliii, F. M. Abel, "Le Siège de Jérusalem par Pompée," *RB*, 54 (1947), pp. 243–255, and M. Aberbach, "The Historical Allusions of Chapters IV, XI, and XIII of the Psalms of Solomon," *JQR*, 41 (Apr 51), pp. 379–396. A. Dupont-

Judea and captured Jerusalem in the mid-first century BCE[18] Of all the candidates, Pompey is the only one who was to die in Egypt (PsSol 2.26), a fact that gives him the distinction.[19]

Recently, however, it has been suggested that if PssSol 2 and 8 portray Pompey,

---

Sommer, *The Essene Writings from Qumran* (London: Blackwell, 1961), p. 348 saw parallels with the Damascus Document (CD) and with the Commentary on Habakkuk (1QpHab) in their references to the Roman attack under Pompey. See also: Kenneth Atkinson, "Toward a Redating of the Psalms of Solomon: Implications for Understanding the *Sitz im Leben* of an Unknown Jewish Sect." *JSOP* 17 (1998): 95–112).

[18] The next-most-popular hypothesis for the time of composition is that of the plundering of Jerusalem under Antiochus IV–Epiphanes in 170 BCE. See G.H.A. von Ewald, *The History of Israel,* 2nd ed., p. 301 (London: Longmans, Green, 1880) and G.F. Oehler, "Messias," in *RE,* ed. J.J. Herzog, G.F. Plitt, and A. Hauck, cols. 641–655 (Leipzig: Hinrichs, 1881). Also, A.P. Stanley, *The History of the Jewish Church,* IV, p. 335 (New York: Schribner, 1879), and A. Dillmann, "Pseudepigraphen des A.T.," *RE,* p. 341–367. M. Aberbach, "Historical Allusions," found references in the PssSol to the entire last half of the Hasmonean dynasty. In addition to Movers, others who dated the PssSol to the time of Herod the Great include: K.Th. Keim, *Geschichte Jesu von Nazara in ihrer Verkettung mit dem Gesamtleben seines Volkes,* vol. I, p. 243 (Zurich: Orell, Fussli, 1867), F.J. Delitzsch (*Biblisher Commentar über den Psalter,* II, p. 381(Leipzig, 1860); and, more recently, E. M. Laperrousaz, "Hérode le Grand est–il «l'ennemi (qui) a agi en étranger», des Psaumes de Salomon?" in *Politique et religion dans le judaïsme ancien et médiéval,* ed. D. Tollet, pp. 29–32 (Paris: Relais-Desclée 7, 1989). E. Bengel, *Opuscula Academica.* ed. J.G. Pressel (Hamburg: Apud Fridericum Perthes, 1834) placed the PssSol after the destruction of Jerusalem in 70 C.E. The earliest dating of the PssSol was made by K. G. Bretschneider, *Die historisch-dogmatische Auslegung des Neuen Testaments,* pp. 121-122 (Leipzig: J. A. Barth, 1806) who saw the hand of Nebuchadnezzar's desctuction of Jerusalem in the PssSol. Heinrich H. Ewald, who placed the PssSiol at 320 BCE and identified the invader as Ptolemy I, *Die jüngsten Propheten des Alten Bundes,* III, p. 269 (Göttingen: Vandenhoeck & Ruprecht, 1868). H. Winckler was alone in seeking to identify the historical psalms (2, 8, 17) with the turbulent political situation under Jason as described in 2 Macc 4–5, "Jason und die Zeit der Psalmen Salomos," *Altorientalische Forschungen* Nr. 2, pp. 556–564 (Leipzig: Eduard Pfeiffer, 1901). J. Tromp identified the "sinners" of PsSol 17 with the Romans but the expected foreign invaders in vss. 7–9 as the Parthians, "The Sinners and the Lawless in Psalm of Solomon 17," *NovT* 35 (1993), pp. 344–361). A fairly thorough analysis of the leading contenders and the evidence available until 1891 was prepared by Ryle and James, *The Psalms of the Pharisees,* pp. xxxix–xliv. The latest comprehensive review of the scholarship is by K. Atkinson, *An Intertextual Study of the Psalms of Solomon Pseudepigrapha* (Lewiston, NY: The Edwin Mellen Press, 2001).

[19] See also K. Atkinson, *I Cried to the Lord: A Study of the Psalms of Solomon's Historical Background and Social Setting,* p. 22 (Leiden: Brill, 2003).

then PsSol 17 better describes Herod the Great and the Roman general Sosius' 37 BCE siege of Jerusalem. This equates Herod with both the "man alien to our race" (PsSol 17:7) and the "lawless one" (PsSol 17:11).[20] The invective "a man alien to our race" is much more a pejorative when applied to Herod than to any foreigner. PssSol 4, 12, and 15 describe inter-Jewish disputes apparently earlier than Pompey. PsSol 7 is reacting to the threat of a possible Roman intervention, and the author pleads that God would not allow the Gentiles to invade, thus clearly predating Pompey's arrival.[21]

If the conqueror of PssSol 2 and 8, indeed, is Pompey, and the "alien" of PsSol 17 describes Herod, then the events alluded to in these psalms span the time between just before Pompey's invasion in 63 B C E, through his death in 48 BCE, to Herod's extermination of the remaining Hasmonean leaders in 30 BCE.

This analysis suggests that there were several authors and probably a redactor involved in the creation of the Psalms of Solomon.[22]

A redactor would have edited the collection and shaped its final form. He selected a core of "historical" psalms composed over three decades, from approximately 65 to 30 BCE, spanning the time from before Pompey through Herod. He appended the first

---

[20] The psalmist anticipates that the Hasmonean line is about to be exterminated, by someone from his own midst. By accusing the conqueror of acting like a Gentile, the author is implying that he was, in fact, Jewish (Kenneth Atkinson, "Toward a Redating of the Psalms of Solomon: Implications for Understanding the *Sitz im Leben* of an Unknown Jewish Sect." *JSOP* 17 (1998): 95-112). This proposal considers that the future tenses, in 17:7–8 were intended to refer to Herod's murders of the surviving members of the Hasmonean family, that occurred between 37 and 30 BCE. The shift to the aorist in vs. 9b (ἐξηρεύνησεν), may convey the author's expectation that God was about to punish these Hasmonean sinners (see also 1 Macc 3:5 and Amos 9:1–3 (LXX) where the verb signifies a search for an enemy, before chasing or killing him). Therefore, vs. 9b would indicate that Herod had begun, but not yet completed, his execution of the remaining Hasmoneans). See also, K. Atkinson, "Herod the Great, Sosius, and the Siege of Jerusalem (37 B.C.E.) In Psalm of Solomon 17, *NovT* 38 (1996), pp. 313-322.

[21] Atkinson, "Toward a Redating," p. 105-106. See also, Atkinson, "On the Herodian Origin of Militant Davidic Messianism at Qumran: New Light from Psalm of Solomon 17." *JBL* 118 (1999), 435-460

[22] Although some scholars have seen a single author behind these psalms , as did J. Brierre-Narbonne, *Exégèse apocryphe des prophéties messianiques* (Paris: P. Geuthner, 1937) p. 5, J. Liver, *The House of David*, p. 141 and M. Stein, "The Psalms of Solomon," in A. Kahana, *The Outside Books,* II, p. 433 (Tel Aviv: Masada, 1959), most discern several hands at work. See R. A. Charles, *A Critical History of the Doctrine of Future Life in Israel, in Judaism and in Christianity,* 2nd ed. p. 267 (London: Adam and Charles Black, 1913) ; G. B. Gray, *APOT*, p. 628; P. Volz, *Die Eschatologie der jüdischen Gemeinde im neutestamentlichen Zeitalter,* p. 26 (Tübingen: J. C. B. Mohr, 1934); A. Bentzen, *Introduction to the Old Testament,* 2, p. 239 (Copenhagen: G. E. C. Gad, 1952); O. Eissfeldt, *Einleitung in das Alte Testament,* p. 756 (Tübingen: J. C. B. Mohr, 1956).

and eighteenth Psalms of Solomon, providing an introduction and conclusion. The redactor would have added the remaining "generic" psalms, from an existing pool of cultic poetry. He arranged the psalms, added liturgical headings in emulation of the biblical Psalter, and attributed the whole to King Solomon.[23]

That Jerusalem has been attacked and desecrated, but not destroyed, suggests that the psalms reached their final form before 70 C.E.[24] Thus, the last half of the first century BCE emerges as the most suitable time for the composition and editing of the Psalms of Solomon, followed by a translation into Greek perhaps about the turn of the era, possibly in Egypt.[25]

ASCRIPTION AND PROVENANCE

The PssSol, by title superscriptions and tradition, are either ascribed or dedicated to Solomon, although there is no reference to him within the poems themselves. The similarity between the most prominent psalm (PsSol 17) and the canonical Psalm 72, already known as a "Psalm of Solomon," may have prompted the editorial ascription to the one who, next to David, enjoyed a reputation as a poet (1 Kgs 4.32–34; Heb: 5.12–14).

Because of its unusual prominence, there is little doubt that Jerusalem is the venue of the Psalms of Solomon.[26] Jerusalem is the locale of many events. The corruption of the Jerusalem leadership (PsSol 4) and the anticipation of God's blessings on the Holy City (PsSol 11) reinforce this conclusion. Jerusalem is addressed (PsSol 11), speaks (PsSol 1), and is the seat of the Sanhedrin (PsSol 4.1).

The authorship of the PssSol has most often been attributed to the Pharisees,[27] but

---

[23] . Blackburn, Rollin J. "Hebrew Poetic Devices in the Greek Text of the Psalms of Solomon." Temple University, 1998.

[24] Few have dated the PssSol to C.E. 70 or later. P. D. Heutius, in 1694, found evidence of a date later than the First Century, C. E. See P.D. Heutius, (AKA: Huet), *Demonstratio Evangelica ad Serenissimum delphinum,* 4th ed., p. 397 (Leipzig: J. Thomam Fritsch, 1694). R. Ceillier saw Titus' destruction of the Temple reflected in the PssSol, *Histoire Générale des Auteurs Sacrés et Ecclésiasgtiques*, I, p. 136(Paris: Luis Vivès, 1858). Later, Bengel agreed with Ceillier (*Opuscula Academica*, p. 395).

[25] See Ryle and James, *The Psalms of the Pharisees*, xc. On the Egyptian venue for the Greek translation, see Denis, *Introduction*, p. 63. On the question of the origin of the Syriac translation, see below.

[26] See Ryle and James, *The Psalms of the Pharisees*, p. lviii–lix.

[27] Ryle and James, *The Psalms of the Pharisees*, p. lix; J. Wellhausen, *Die Pharisäer und die Sadducäer*, p. 139 (Greifswald: L. Bamberg, 1874); E. Schürer, *A History of the Jewish People in the Time of Jesus Christ*, p. 21 (Edinburgh: Clark, 1894); Gray, *APOT*, II, p. 630; S. Mathews, "Psalms of the Pharisees," in *A History of New Testament Times in Palestine*, pp. 96–98 (New York: Macmillan, 1899, 1918); T. W. Manson, *The Servant-Messiah*, p. 21 (London: Cambridge (England) University Press, 1956); and R. B. Müller, "Messias und Menschensohn in jüdischen Apokalypsen und in der Offenbarung des Johannes," *SNT*, 6 (1972) p. 76, n. 58. See also J. Klausner,

that identification must now be abandoned.[28] Other scholars have linked the PssSol to the Hasidim,[29] to the Essenes,[30] or, if one stays with the evidence available to date, to

---

The Messianic Idea in Israel from Its Beginning to the Completion of the Mishnah, p. 392. (New York: Macmillan, 1955) These identifications, it now seems, were driven by the obvious realization that these psalms could not have been composed by Sadducees. G.E.W. Nickelsburg, after surveying the evidence, concludes that there is much in the PssSol that fits what is known about the Pharisees and nothing that does not. He locates the PssSol, then, in circles close to the Pharisees *(Jewish Literature between the Bible and the Mishnah: A Historical and Literary Introduction,* pp. 204, 212 (Philadelphia: Fortress, 1981), a conclusion echoed by K.E. Pomykala, *The Davidic Dynasty Tradition in Early Judaism: Its History and Significance for Messianism,* SBLEJL (Atlanta: Scholars Press, 1995). For a vigorous defense of a pharisaic origin, see J. Schüpphaus, *Die Psalmen Salomos: Ein Zeugnis Jerusalemer Theologie und Frömmigkeit in der Mitte des vorchristlichen Jahrhunderts,* ch. 1 *ALGHJ* 7 (Leiden: Brill, 1977). See also the review of Schüpphaus by R.B. Wright in *CBQ* 41 (1979) pp. 657–658. Most recently, M.Winninge, *Sinners and the Righteous: A Comparative Study of the Psalms of Solomon and Paul's Letters* (Stockholm: Almqvist & Wiksell, 1995). See, e.g., p. 180..

[28] See the thorough analysis and refutation of the arguments in favor of Pharisaic authorship in J. O'Dell, "The Religious Background of the Psalms of Solomon Re-evaluated in the Light of the Qumran Texts," *RevQ* 3 (May, 1961) pp. 241–257. For other objections see: O. Eissfeldt, *The Old Testament: An Introduction,* tr. P. R. Ackryod p. 613 (New York: Harper and Row, 1965), and A. Bentzen, *King and Messiah,* ed. G. W. Anderson (Oxford: Basil Blackwell, 1970). As G. Stemberger, *Jewish Contemporaries of Jesus: Pharisees, Sadducees, Essenes* (Minneapolis: Fortress Press, 1995) reminds us: "...The designation Pharisee is not found before Paul, or the name Sadducee before Mark's Gospel....This means that the earliest explicit statements about Pharisees and Sadducees were first written at a time when they had ceased to exist."

[29] J. Liver insisted in 1959 that the author of the PssSol must have been a "Chasid" or one of the "Chasidim of the Pharisees," who, contrary to most Pharisees, were opposed to any regime not of the House of David (J. Liver, *The House of David from the Fall of the Kingdom of Judah until the Destruction of the Second Temple of Jerusalem* (in Hebrew), p. 143 Jerusalem: Magnes and Hebrew University, 1959. See also O'Dell, "Religious Background"; H.R. Moeller, *The Legacy of Zion: Intertestamental Texts Related to the New Testament,* pp. 44–47, 131–151, 199–203 (Grand Rapids: Baker, 1977), and O. Plöger, *Theokratie und Eschatologie,* p. 16 (*WMANT*).

[30] As early as 1887, J. Girbal suggested that the PssSol were written by a pietist group of the first Essenes, the "Khassidim:" *Essai sur les Psaumes de Salomon,* (Toulouse: A. Chauvin et Fils, 1887). J. E. H. Thompson firmly identified these psalms with the Essenes (Thomson, *Books Which Influenced Our Lord and His Apostles: Being a Critical Review of Apocalyptic Jewish Literature,* , pp. 268ff, 423ff (Edinburgh: T. & T. Clark, 1891). See also A. Dupont–Sommer, *Essene Writings,* p.

"some unknown eschatological group in Jerusalem."[31] While few have suggested
Qumrân as a locale for the PssSol, many have pointed out similarities to various Dead
Sea Scrolls.[32] The PssSol have been attributed to the Sadducees[33] or even to the

---

12; O'Dell, "Religious Background"; and H.L. Jansen, *Die Spätjüdische
Psalmendichtung: ihr Entstehungskreis und ihr 'Sitz im Leben'* (Oslo: Norske
Videnskap–Akademie, 1937)

[31] R.B. Wright, "The Psalms of Solomon, the Pharisees and the Essenes," in *SBLSCS
2*, pp. 136–154, ed. R. A. Kraft (Missoula, MT: Scholars Press, 1972); R.R. Hann,
"The Community of the Pious: The Social Setting of the Psalms of Solomon" (*SR*
XVII, No. 2, 1988) pp. 169–189. For a critique of both O'Dell and Wright, see M.
Delcor, "Psaumes de Salomon," *DBSup*, fasc. 48, cols. 239–242 (Paris: Letouzey and
Ané, 1973).

[32] A.Jaubert, "La notion d'alliance dans le judaisme aux abords de l'ère chrétienne,"
Patristica Sorboniensia, 6, p. 255 (Paris: Editions du Seuil, 1963); S.Holm-Nielsen,
"Erwägungen zu dem Verhältnis zwischen den Hodajot und den Psalmen Salomos,"
Bibel und Qumran Wissenschaft, ed. S. Wagner, pp. 112–131 (Berlin: Evangelische
Haupt–Bibelgesellschaft, 1968); J. O'Dell, "The Religious Background"; D.Rosen and
A. Salvesen, "A Note on the Qumran Temple Scroll 56:15–18 and Psalm of Solomon
17:33," *JJS* 38 (1987) pp. 99–101; D. Dimant, "A Cultic Term in the Psalms of
Solomon in the Light of the Septuagint,"(in Hebrew), *Textus* 9 (1981) pp. 28–51; D.
Flusser, "Psalms, Hymns, and Prayers," *Jewish Writings of the Second Temple Period:
Apocrypha, Pseudepigrapha, Qumran Sectarian Writings, Philo, Josephus* (*CRINT*,
II, (1984), pp. 551–577); A. S. Van der Woude, *Die messianischen Vorstellungen der
Gemeinde von Qumran* (Assen: 1957); G. Morawe, "Vergleich des Aufbaus der
Danklieder und hymnischen Bekenntnislieder (1QH) von Qumran mit dem Aufbau der
Psalmen im Alten Testament und im Spätjudentum," *RevQ* 4 (1963) pp. 233–254; S.
Fujita, "The Metaphor of Plant in Jewish Literature of the Intertestamental Period," *JSJ*
(1976), p. 30.

[33] F. Hitzig, *Geschichte des Volkes Israel von Anbeginn bis zur Eroberung Masada's
im Jahre 72 nach Christus*, p. 502 (Leipzig: S. Hirzel, 1869); J. Le Moyne, *Les
sadducéens* (Paris: Lecoffre, 1972).

Christians,[34] although there is slim evidence for these attributions.[35] As Kenneth Atkinson observes: "Because at least a third of the Dead Sea Scrolls did not emanate from the members of the Qumran sect, but were apparently written by other as yet unidentified authors, it is not necessary to assign a composition such as the Psalms of Solomon to a known Jewish sectarian community."[36] Locating these psalms would be easier if we had a better understanding of the complex of religious coalitions active during this period,[37] and persistent attachment to a rigid classification into only the traditional groups may not serve us well.

There are some indications of a synagogue venue for the Psalms of Solomon. The community apparently worshiped apart from the Temple, without sacrifices. Piety had become a substitute for sacrifice,[38] so that sins were now cleansed through confession and penance in the "synagogues of the devout" (PsSol 17:16; 10:7), where they give thanks to God (PsSol 10:6). They were forced to flee during Herod's siege of Jerusalem, and were dispersed (PsSol 17:16-18). These allusions and the explicit communal identity throughout the psalms suggest that a synagogue setting may be most appropriate for these psalms.

The appearance of several rubrics for musical settings (εἰς νῖκος [8.tit.], διάψαλμα [17.29; 18.9]), that echo the biblical Psalter, is further evidence that these

---

[34] H. Graetz, *Geschichte der Judäer von den Ältesten Zeiten,* 2nd ed, III, p. 489. (Leipzig: O. Leiner, 1888) attributed the PssSol to a Christian author, an ascription he omitted in the third edition (III, p. 621). See also J. Efron, "The Holy War and Visions of Redemption," SJLA 39, pp. 219-286, Ed. J. Neusner (Leiden: Brill, 1987), and "The Psalms of Solomon, The Hasmonean Decline and Christianity," (pp. 219–286), both in *Studies on the Hasmonean Period* (Brill: SJLA, vol. 39: 1987). P. A. Alpe saw the PssSol as a product of the Pharisees and believed that, because of their use of messianic imagery drawn from the Hebrew Bible, they are to a degree higher than all other apocrypha to be understood as a bridge between the Old Testament and the New Testament, "Christologia in Psalmis Salomonis," *VD* 11 Fasc. 2–4. 1931, pp. 56–59, 84–88, 110–120). Despite its title, the article is a general discussion of the PssSol and their importance for understanding the function of Christology in the NT.

[35] MS 769 had a marginal note, now lost, of indeterminable date, at 2:25 that appears to be a Christian comment on a verbal link between the dragon of this verse and that of the *Book of the Revelation*. Von Gebhardt preserved the text of this note in his major edition, *Die Psalmen Salomo's*, O.L. von Gebhardt (1844–1906), ΨΑΛΜΟΙ ΣΟΛΟΜΩΝΤΟΣ: *Die Psalmen Salomo's zum ersten Male mit Benutzung der Athoshandschriften und des Codex Casanatensis.* Texte und Untersuchungen zur Geschichte der altchristlichen Literatur, XIII, pt. 2, p. 96, note 1 (Leipzig: J. C. Hinrichs, 1895).

[36] Atkinson, *I Cried to the Lord,* p. 7.

[37] A. Geiger ("Aus Briefen," *Jüdische Zeitschrift für Wissenschaft und Leben,* VI, 1868, p. 240), could not decide on the group responsible for the PssSol and saw them as the product of the controversy between Pharisees and Sadducees.

[38] See Wright, "The Spiritualization of Sacrifice."

hymns were used in synagogue services.[39] Of course, these liturgical directions, too, may be from the pen of a redactor, in emulation of the Biblical Psalms.

In terms of genre, apart from the obvious echos of the biblical Psalter, has been the assertion that the PssSol were in conscious imitation of the "City-Lament" form to be found in Lamentations, itself reflective of Ancient Near Eastern models.[40]

ORIGINAL LANGUAGE

The Psalms of Solomon, according to most scholars, were composed in Hebrew, very soon afterwards translated into Greek,[41] and sometime later into Syriac.[42] There are no

---

[39] P. Winter, "Psalms of Solomon," *IDB*, 4, pp. 958–960.

[40] D. J. Spink, "A City-Lament Genre in the Psalms of Solomon," pp. 31-32 Philadelphia: Temple University dissertation, 2001. For a further discussion of prose and poetry in the PssSol, see Atkinson, *I Cried to the Lord*, and R.J.Blackburn, "Hebrew Poetic Devices in the Greek Text of the Psalms of Solomon." Temple University doctoral dissertation (Temple University Department of Religion, 1998). Also, see Donald L. Scott, "The Role of Remembrance in The Psalms of Solomon." Chicago Theological Seminary, 1995 (R.B.Wright, External Examiner).

[41] The Greek translation is most often placed in the early first century C.E. "The historical references were still relevant and understandable for the Jews in the diaspora and the text is free from Christian interpolations, which might suggest a date when Christianity was not yet widespread." (D. Jongkind, "Psalms ofSolomon: Introductory Notes," Cambridge (England) University New Testament Seminar, 2001-2002 (Last accessed 11/2006. Online, URL: http://www.tyndale.cam.ac.uk/Tyndale/staff/Head/PssSol.htm)

[42] The Syriac version of the Psalms of Solomon is preserved in four manuscripts, dating from the tenth to the sixteenth centuries (a six-verse Syriac fragment, so-called MS "S" found in a marginal note on a seventh-century manuscript (British Library MS 17143), now known to be not a part of the textual tradition [see following note]) none of which preserves a complete text. The latest critical edition is found in W. Baars, "Psalms of Solomon" *The Old Testament in Syriac According to the Peshitta Version*, ed. The Peshitta Institute, Part IV, Fascicle 6 (Leiden: E. J. Brill, 1972). Earlier editions include J. Rendel Harris, *The Odes and Psalms of Solomon*; J. R. Harris and A. Mingana, *The Odes and Psalms of Solomon, Vol. I, The Text with Facsimile Reproductions*. Manchester: University Press; London; New York: Longmans, Green & Co.,1916, ; *Vol. II, Translation with Introduction and Notes* (Manchester: Manchester University Press; London/New York: Longmans, Green & Co., 1920). For examinations of the relationship of the Hebrew, Greek, and Syriac versions, see K.G. Kuhn, *Die älteste Textgestalt der Psalmen Salomos insbesondere auf Grund der syrischen Übersetzung neu untersucht*, BWANT, 21 (Stuttgart: Kohlhammer, 1937); J. Begrich, "Der Text der Psalmen Salomos, ZNW 38 (1939), pp. 131–164; J. Trafton, *The Syriac Version*, and "The Psalms of Solomon: New Light from the Syriac Version?" *JBL* 105 (1986) pp. 227–237.

surviving Hebrew manuscripts, and the extant Greek and Syriac manuscripts are no earlier than the tenth century C E.[43] Clearly the Greek text is a translation. Ryle and James and G.B.Gray noted features in common with other translations: characteristic translational errors from Hebrew, "semiticisms" in the Greek, etc.[44] More recently, R. Hann confirmed by syntactical analysis that our text is indeed "translation Greek,"[45] a phenomenon identifiably distinct from writings originally composed in Greek, even those written in conscious imitation of the Septuagint.[46] The Greek of the Psalms of Solomon is written with a modest vocabulary. In several passages the meaning is obscure and has been subject to conjecture by both medieval scribes and modern editors.

Adolph Hilgenfeld, but few others, has argued for a Greek original.[47] Evidence for a Greek prototype is based largely on quotations from the Septuagint, especially the *Wisdom of Solomon*. However, the use of the Septuagint merely shows an acquaintance with that version or a conscious or unconscious harmonization with its readings by a translator. Several attempts have been made to reconstruct a Hebrew original, a so-called "retranslation," or "back-translation" from the Greek,[48] but such efforts have little

---

[43] The Syriac fragment, MS "S", is a marginal note on a seventh-century copy of the "Hymns of Severus." The earliest Syriac fragment has usually been seen in this marginal note. It has now been determined that this intertextual note was made by Jacob of Odessa, sometime later, probably from memory. This fragmentary marginal note is therefore not regarded as part of the textual history of the PssSol. (Prof. Sabastian Brock, Oxford University, personal correspondence, January 8, 2002)

[44] Ryle and James, *The Psalms of the Pharisees*, pp. lxxviii–lxxxi; Gray, *APOT*, p. 627. See also R.J.Blackburn, "Hebrew Poetic Devices in the Greek Text of the Psalms of Solomon." Temple University doctoral dissertation (Temple University Department of Religion, 1998).

[45] Hann, *The Manuscript History*, pp. 36–40.

[46]   R.A. Martin, *Syntactical Evidence of Semitic Sources in Greek Documents*, *SBLSCS* 3, 1974.

[47] A. Hilgenfeld ("Die Psalmen Salomo's und die Himmelfahrt des Moses, griechisch hergestellt and erklärt," ZWT *11* [1868] pp. 133–168; and *Messias Iudaeorum*, "Prolegomena"), refuted by J. Wellhausen (*Die Pharisäer und die Sadducäer*, pp. 135f) and by Ryle and James *(The Psalms of the Pharisees*, pp. lxxxiv–lxxxvii); O. Zöckler, "Die pseudepigraphische Lyrik: Der Psalter Salomos," in his *Die Apokryphen des Alten Testaments nebst einem Anhang über die Pseudepigraphenliteratur,* ed. H. Strack and O. Zöckler, I, pp. 9, 405–420 (Munich: Beck, 1891). Earlier, P. D. Huetius, (*Demonstratio Evangelica*, and G. Janenski, *Dissertatio historico-critica de Psalterio Salomonis præside Neumann publicæ disquisitionis*, ed. J. G Neumannus, 8, p. 274 (Wittenberg: Neumann, 1687) had assumed, but not argued for, a Greek original.

[48] W. Frankenberg, *Die Datierung der Psalmen Salomos. Ein Beitrag zur jüdischen Geschichte*, BZAW, 1, 1896). Apparently, Wellhausen attempted a Hebrew back-translation, but either he had "not committed it to writing" (Ryle and James, *The Psalms of the Pharisees*, p. xvii), or it was "not printed" (J.H. Miller, "The Psalms of

historical or linguistic value.

The Syriac has usually been seen as a translation from the Greek text,[49] although some have suggested that there is evidence that the Syriac may have been influenced by a Hebrew text.[50] New philological research now strongly suggests that the Syriac is indeed a direct translation from an early Hebrew text,[51] perhaps with some reference to the Greek.

The most notable feature of the Syriac is its attempt to smooth difficult readings. In many passages where the Greek text is troublesome and the MSS readings diverge, the Syriac gravitates toward Greek MS 253 and its group.[52] The texts of Wisdom and Sirach that are also preserved in MS 253 and its group are part of the Syro-hexaplaric text tradition. This fact may reinforce similarities between this group of MSS and the Syrian Christian community that preserved these Syriac Psalms and attached them to the Odes of Solomon.

THE GREEK MANUSCRIPTS

The Psalms of Solomon are preserved, in whole or in part, in twelve Greek manuscripts, one dating from the fifth century C.E., the rest from the tenth to the sixteenth centuries C.E. The numerical designations used here conform to those assigned by Rahlfs and his successors in the Göttingen *Verzeichnis*.[53] Von Gebhardt's

---

Solomon,", p. 10 (New York: Hebrew Union College), unpublished, handwritten master's thesis, 1906); see also Ryle and James, *The Psalms of the Pharisees*, p. xvii). F. Delitzsch made a Hebrew translation (now in the library of the University of Leipzig, "Rückübersetzung der Psaumes Salomon ins Hebräische" (unpublished manuscript number 01503 in the Universitätsbibliothek, Leipzig, ca. 1860). Also, see Viteau, *Psaumes de Salomon*, p. 243, and A.S. Kamenetzki, *Eine hebräische Übersetzung der PsS mit Einleitung und Anmerkungen in neuhebräischer Sprache* (Cracow: n. p. 1904).

[49] See also Gray, *APOT*, p. 626; and Harris, *The Odes and Psalms* (1909) pp. 37–39. Ryle and James (*The Psalms of the Pharisees*, p. xxvi) suggested that because three of the early references to the PssSol are from Latin writers (particularly the MSS of Lactantius) an early Latin version existed at one time. There is no known evidence of the existence of this or of any other versions.

[50] Kuhn, *Die älteste Textgestalt;* Trafton, *The Syriac Version*, "New Light " and "Solomon, Psalms of," in *ABD*, VI, pp. 115–117; P. Winter, "Psalms of Solomon."

[51] G. Ward, *A Philological Analysis of the Greek and Syriac Texts of the Psalms of Solomon* (Philadelphia: Temple University Dissertation, 1996). See also W. Baars, "A New Fragment."

[52] See J. Begrich, "Der Text der Psalmen Salomos," pp. 131–164, where he argues that the Syriac and MS 253 come from a common Greek *Vorlage*.

[53] Rahlfs, *Verzeichnis*. Previously editors created their own unique set of sigla, often the initial letter of the name of the city or library holding the particular MS.

and others' sigla are shown in curved brackets.[54] The contents of the MSS discussed here include only their biblical, Apocrypha, and Pseudepigraphic texts; the MSS often contain other later religious writings not herein listed.[55]

Three of the manuscripts (MSS 769, 471, and 336) are known to have originated from the monasteries of Mt. Athos, 336 and 471 both from Iveron. MS 336 remains in their library. MS 769 probably originated from the Laura Monastery, at least that is from where it was reportedly stolen at the beginning of the 20th Century. MSS 260 and 149 are clearly by the same hand. MSS 655 and 659 are not only copied by the same scribe, but we know the name of the copyist who held the pen: Ἰωάννης Μαυρομάτης, who worked in the third quarter of the sixteenth century.[56] Others, if not most, of the MSS may have been produced at ths center of Orthodox monastic life on Mt. Athos.

The manuscript groups, and the *stemma* deduced from them, were determined initially by von Gebhardt and confirmed and refined by Hann,[57] the latter partly based on an application of the Claremont Profile Method[58] to the text readings.

MS Group 253 (includes 253, 655, 659)

MS 253 (= von Gebhardt [vG] "R," "Codex Romanus") is *Vaticani Graeci 336* of the Biblioteca Apostolica Vaticana in Rome. It is dated to the eleventh century.[59] The

---

[54] *Die Psalmen Salomo's*, p. 39.

[55] Words added in lower right margins to match folio assembly are not noted unless problematic for some reason. Standard manuscript abbreviations are not noted separately. Unique or questionable characters are recorded.

[56] E. Gamillscheg, *Repertorium der Griechischen Kopisten 800-1600*, Vol. 3, p. 106 (Vienna: Verlag der Österreichischen Akademie der Wissenschaften, 1997). (Appreciation to Fr. Paul Canart of the Vatican Library for locating this reference).

[57] Von Gebhardt, *Psalmen Salomo's*, pp. 14–42; Hann, *Manuscript History*, pp. 35–51.

[58] P.R. McReynolds, "The Claremont Profile Method and the Grouping of Byzantine New Testament Manuscripts" (Claremont Graduate School, Ph.D. Dissertation, 1968); F. Wisse, "The Claremont Profile Method for the Classification of Byzantine New Testament Manuscripts: A Study in Method" (Claremont Graduate School, Ph.D. Dissertation, 1968). See E.J. Epp, "The Claremont Profile Method for Grouping New Testament Minuscule Manuscripts," in E.J. Epp and G.D. Fee, *Studies in the Theory and Method of New Testament Textual Criticism* pp. 211–220 (Studies and Documents 45, ed. Irving Alan Sparks (Grand Rapids: Eerdmans, 1993).

[59] The MS is listed in Rahlfs' *Verzeichnis* on p. 249. The date is attested in *Bibliothecae Apostolicae Vaticanae Codces manuscripti Recensiti*, Codices Vaticani Graeci Tomus II, Codices 330-603, p. 8. Recdnsivit Robertus Devreesse. (Vatican City: Bibliotheca Vaticana, 1937). See the chart of traditional names of the MSS and their present locations, on p. 31.

parchment codex is mostly in good condition,[60] with some discoloration, and a few pages with torn corners. The 194 folios[61] measure 25.0 x 19.0 cm with 16.0 x 12.0–13.0 cm of inscribed surface[62] in one column. The color of the parchment is Pantone[63] 12-1006 (Cream Pearl). The text ink is Pantone 16-1317 (Brush), and the engrossing[64] is Pantone 18-1449 (Catchup). The MS contains *Job, Proverbs, Ecclesiastes, Canticles, Wisdom of Solomon*, the *PssSol*, and selections from *Sirach*. It contains the PssSol on folios 122v–136v with the superscription "Σοφία Σολομῶντος." The superscription to *Wisdom* refers to *Wisdom*, the *PssSol*, and *Sirach* as "Ἀδιάθετα." No *iota* subscripts or adscripts are used but omissions are not regarded as variants[65]. The heading for PsSol 9 appears at the bottom of folio 129r and also at the top of folio 129v. There are several erasures. Usually the erased text is not recoverable; occasionally an erasure is overwritten with new text. A personal marginal note at the end of Job dates from the beginning of the fifteenth century.[66] The manuscript appears to have been written by one hand. Von Gebhardt himself collated this manuscript for his edition.

MS 655 is *Ottoboniani Graeci 60* of the Biblioteca Apostolica Vaticana. It is dated to the late sixteenth century.[67] The paper codex of 363 folios is in generally good condition, and measures 24.0–24.5 x 16.5–17.5 cm with 15.5 x 10.0 cm of inscribed surface in one column. The paper is Pantone 11-0603 (Pastel Parchment). The text ink

---

[60] Judgments of the condition of manuscripts usually include: "Excellent" (fine, almost pristine), "Good" (codex and leaves intact and completely readable, minor discoloration), "Fair" (wear, tears, considerable discoloration, but text readable), "Poor" (binding and leaves torn or missing, with heavy discoloration; the text illegible in places).

[61] A *folio*, by one common definition, is a leaf in a book, containing two or four pages. They are normally numbered only on the front (*recto*) side, but not on the back (*verso*) side. A *quarto*, specifically, is a sheet folded into four leaves. A *quire* contains 24 or often 25 leaves.

[62] The measure of inscribed surface includes the body of the text but not headings or engrossed marginal letters.

[63] Manuscript media and ink colors of all the MSS were personally measured by this editor using the Pantone® Professional Color System, an international standard in the graphic arts. A color is identified by its Pantone reference number, and its Pantone descriptive name. L. Eiseman and L. Herbert, *The Pantone Book of Color* (New York: Harry N. Abrams, 1990). Occasionally, when the technical color name is not visually descriptive, a more commonplace color name is also suggested.

[64] Engrossing refers to large initial letters appearing usually in the left margin. It also may refer to titles, running headers, and other decorative elements in a manuscript.

[65] If it is necessary to locate *iotas* (or any other features) in the MSS, one may use the transcription files that are line and word matched to the photographs, on the CD mentioned at the end of this book.

[66] See von Gebhardt, *Psalmen Salomo's*, p. 27, n. 1.

[67] Rahlfs, *Verzeichnis*, p. 240.

is Pantone 19-1314 (Seal Brown) and the engrossing is Pantone 16-1541 (Camellia). It contains the PssSol on folios 201r–220v with the superscription: "Σοφία Σολομῶντος." It was copied from a near relative of MS 253,[68] by the same modestly skilled scribe who reproduced MS 659. The scribe of these two MSS was Ἰωάννης Μαυρομάτης, who worked in the third quarter of the XVI Century[69] This MS was not available to von Gebhardt. The present codex has perhaps a dozen numbering systems, as the volume is an assemblage from parts of other manuscript collections. The PssSol itself displays six separate pagination schemes. What appears to be the latest, and the one that includes the entire codex in its present configuration, is the one used here. The ink has soaked through to the back in many places, appearing as a tan shadow with orange-pink shading. The text uses few *iota* sub- or addscripts. Unique among this group of MSS, the text uses hyphens when words are split between lines.

MS 659 is *Ottoboniani Graeci 384* of the Biblioteca Apostolica Vaticana.[70] It is dated to the late sixteenth century. The paper codex of 354 folios measures 22.5 x 15.5 cm with 15.5 x 9.5-10.0 cm of inscribed surface in one column. The codex is in good condition with only some staining on the bottoms of the pages. The ink has often bled through from the back of the pages. Often later corrections were added to the text in a somewhat more viscous ink, that did not bleed through, a feature that, in some cases, allows later emendations to be distinguished from the original text. The paper is the color of Pantone 11-0603 (Pastel Parchment). The text ink is Pantone 19-1314 (Seal Brown) and the engrossing is Pantone 16-1541 (Camellia). The MS preserves the PssSol on folios 208r–226v with the superscription: "Σοφία Σολομῶντος." It was copied from the same intermediary cousin of MS 253,[71] by the same scribe who copied MS 655.[72] This MS was not available to von Gebhardt.

The 253 texts of Wisdom and Sirach have been judged to preserve the hexaplaric recension traced back to Origen in the third century.[73] R. Hann has argued that the best representation of the earliest text form is preserved by the 253 MS group. It conserves

---

[68] Hann, *Manuscript History*, p. 61.

[69] E. Gamillscheg, *Repertorium der*, p. 106.

[70] Rahlfs, *Verzeichnis*, p. 241.

[71] Hann concluded that "it is not possible that one of these MSS (655 or 659) was copied from the other, since each preserves a number of readings not found in the other," and that "the exemplar of 655-659 could not have been 253" directly, but through a common intermediary, "an uncial MS closely resembling the present MS 253" (*Manuscript History*, pp. 61–63).

[72] The scribe of this MS and of MS 655 was Ἰωάννης Μαυρομάτης, who worked in the third quarter of the XVI century. (See E. Gamillscheg, *Repertorium der*, p. 106). This MS uses the same colors of parchment and ink as its near-twin, MS 659.

[73] J. Ziegler, *Sapientia Salomonis*, pp. 50–53 (Göttingen: Vandenhoeck & Ruprecht, 1962); *Sapientia Iesu Filii Sirach*, pp. 57–63. (Göttingen: Vandenhoeck & Ruprecht, 1965)

the apparent earliest form of the text and appears to have the largest number of readings judged to be early.[74] Other MSS also contain early readings, and these have been examined for incorporation into this edition.

MS Group 260 (includes 260, 149, 471, 606, 3004)

MS 260 (= vG "H"; = Ryle & James "K,"[75] "Codex Havniensis"[76]) is *Gamle Kongelige Samling 6* of the Kongelige Bibliotek of Copenhagen.[77] It is dated to the tenth or eleventh centuries.[78] The parchment codex of 232 folios (ten quires have been lost from the beginning of the MS) measures about 36.5 x 27 cm with about 21.5 x 14.25 cm of inscribed surface in one column (folios 2r–82v), and in two columns (from folio 84r to the end of the MS). The manuscript is in excellent condition with some minor staining on the parchment. The color of the parchment is Pantone 12-0605 (Angora). The text ink is Pantone 19-1314 (Seal Brown). Unique among this group of MSS, the engrossing is in gold ink, Pantone 16-0836 (Rich Gold), in places faded to Pantone 16-1325 (Copper). It contains the book of *Job* with a *catena* in the margin, *Proverbs, Ecclesiastes, Canticles* (all with marginal commentaries), *Wisdom of Solomon, PssSol,* and *Sirach* with a Prologue.[79] Folio 83r is blank, and folio 83v contains a full-page colored illustration representing King Solomon.[80] The text of the PssSol is found on

---

[74] Hann, *Manuscript History*, pp. 76–79, 91–92, 107, 110.

[75] Ryle and James, *The Psalms of the Pharisees*, p. xxviii; Rahlfs, *Verzeichnis,* p. 91.

[76] See Gray, *APOT*, p. 625; Ryle and James, *The Psalms of the Pharisees*, p. xxviii.

[77] The MS was mentioned first by C. Graux in a review of C.W. Bruun's *Aarsberetningen og Meddelelser fra det Store Kongelige Bibliothek Udgivne,* Annual of Communication of the Great Royal Library of Copenhagen), 2nd ed. pt. 3 (Copenhagen: Gyldendalske, 1877) in *RC,* 1877, pp. 291–293), who briefly described the MS. He later delineated it more completely in his *Notices sommaires des MSS. grecs de la Grande Bibliothèque Royale de Copenhague,* pp. 1–4 (Paris: Imprimerie nationale, 1879). The MS was bought in Venice in 1699 by Frederick Rostgaard, subsequently sold to Count Danneskjold in 1726, and in 1732 it came to the Royal Library (Ryle and James, *The Psalms of the Pharisees,* pp. xxviii f).

[78] Graux, *Notices Sommaires,* p. 1.

[79] These are the contents according to M. Mackeprang, V. Madsen, and C.S. Petersen, in *Greek and Latin Illuminated Manuscripts of the X to the XIII Century in Danish Collections,* p. 1 (Copenhagen: A. Marcus, 1921). But, according to Rahlfs' *Verzeichnis,* (p. 91) the contents are "Cat. in Iob, Cat. in Prov., Eccl. com comm. marg., Cant. cum comm. marg., Sap., Ps.Sal., Sir."

[80] The illustration is captioned above his head as: "ΣΟΛΟΜΩΝ." He is seated on a throne in front of a colonnaded balustrade, in royal robes, with a crown and red shoes. His right hand gestures in the manner of a Greek ecclesiastical benediction, and in his left he holds a scroll tied with two red and white ribbons. Sitting on a stool in front and to Solomon's right is an old man, similarly gesturing and with a scroll bound with one ribbon. Behind the railing is the figure of a woman, visible to the waist,

folios 170v–183r. A collation of the MS was made by Charles Graux and given to von Gebhardt in 1879. It was identified by von Gebhardt as the exemplar for MS 149.[81] Hann has confirmed this relationship.[82] MS 260 appears to have been written by the same hand as MS 149.[83] At the end of the MS, there are two pages of notes of the history of the MS, referencing dates from 1453 to 1732[84]

The scribe engrossed one or two letters per column, usually whatever letters happened to fall into the left margin. On folio 142v, col. 2, at the beginning of *Canticles*, the initial "A" in "Αισμα" is missing, marked by a dot. The gold letters occasionally imprinted on the facing page. The text uses *iota* addscripts.

MS 149 (= vG "V," "Codex Vindobonensis," "Venice Codex") is *Theologici Graeci 11* of the Vienna Österreichische NationalBibliothek (formerly the Kaiserlich-

---

holding another scroll with both hands. As the illustration is positioned in the MS immediately before the group of five "Solomonic" writings, it is often interpreted to pertain to the collection of works traditionally identified with him: The old man may be one of the men of Hezekiah, who, according to Proverbs 25, copied the proverbs of Solomon. In this interpretation, the woman would be Παροιμία personified. But because the old man is gesturing with a motion similar to that of Solomon, as if he were his near equal, some have suggested this figure represents Jesu Sirach, whose writing follows those of Solomon in this MS. In this case, the woman would represent Σοφία personified (See Mackeprang, *Greek and Latin Manuscripts*, p. 2, and Bruun, *Aarsberetningen*).

[81] Von Gebhardt, *Psalmen Salomo's*, pp. 19, 23.

[82] Hann, *Manuscript History*, p. 64.

[83]B. Schartau,. *Codices Graeci Haunienses: Ein deskripiver Katalog des griechischen Handscriftenbesandes der Königlichen Bibliothek Kopenhagen* , p. 53 (Copenhagen: Museum Tusculanum, 1994).

[84] From a series of subscriptions on folio 232r, one can reconstruct some of the history of this manuscript: "ἀπό τινος καλοθέτου," "(acquired) from (a member of the family) Kalothetes." The manuscript came into the possession of Lukas Notaras, Duke of Constantinople in the fifteenth century (Rahlfs, *Verzeichnis*, p. 91). He was commander–in–chief of the Byzantine fleet and was executed by Sultan Mohammed II after the fall of Constantinople in 1453. The MS then was obtained by one Georgios Kantakuzenos (d. 1456), to whom the family Notaras was related by marriage. He took it from Constantinople in 1453 to Smendervo (Semendria) [σμεντορόβω] in Serbia. The next note is indistinct (perhaps unfinished), and may have told how the MS arrived in Venice. While in that city, it came into the possession of Urganus, a monk in the monastery of St. Nicola, in Venedig (Venice), who is described in the note as a "grammarian." The MS was purchased at Venice in 1699 by a Frederik Rostgaard (1671-1745), and acquired at auction in 1726 by Graf Christian Danneskjold Samsøe. In 1732, the Royal Library in Copenhagen acquired the MS (Mackeprang, *Greek and Latin Manuscripts*, p. 2).

Königliche Hofbibliothek).[85] It is dated to the tenth or eleventh century.[86] The parchment codex of 166 folios measures 35.75 x 27.5 cm with 20.25 x 14.5 cm of inscribed surface in two columns, each 63 mm wide. The parchment is colored Pantone 12-0605 (Angora). The text ink is Pantone 15-1512 (Misty Rose [tan]), and the engrossing is Pantone 16-1526 (Terra Cotta). Twenty-two pages are lost between folios 33 and 44. The MS was rebound in white parchment in 1755. The MS contains *catenae* on *Job* and *Proverbs*, then *Ecclesiastes* and *Canticles* (with marginal commentaries), *Wisdom*, the *PssSol,* and *Sirach*. The text of the PssSol is found on folios 105v–118r.[87] The text of PssSol in this MS is a close replica of MS 260, written in the same hand.[88] The MS was collated by von Gebhardt himself who identified it as a copy of MS 260. *Iota* addscripts are used. They are not regarded as variants and appear in our collation as subscripts.

MS 471 (=vG "M," "Codex Mosquensis") is *Bibliotheca Sanctissimae Synodi 147*[89] of the State Historical Museum in Moscow. It is dated to the last quarter of the thirteenth century.[90] The parchment codex of 225 folios measures 34.5 x 27.5 cm with 18.5 x 16.0 cm of inscribed surface in two columns. The parchment is colored as Pantone 12-0605 (Angora). The text ink is Pantone 16-1220 (Café Creme) and the engrossing is Pantone 16-1340 (Brandied Mellon [red faded to light brown]). It contains *catenae* on *Job* and *Proverbs*, then *Ecclesiastes* and *Canticles* (with marginal commentaries), *Wisdom,* the *PssSol,* and (in the same hand as PssSol) *Sirach*. The text of the PssSol is found on folios 168v–179v. The MS was formerly in the Ἰβήρων

---

[85] Rahlfs, *Verzeichnis*, 318. The MS is first discussed by P. Lambeck in his *Hamburgensis Commentariorum de augustissima Bibliotheca caesarea vindobonensi*, liber primus–octavus (Vienna: I. Thomae, 1716) III. It was originally cataloged as Lambecii # 7.

[86] H. Hunger and O. Kresten, *Katalog der griechischen Handschriften der Österreichischen National Bibliothek, Teil 3/1: Codices Theolog. 1-100*, (Vienna: Brüder Hollinek, 1976).

[87] There are, in fact, two page-numbering schemes: the first has been lined through and replaced by the second. The folios containing the PssSol are numbered 127v–140r in the old numbering system and 105v–118v in the new tallying.

[88] See Hann, *Manuscript History*, pp. 63f, for an analysis of the single difference that has been the subject of successive scribal emendations.

[89] Also called "Codex Mosquensis Sanctissimae Synodi Bibliothecae Graecae N 147." It was formerly in the Library of the Holy Synod at Moscow. The MS was taken from the Iveron Monastery on Mt. Athos in 1653 (Gray, APOT, p. 625).

[90] Б. Л. Фонкич Ф. Б. Поляков (B. L. Fonkich, F. B. Polyakof), *Греческие Рукописи Синодальной Библиотеки (Grecheskye Rukopisi Sinodal'noy Biblyoteki)*. Moscow: Sinodal'naya Biblyoteka, 1993, p. 34.

(Iveron) monastery on Mt. Athos.[91] The MS was collated by von Gebhardt himself.[92]

A large number of characters are missing among the engrossed letters and titles; numerous are invisible in monochrome photographs, but appear in the color images. Many letters or locations of engrossing are marked with a black dot. There are no individual psalm titles except for PsSol 3. However, on folio 175r space is left at the top of the second column for the superscription to PsSol 12. Therefore, these missing letters and titles are regarded not as variants, but as omissions resulting from an incomplete production process. The spaces were intended to be filled by psalm titles, perhaps by another scribe. Tandem black dots appear above some letters, not always on characters that appear in our variant notes. Often in MS 471 and also in MS 606 an initial large vowel is followed, rather than preceded, by the diacritical. Also, where the first letter of an initial diphthong is enlarged and in red, the breathing or accent mark that immediately follows it is also in red, as if the diacritical mark is on first letter, not the second. There are no enlarged, engrossed letters in folios 172^v to 177^r.

---

[91] Rahlfs, *Verzeichnis*, p. 145.

[92] MS 471 has many lines with the first word lacking its initial letter. The missing letters always fall in the left margin, often in mid-word, but with no other discernable linguistic or graphic patterns. Most often the location of the missing letter is marked with a dot. There are eight examples of the same phenomenon in MS 336 (see below in the description of MS 336), one in MS 260, and one in MS 606. These are likewise all at the left margin, all at the beginning of lines. The only superscription in MS 471 is for PsSol 3. Where superscriptions would be expected to appear, sufficient space is left for them. The space left for a superscription above PsSol 12 falls at the top of the second column suggesting that the spaces were not provided just to separate the psalms. The best explanation for these anomalies appears to be that MS 471's condition is the result of an incomplete production process: the text was inscribed, space was left for superscriptions and the locations for the rubricated illuminations of letters were often marked, but many of the illuminated marginal letters and all but one of the superscriptions were never added. Therefore, this collation assumes the missing letters are a production mistake, not an intended scribal or editorial alteration of the text. They are not considered to be textual variants and are included in the apparatus only where noting them is needed to clarify an ambiguity in the text.

"Cassiodorus (ca. 487-ca. 580 CE), a Roman nobleman, established a monastery on his estates in southern Italy at Vivarium around 540 CE. that placed great emphasis on education and book production. In 562 CE he wrote his *Institutiones* which set out his educational program that had specific guidelines for book production. Within the monastic community scribes had great status. Above the scribe, was an editor who compared the copy with the original, furnished marginal notes in red ink, and supplied punctuation." ("Medieval and Renaissance Book Production: Manuscript Books," in *ORB: the Online reference Book for Medieval Studies*, Online: http:/: http://www.ukans.edu/~bookhist/medbook1.html, p. 5. Last accessed: 5/2004)

If this description of Cassiodorus' manuscript factory was at all adopted by other *scriptoria*, then this may confirm our suggestion about the incomplete production of MS 471: there was a division of scribal labor.

MS 606 (=vG "P," "Codex Parisinusi) is *Grec 2991A* of the Bibliothèque nationale de France, in Paris. It is inscribed with the date 1419. The paper codex of 495 folios is in excellent condition and measures 21.25 x 14.5 cm with 15.5 x 8.0 cm of inscribed surface in one column. The color of the paper is Pantone 12-1006 (Cream Pearl). The ink, partially faded, ranges from Pantone 17-1430 (Pecan Brown) to Pantone 16-1439 (Caramel). Titles, marginal capitals, and running heads are all Pantone 14-1318 (Coral Pink). In addition to non-biblical texts, the MS contains *Wisdom, PssSol*, and *Sirach*. The text of the PssSol is found on folios 224v–243v. In the first word in PsSol 13, the initial letter of Δεξιά is lacking, marked by a dot. There are running headers on every page (except 235v): "ψαλμοὶ σολομῶντος". At folio 228r, the original header begins: "σοφια," in red, and is written over in black: "ψαλμος," in a different hand. Diacritical marks often follow capital letters, as in MSS 471 and 606 (see above). The MS was brought from Istanbul to Paris by unknown persons in 1730.[93] The MS was collated by von Gebhardt himself in 1877.

MS 3004 is *Vossius Miscellaneous 15* of the *Bibliotheek der Rijksuniversiteit* of Leiden. It is dated from the twelfth to the sixteenth centuries. The paper codex of 83 folios measures 22.5 x 16.25 cm with 14.5 x 9.25 cm of inscribed surface in one column in the section containing the PssSol. MS 3004 Folios containing PssSol 1.1 - 17.1 are missing. The codex is in good condition, with some page edge discoloration. The color of the paper is Pantone 12-1006 (Cream Pearl) and has numerous inclusions of fine black and brown threads and particles. The text ink is Pantone 19-3903 (Shale [dark gray, short of black]). Running headers are Pantone 17-1564 (Fiesta [orange red]) as are the two "Διαψαλμα," and the initial letter of what the scribe felt was each new sentence.[94] The MS contains an extended commentary on *Canticles* and a fragment of *PssSol*. The text of the PssSol remnant is found on folios 79r–82v and preserves only PssSol 17.2b (from καὶ ἡ ἐλπίς...) to the end at 18.12. Although it appears in Rahlfs' index, it is incorrectly identified there as "Comm. in Ps. Fragm,"[95] and the text was not discovered there until 1961 when W. Baars published his collation.[96] MS 3004 forms a nineteenth psalm from PsSol 18.10–12, following the break marked by the

---

[93] Rahlfs, *Verzeichnis*, p. 213. There is a colophon on folio 446v that indicates that the codex was prepared under the patronage "τοῦ πανευγενεστάτου κυριοῦ Ματθαίου Παλαιολόγου τοῦ Λασκάρι," "Of the most noble Lord Matthew Palaiologos of the Laskaris (family)." (Ryle and James, *The Psalms of the Pharisees*, p. xx). The royal Palaiologos and the prominent Laskaris families were influential Byzantine names dating from as far back as the 11th century.

[94] These initial letters were originally written in red, and then many were overwritten in black. The black of these bi-color letters is not always a complete letter. Thus it is less likely that the letters were black, overwritten in red. The black-over-red combination color is Pantone 18-1443 (Redwood).

[95] Rahlfs, *Verzeichnis*, p. 95.

[96] W. Baars, "A New Fragment," p. 441.

"Διαψαλμα," with the title: "ψαλμος τω σαλομων ιϑ."[97] A series of corrections was made on the MS based on de la Cerda's text by a Fr. Junius.[98] The psalms are numbered, possibly by the same Fr. Junius. These corrections and emendations are not to be considered for inclusion in this critical text, but are noted as later annotations. This MS was not available to von Gebhardt.

The MSS of the 260 group are also a text group in Wisdom and in Sirach, and have been identified with the Lucianic recension.[99]

MS Group 629 (includes 629 and 769)

MS 629 (=vG "C" =Swete "c"), "Codex Casanatensis," is number 1908 of the Biblioteca Casanatense in Rome.[100] It is dated to the twelfth to the fourteenth centuries. The paper codex of 310 folios now measures 37.5 x 24 cm,[101] with 27 x 11.5 cm of inscribed surface in one column. The original folio size was, apparently, ca. 20.75 x 33.5 cm. Among many other texts, the MS contains a *catena* on the canonical *Psalter*, and the *PssSol*. The text of the PssSol is badly preserved and the folios containing 1.1 - 2.26 and 16.9 - 18.12 are missing. The remaining leaves contain only PssSol 2.27–16.8, found on folios 303r–307v.[102] Color readings of the MS show the original leaves to be Pantone 14-1213 (Toasted Almond), the ink of the text to be 17-1430 (Feather Gray), and the engrossing to be 17-1818 (Red Violet). The now darkened areas are 18-1031

---

[97] The earliest extant manuscript fragment of the PssSol, the index entry of the title in the Codex Alexandrinus, gives the count as "IH"= "18." MS 3004, alone among the MSS, has verse numbers that, however, match none of the printed editions. Because these numbers ignore the superscription for PsSol 19, and continue the numbering for Psalm 18, they are judged to be secondarily added by someone who had access to another MS (no longer extant) that had such a verse-numbering scheme, but one that did not divide Psalm 18. The verse numbering in MS 3004 also divides PsSol 17 into 51 verses (we now recognize 46) and the twelve verses of PsSol 18 into eighteen. This, of course, simply describes manuscript 3004. How earlier copies further up on the genealogical tree divided the PssSol is another question.

[98] K.A. de Meyier, *Codices Manuscripti VI Codices Vossiani Graeci et Miscellanei*, p. 254 (Leiden: Bibliotheek der Rijksuniversiteit, 1955). A marginal note at PsSol 18.6 reads: "Cerda interpretatur, regno: ⌒." The corrector also made three emendations himself (see Baars, "A New Fragment," p. 29).

[99] Ziegler, *Sapientia Salomonis*, p. 48; *Sirach*, pp. 56, 70.

[100] Rahlfs, *Verzeichnis*, p. 234.

[101] One manuscript index measured the folios at 384 x 249 mm (Francesco Bancalari, "Index codicum graecorum bibliothecae Casanatensis," in *Studi Italiani di Filologia Classica*, ed. F. le Monnier, vol. 2, pp. 161–207, ref. on 203 (Florence: Sansoni, 1894).

[102] The MS has two schemes of page-numbering: a handwritten enumeration in the upper right corners of the recto sides and a later series stamped in the lower right of the same leaves. The written numbers of the leaves containing the PssSol run from 302r to 305v. The stamped numbers are consistent with the present binding and are used here.

(Toffee).

Von Gebhardt used a collation provided to him by Johannes Tschiedel of Rome prepared against Fritzsche's edition.[103]

The MS is in poor condition, torn, stained into illegibility in many places, often with whole leaves nearly unreadable.[104] The badly worn leaves have been subjected to a restoration.[105] They have been remounted, renumbered, and the whole rebound. Modern photographic techniques allow us to now read nearly the entire text.[106] On folio 307r, a portion of its text of 14.1-14.4a is reproduced in the right margin.[107]

MS 769 (=vG "L"), Codex 5 of the Benaki Museum in Athens, is listed in Rahlfs' *Verzeichnis*[108] as number 1485 of the Great Lavra monastery on Mt. Athos.[109] It is dated to the twelfth to the fourteenth century. The paper codex is in fair but fragile condition,

---

[103] Von Gebhardt, *Psalmen Salomo's*, p. 30.

[104] According to von Gebhardt: "Viele Blätter und ganze Lagen sind verbunden, die Schrift oft durch Nässe beschädigt und unleserlich" (*Psalmen Salomo's*, p. 30).

[105] The difference between the condition of the manuscript Tschiedel consulted for von Gebhardt and that available to us today, is the result of a restoration attempted in the 1950's. The MS was sent to the monastery Abbisa di' Gottoferrofi. There the MS folios were inlayed into larger sheets that formed "frames" for the damaged pages. Chinese rice paper was applied to both sides, and the whole was compacted and varnished. The rice paper produces a haze effect that obscures detail, and the varnish has badly discolored and occluded the text on parts of every leaf, and the whole of several of the folios (f. 304r - 304v). Legibility in some places is marginally improved when viewed with ultraviolet light. The folios are out of order: folio 303 belongs in between folios 305 and 306.

[106] *The Center for the Preservation of Ancient Religious Texts* at Brigham Young University, Provo, Utah, has successfully restored most of the obscured text by using their "Multi-Spectral Imaging." The text is now 80-90% recoverable.

[107] MS 629, on folio 307r, has a marginal note that copies the same text of 14:1–4 in a different hand. The leaf of the manuscript has been torn from upper right to lower center, through the note, leaving a jagged remnant of 13 partial lines of text. The note is not mentioned by von Gebhardt (another note at 2:25 on MS 769 does elicit his comments) and so may be a later addition. There are no other known references to this note.

[108] Rahlfs, *Verzeichnis*, p. 20.

[109] According to personal correspondence dated May 17, 1972, from Marcel Richard, Chief of the Greek Section of the Institut de Recherche et d'Histoire des Texts of the Centre National de la Recherche Scientifique in Paris, the MS was stolen from the Laura monastery about the turn of the 20th century. A letter dated June 28, 1973, from E. Hadjidakis, Director of the Benaki Museum, confirms the account of the theft from Laura and adds that MS 769 was acquired by the Benaki Museum in 1931.

with frayed edges, worm or acid holes, and other damage.[110] The codex of 311 folios measures 22.0 x 18.0 cm with 18.0 x 14.5 cm of inscribed surface in a single column. The paper is Pantone 13.1010 (Gray Sand). The text ink is Pantone 19-1217 (Mustang [dark brown to black]) and the engrossing, only the title of the MS, is Pantone 18-1441(Baked Clay). The MS contains a commentary on the canonical *Psalms*, the *Odes of Solomon* with a marginal commentary on the first ode, the *PssSol*, and a commentary on *Canticles* by Cyril of Alexandria. The PssSol are found on folios 294r–304v. Von Gebhardt used a collation prepared by a Mr. Alexandros made against Hilgenfeld's text.[111] That the manuscript has been rebound since von Gebhardt's time is evident from the incomplete remnants of a note in the outside margin at 2.25 on folio 295r, a note that von Gebhardt quotes in full.[112] The leaves have been renumbered (1r to 11v) and trimmed, and the vestige of the note is now but a column, two or three characters wide. The MS was stolen from the Lavra Monastery on Mt. Athos at the turn of the twentieth century and auctioned to the Benaki museum in 1931.[113] The text uses *iota* addscripts.

MS 336

MS 336 (=vG "J"; =Swete "I") is number 555[114] of the Iveron[115] monastery of Mt. Athos. It is dated to the fourteenth century. The paper codex of 327 folios is in good condition, with only a few worm (?) holes. It measures 24.5 x 17.0 cm with 19.5 x 12.5 cm of inscribed surface. The paper is the color of Pantone 12-1006 (Cream Pearl). The text ink is Pantone 19-0000 (Raven) and the engrossing is Pantone 17-1558 (Grenadine). It contains most of *Job, Proverbs, Ecclesiastes, Canticles, Wisdom, Sirach*, the *PssSol*, and *scholia* on *Ecclesiastes, Canticles*, and *Proverbs*. The text of the PssSol is found on 227r–245v. Two leaves are missing (between folios 233 and

---

[110] When Medieval inks were improperly mixed they produced a highly acidic, or *encaustic*, ink which over the centuries has slowly burned its way through a great many manuscripts. (See: "Medieval and Renaissance Book Production: Manuscript Books," by R.W. Clementin *ORB: the Online reference Book for Medieval Studies*, at: http://www.ukans.edu/~bookhist/medbook1.html. Last accessed 6/1/04) This apparently explains some of the damage to the parchment of MS 769 where at the beginning of the PssSol the internal part of the initial "E" is missing, indeed it is a hole. One might easily attribute this damage to worms with a literary taste. But it is more likely from acidic ink that burned away the initial, engrossed letter. Thus, the black ink, that shows no such erosion was of more stable formula, and the red ink used for the decorative engrossing, was more caustic and has damaged the parchment.

[111] Von Gebhardt, *Psalmen Salomo's*, p. 29

[112] Von Gebhardt, *Psalmen Salomo's*, p. 96, note 1. It appears to be a Christian catena between this psalm and the *Book of the Revelation*.

[113] A note in French suggests: "anciennement, Lavra ⊖ 70." This was confirmed by Rita Tsakona, Librarian of the Benaki Museum, Athens.

[114] Also called "Codex Iberiticus" (Gray, *APOT*, p. 625).

[115] Also spelled "Iberon" (Rahlfs' *Verzeichnis*, p. 13, 413).

234) that contained PssSol 5.14b–8.12a.[116] The text of the PssSol ends at 18.4 (with: "...ἐν ἀγνοίᾳ") and is immediately followed, without break and in the same hand, by a unique text of Sirach 33.1–13.[117] A copy of this text of the PssSol was provided to von Gebhardt by Philipp Meyer in 1886, who had discovered it.[118] Von Gebhardt noted the end of the text of the PssSol, but neither he nor his informant recognized the following text as being of Sirach. MS 336 does not employ either *iota* subscripts or *iota* addscripts. Often the red ink of the engrossing imprints from the facing page.

MS A (Codex Alexandrinus)

This fifth century uncial codex of the Septuagint and the New Testament is the oldest direct historical evidence we have of the *Psalms of Solomon*. Although the text of the PssSol has now gone missing, the title appears in the index of the MS's contents: Ψαλμοὶ Σολομῶντος ιη. As the oldest fragment of the text of the PssSol by half a millennium, it give us the base text for the title of the collection, and an early count for the total number of poems in the collection.[119]

STEMMA

The first published *stemma* was prepared by Ryle and James[120] and showed the relationships of four manuscripts. Von Gebhardt's edition used eight,[121] and Begrich

---

[116] Rahlfs' *Verzeichnis* (p. 13) lists the lacuna as from 5.10 to 8.13. The text, in fact, ends at 5.14 with "...μετὰ χρηστότητος," and resumes at 8.12 with "καὶ ἐν ἀφέδρῳ...." Thirty-two verses are missing, approximately the equivalent of two leaves (four pages). Ink-blot impressions from the *recto* of the following sheet (beginning at 8.12b) do not appear on the *verso* of the preceding sheet (as is common elsewhere), and the ink blots appearing on the preceding sheet are different from the now-facing sheet. This means that the missing sheets were in the original MS, and that the lacuna was not a scribal omission, but that the sheets were lost before the leaves were secured in their present binding. The folios were numbered after rebinding without regard for the missing leaves. There are eight instances where the initial letter of a line of script has been omitted (3.12, 9.6, 11.7, 13.8, 13.10, 13.11, 15.0, 17.4). For reasons discussed above for MS 471, these omissions are considered to be production errors, not textual variants and thus are not included in the apparatus of this edition.

[117] Discovered in 1974 by Robert B. Wright and Robert R. Hann. See "A New Fragment of the Greek Text of Sirach," *JBL* 94:1 (1975) pp. 111–112.

[118] Von Gebhardt, *Psalmen Salomo's*, p. 28.

[119] Codex Alexandrinus is British Library Royal 1 D.v-viii. Volumes v, vi, and vii (as presently bound) contain the Old Testament, volume viii the New Testament. Originally given to the English by Cyril Lucar, at various times patriarch of Alexandria and Constantinople.

[120] Ryle and James, *The Psalms of the Pharisees*, p. xxiv.

[121] Von Gebhardt, *Psalmen Salomo's*, p. 39.

slightly modified von Gebhardt's *stemma*, adding two Syriac text traditions.[122] A thorough analysis of the characteristics and relationships of all the extant Greek manuscripts was done by Hann from which examination the following *stemma* was produced. Existing manuscripts are encased in rectangles; lost but extrapolated texts are in ovals. The intent in this edition is to reproduce, as far as is possible from the available manuscript evidence, the state of the text as represented on the *stemma* by the manuscript designated as "y," a manuscript of yet unknown date and provenance.

---

[122] J. Begrich, "Der Text der Psalmen Salomos," p. 162.

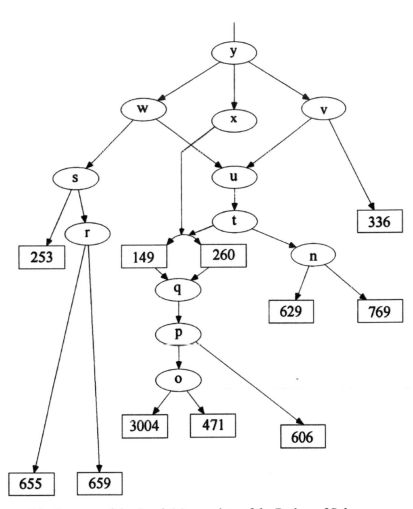

The Stemma of the Greek Manuscripts of the Psalms of Solomon

Traditional MSS Names Used in the Literature
and the Present Locations of the MSS

Rahlfs	von Gebhardt	Ryle & James	Date	Location	Library	MS #	Traditional Name
—	—	A	—	—	—		Augustanus (Augsburg)
149	V	V	10–11	Vienna	Nat. Bibliothek	Theol. Graeci 11	Vindobonensis
253	R	—	11–12	Rome	Vatican Library	Vat. Graeci 336	Romanus
260	H	K	10–11	Copenhagen	Kongelige Bibliotek	Old Royal Coll. 6	Havniensis
336	J	—	14	Mt Athos	Iveron	Iveron 555	Iberiticus
471	M	M	12–14	Moscow	State Historical Museum	Gr. Codex 147	Mosquensis
606	P	P	1419	Paris	Bibliothèque Naionale	Gk 2991A	Parisinus
629	C	—	12–14	Rome	Biblioteca Casanatense	1908	Casanatensis
655	—	—	16	Rome	Vatican Library	Ottoboniani Graeci 60	
659	—	—	16	Rome	Vatican Library	Ottoboniani Graeci 384	
769	L	—	12–14	Athens	Benaki Museum	1485 (Benaki 5)	Laura Monastery
3004	—	—	12–16	Leiden	Bibliothek der Rijksuniversiteit	Vossius Miscl. 15	

NUMBERING OF THE PSALMS OF SOLOMON

The following chart represents the differing numbering schemes of the manuscripts of the PssSol that display psalm or chapter numbers:

MSS →	149	253	260	336	606	629	769	3004
↓ Psalms								
1.	A	--	A	πρῶτος	A	--	A	
2.	B	B	B	B	B	--	B	
3.	--	Γ	--	--	--	Γ	Γ	
4.	Γ	Δ	Γ	τέταρτος	Γ	Δ	Δ	
5.	Δ	E	Δ	πέμπτος Δ		E	E	
6.	E	--	E	--	E	Ϛ	Ϛ	
7.	Ϛ	Z	Ϛ	--	Ϛ	Z	Z	
8.	Z	Θ	Z	--	Z	H	H	
9.	Θ	Θ	Θ	Θ	Θ	Θ	Θ	
10.	I	I	I	I	I	I	I	
11.	IA	IA	IA	IA	IA	IA	IA	
12.	IB	IB	IB	--	IB	IB	IB	
13.	IΓ	IΓ	IΓ	τρίτος καὶ δέκατος	IΓ	IΓ	IΓ	
14.	IΔ	IΔ	IΔ	IΔ	IΔ	IΔ	IΔ	
15.	IE	IE	IE	IE	IE	IE	IE	
16.	IϚ	IϚ	IϚ	IϚ	IϚ	IϚ	IϚ	
17.	IZ	IZ	IZ	IZ	IZ	--	IZ	
18.	IH	IH	IH	--	IH	--	IH	IH
19.	--	--	--	--	--	--	--	IΘ

Only MS 769 counts and marks all its psalms in the numbering and divisions adopted by the printed editions. No manuscript has paragraph divisions. MSS 471 (except for Psalm 3), 655, and 659 have no psalm or chapter numbers. The numbered leaves of MS 336 between 5.14b and 8.12a are missing, but the numbering is otherwise intact, suggesting the MS was originally complete. PsSol 13, lacks a number, but the correct count continues.

MS 336 numbers the first psalm "Πρῶτος," the fourth as "τέταρτος Δ," the fifth as "πέμπτος," and the thirteenth as "τρίτος καὶ δέκατος." MS 149 and 260 appear to count PssSol 2 and 3 together as number "B," with no numeric character at Psalm 3. MS 253 identifies PsSol 5 as "E," skips the count for Psalm 6, and marks PssSol 8 and 9 both as "Θ." MSS 149 and 260 employ the *stigma* "Ϛ" for Psalm 7 and MS 769 uses it for Psalm 6 (all numbered MSS use "IϚ" for Psalm 16). All the MSS pick up a common numbering at Psalm 9, "Θ." MS 253 at Psalm 10 has a small sketch of a bird where the psalm number would have appeared. The deteriorated state of MS 629 makes identifying the psalm numbers difficult, so, as suggested above, von

Gebhardt's text has been consulted where the MS is unclear. MS 3004 begins its text at 17:2b, numbers PsSol 18 as "IH," and marks its unique division of this psalm, after vs. 9 "διάψαλμα," to form PsSol 19, as "IΘ." Whether or not they have superscripts or psalm numbers, all of the manuscripts have the initial letter of each psalm capitalized, often in a color contrasting with the body text. MSS 655, 659, 769 and 3004 have only these capitalizations, with no paragraph divisions. MS 336 has enlarged marginal letters placed every two or three lines, often in mid-word, apparently solely for the sake of ornamentation.

The PssSol, like many early manuscripts, originally had no paragraph divisions. As noted above, a few of the MSS have capital letters in the left margins of the body of the psalms that may be indications of sense divisions. In the 260 group, MSS 260 and 149 have many of these internal capital letters, some fifty-one in all, occasionally with a logical connection to the sense of the text. However, in other places there appears to be little concern if the marginal letters occur in the middle of a sentence, or even in the middle of a word, a practice apparently common in manuscripts from this period. MS 471, as was observed above, has locations for many marginal letters marked, but the engrossing is incomplete. What capital letters exist, and where marks for the missing letters are discernible, the pattern follows that of MSS 260 and 149.

MS 606 has far fewer internal capital initials (sixteen) and with one exception (11.7), these are always among those to be found in MSS 260 and 149. The similarities between these manuscripts in their use of enlarged marginal letters conform with the thesis of the identity of Manuscript Group 260.

The first extant published edition of the PssSol, the 1623 text of Johannes Ludovici de la Cerda,[123] has no paragraph divisions. Without precedent in the manuscripts, all editors apparently have divided the psalms according to their understanding of the logical sense of the text. This edition has generally followed these common agreements, but occasionally has made its own judgments.

The division of verses and the numbers assigned to them in this edition are aligned with those of Rahlfs' *Septuaginta*, that itself follows von Gebhardt.[124] The earlier enumeration of de la Cerda's edition, appearing in the Syriac editions of Harris and Mingana, and later in Baars' was used by Ryle and James, and by Gray, and is found in small figures in the left margin of von Gebhardt's text. Gray's edition prints von Gebhardt's verse numbers within parentheses.

The superscriptions to the psalms are of unknown date and provenance. The

---

[123] J.L. de la Cerda, *Adversaria Sacra. Opus varium ac veluti fax ad lucem quam multorum locorum utriusque Testamenti Patrumque et Scriptorum quorumcumque: Christianæ antiquitatis et sacrorum rituum pancarpia; politioris denique litteraturæ thesaurus multiplex. Accessit eodem auctore Psalterii Salomonis ex graeco MS codice pervetusto latina versio et ad Tertulliani librum de Pallio Commentarius auctior. Produnt omnia nunc primum. Cum privelegio* (Lyon: Ludovici Prost Haeredis Roville, 1626).

[124] A. Rahlfs, *Septuaginta. Id est Vetus Testamentum graece iuxta LXX interpretes*, 2 vols (Stuttgart: Württembergische Bibelanstalt, 1962). "Psalmi Salomonis," II, pp. 471–489. "Optima editione Oscari de Gebhardt," p. 24.

orthography, even of the name "Solomon" varies within individual manuscripts[125]. These titles could have come from the Hebrew collator, or added by the Greek translator, or, more likely, added by later scribes.

At the end of several manuscripts scribes have added notes:[126]

149, 260	Ψαλμοι σολομῶντος ΙΗ ἔχουσιν ἔπη Α
253	σολομῶντος ψαλμοὶ στίχ ψν
606	ψαλμοὶ σολομῶντος δεκαοκτω ἔχουσιν ἔπη
	τριάκοντα
655 659	ψαλμοὶ στίχ ψν̄ —
769	ψαλμὸι σαλομῶντος ιη
3004	ἔχουσιν ὁ ἔπη ἀ

The phrase, τέλος σὺν θεῷ, is a codicil, perhaps even a prayer, that was often added by Höschel at the end of his manuscripts. De la Cerda copied it into his edition. This editor, with much the same feelings as these early publishers, echoes the phrase.

---

[125] For example: in MS 253 the first superscription reads: σοφια σολομωντος, whereas that of PsSol 2 is ψαλμος τω σαλωμον. In MS 149 the first superscription includes the spelling: σολομωντος, and those of PssSol 2,3 are σαλομων.

[126] See Graux, "Nouvelles recherches," p. 117.

Titles of the Collection and of the Individual Psalms:

The Hebrew version of the PssSol probably had no individual titles. These most likely were added some time later, in further imitation of the biblical Psalter. Likewise, the early Greek texts either translated the Hebrew superscriptions, or created their own. Few of the titles echo anything going on within the psalms themselves. The connection with the "Son of David," found in PssSol 17.21 probably inspired the original author or the Greek translator to caption most of the psalms as "Of Solomon." Certainly he selected the name of Solomon because of 1 Kings 4.32 where it says that Solomon composed several thousand proverbs and songs. So, Solomon's name became attached to the collection. This was part of the "cover story" for these political poems that could deflect the authorities' wrath, much as the authors of Daniel and The Revelation and other political writers hid their attacks under famous names.

We know from the biblical Psalms that many times the Hebrew preposition *lĕ-* appears ahead of a name or a title. As the preposition can mean "by," "of," "to," "in honor of," "for,"or "belonging to," the sense of the title is not always clear. The preposition *lĕ-* occurs in the expressions "to the choirmaster" or "for the leader" in 55 psalms, and in these cases it probably indicates a liturgical instruction, not authorship. In the Hebrew text, 73 psalms include in the title, *lĕ dvd* from which we get the traditional ascription of authorship: "Of David."

At the end of the 19th Century, Ugaritic tablets from Ras Shamra were discovered containing poems having the title: *le-Ba'al,* translated: "to Ba'al." This was understood as dedication, not authorship. Clearly the Canaanite deity was no lyricist. On the other hand, as Moses is traditionally credited with not only the Commandments on Sinai, but with the entire Torah, and David has been connected with the entire Psalter, so these poems have been attributed to David's Son, the Great and Wise Solomon. Certainly the author and/or editor knew these poems, describing contemporary national and world events, did not come from the king, then a thousand years distant. By attaching the King's name to these psalms he created a "Pseudepigraphon." If this was the editor's intent, we can translate the phrase: "Of Solomon."

If the editor was inconsistent with his spelling of "Solomon/Salomon" we may not be able, nor even need, to determine why. It is said that Shakespeare, in his own hand, spelled his surname fourteen different ways.[127]

---

[127] E.K. Chambers. *William Shakespeare: A Study of the Facts and Problems.* Oxford University Press, 1988.

1. Ψαλμοὶ Σολομῶντος is the title of the collection, taken from the reading of Codex Alexandrinus, the oldest extant reference to the PssSol. Three related MSS, 253, 655, and 659, have the title: Σοφία Σολομῶνος. PsSol 1 usually has no separate title however MS 336 reads: Ψαλμὸς τῶ Σαλομών πρῶτος. MS 471 has a title only for PsSol 3.

2. Ψαλμὸςτῷ Σαλομών περὶ Ἰερουσαλήμ: A Psalm of Solomon about Jerusalem.

3. Ψαλμὸς τῷ Σαλωμών περὶ δικαίων: A Psalm of Solomon about the Righteous.

4. Διαλογή τοῦ Σαλωμών τοῖς ἀνθρωπαρέσκοις: A Dialogue of Solomon with Hypocrites.

5. Ψαλμὸς τῷ Σαλωμών: A Psalm of Solomon.

6. Ἐν ἐλπίδιτῷ Σαλωμών: In Hope, Of Solomon.

7. Τῷ Σαλωμών· ἐπιστροφῆς: Of Solomon. Restoring.

8. Τῷ Σαλωμών· εἰς νῖκος: Of Solomon: On to Victory.

9. Τῷ Σαλωμών· εἰς ἔλεγχον: Of Solomon: In Proof.

10. Ἐν ὕμνοις· τῷ Σαλωμών: With Hymns: Of Solomon.

11. Τῷ Σαλωμών· εἰς προσδοκίαν: Of Solomon: In Expectation.

12. Τῷ Σαλωμών· ἐν γλώσσῃ παρανόμων: Of Solomon: about the Discourse of Those who Manipulate the Law.

13. Τῷ Σαλωμών ψαλμός· παράκλησις τῶν δικαίων: A Psalm of Solomon: Encouragement to the Righteous.

14. Ὕμνος τῷ Σαλωμών: A Hymn of Solomon.

15. Ψαλμὸς τῷ Σαλωμών μετὰ ᾠδῆς: A Psalm of Solomon with Song.

16. Ὕμνος Τῷ Σαλωμών· εἰς ἀντίληψιν ὁσίοις: A Hymn of Solomon. Protection for the Devout.

17. Ψαλμὸςτῷ Σαλωμών μετὰ ᾠδῆς· τῷ βασιλεῖ: A Psalm of Solomon, with Song, For the King.

18. Ψαλμὸς τῷ Σαλωμών· ἔτι τοῦ Χριστοῦ Κυρίου: A Psalm of Solomon: About the Lord's Messiah.

HISTORY OF SCHOLARSHIP IN THE PSALMS OF SOLOMON

The modern history of the Psalms of Solomon[128] begins sometime before 1604 when the Augsburg librarian David Höschel discovered a text of the PssSol in a manuscript that he had obtained from the Vienna library (that ostensibly had been obtained from Constantinople[129]). This was evidently our MS 149, for Höschel reportedly used it for his 1604 publication of Ecclesiastes, leaving notes in his handwriting in the margins of that MS. Höschel wrote to the Vienna library several times between 1609 and 1614 reporting on his work and telling them that he intended to make a copy of their MS of the Psalms of Solomon. Höschel ended his prodigious publication career in 1614, apparently because of ill health,[130] and offered several manuscripts to his friend and collaborator, Andreas Schott.[131] Schott reported in correspondence dated September 24, 1616, that Höschel had offered a text of Cyril of Alexandria (in which Schott was greatly interested)[132] and a "transcript copy" of Solomonic writings, including 18 Psalms of Solomon. This copy contained a "personal mark" of Höschel's, that suggested its source.[133]

This reconstruction of the complex history of the early texts of the PssSol, particularly the problem of the exemplar of de la Cerda, is based on an essay by Joseph McGovern, "The Status of MS A of the Psalms of Solomon: A Re-Examination of Von Gebhardt's Thesis."[134] In 1713, Fabricius reported that the MS that we now know as number 149 was back in the Vienna library.[135]

Some had argued that de la Cerda used a now-lost "Augsburg" manuscript as the basis for his edition of the PssSol.[136] Yet the series of catalogs of the great Augsburg

---

[128] A thorough chronicle of general scholarly references to the PssSol until the beginning of the twentieth century may be found in Viteau's *Psaumes de Salomon*, pp. 192–239.

[129] The codex was among those acquired in Constantinople by Augustus Gislain v. Busbecke in 1592 (see von Gebhardt, *Psalmen Salomo's*, pp. 1,7).

[130] See J.E. Sandys, *A History of Classical Scholarship,* Vol. II, p. 272 (Cambridge (England): Cambridge University Press, 1908).

[131] See J. van Meurs, *Operum* (vol.11), ed. by Ioannis Lami, col 249 (Florence: Regis Magni Etruriea Ducis Typis, 1763).

[132] See, also, *Operum*, cols. 248, 250–251, 253.

[133] As mentioned above, Höschel was given to add a note including the phrase: τέλος σὺν θεῷ, to his writings (von Gebhardt, *Psalmen Salomo's*, p. 8). This "trade-mark" also appears at the end of de la Cerda's text, suggesting the source of his exemplar. It does not appear on any other extant MSS of the PssSol. It appears empathetically at the end of this edition.

[134] An unpublished research report, Department of Religion, Temple University, 1989.

[135] De Meyier, *Codices Manuscripti*, p. 914.

[136] Ryle and James accepted the existence of this "Augsburg" MS and used de la Cerda's text, cited as MS "A," to argue its readings against the other MSS available to them (*The Psalms of the Pharisees*, pp. xxvii–xxxvi). Gray (*APOT*, p. 625) refers to Ryle and James' use of "A," but incorrectly refers to the source MS as "II,"

library from 1575, 1600, 1633, and 1812 contain no references to any MS of the PssSol.[137] This reconstruction by von Gebhardt and McGovern appears to resolve most of the difficulties in tracing the source of de la Cerda's exemplar. Because de la Cerda's text does not represent a tradition different from the extant manuscripts (except for his errors and idiosyncratic emendations), his variants are not included in the present edition. De la Cerda's text may be seen in the available CD of MS photographs.

Johannes Eusebius Nieremberg published PssSol 1, 18, and part of 17 with a Latin translation and a brief preface in 1641.[138] G. Janenski issued the text of PssSol 1 and 11 with the Latin text of de la Cerda in 1687.[139] In the same year Jo. Georgii Neumann edited a text in Wittenburg.[140]

Johannes Albertus Fabricius brought out an edition in 1713[141] that reproduced both de la Cerda's Greek text and his Latin translation and corrected a few of his more egregious misprints. Fabricius noted the existence of MS 149 in Vienna[142] but apparently failed to use it. He published a second edition in 1722, only slightly changed.[143] William Whiston produced the first English translation that appeared in "The Psaltery of Solomon,"[144] An anonymous German translation appeared in 1742 in the *Berlenburgische Bibel.*[145] For a century and a half, these limited editions were

---

elsewhere the designation for MS 260.

[137] J. McGovern, "The Status of MS A," p. 1.

[138] J.E. Nieremberg, "Sacrae Scripturae,"in *De Origine Sacrae Scripturae,* vol. xii, pp. 336–339 (Lyon: Sumptibus Petri Prost, 1641). He printed PssSol 1 and 18 in Greek and Latin, and PsSol 17.23–51 in Latin only.

[139] G. Janenski, *Dissertatio historico-critica de Psalterio Salomonis,* VIII, pp. 274ff.

[140] Mentioned by J.A. Fabricius, "Psalterium SALOMONIS cum Io. Ludovici de la Cerda notis & brevibus castigationibus editoris." *Codex Pseudepigraphus Veteris Testamenti, Collectus Castigatus, Testimonüsque, Censuris & Animadversionibus illustratus,* first ed, p. 915 (Hamburg and Leipzig: Christiani Liebezeit, 1713; second ed. 1722) and by Viteau, *Psaumes de Salomon,* p. 194.

[141] Fabricius, *Codex Pseudepigraphus.*

[142] Reported in Fabricius, *Codex Pseudepigraphus,* p. 914.

[143] A second edition in two volumes was published in 1722. Printing errors of the first edition were not all corrected; indeed, new errors appeared (see von Gebhardt, *Psalmen Salomo's,* p. 9).

[144] W. Whiston, "The Psaltery of Solomon," in *A Collection of Authentick Records Belonging to the Old and New Testaments,* I, pp. 117–161 (London: Printed for the Author. 1727).

[145] Berlenburgische Bibel, Section VIII, pp. 271–279 (Berlenburg: J. F. Haug, 1742); anonymous, but some have attributed it to Fabricius. See also, Viteau, *Psaumes de Salomon,* p. 242, n. 2, and Carrière, *De psalterio Salomonis.* The same translation with corrections appeared in *Auswahl der besten apocryphischen Schriften, welche noch ausser der biblischen vorhanden sind,* First Collection (Corburg: Sammlung, 1776).

the only printed texts available of the PssSol.[146]

In 1868, Adolph Hilgenfeld printed a Greek text in an article[147] and then in 1869 republished the text,[148] for both of which he used de la Cerda's edition. His second version was supplemented by readings from Haupt's collation of MS 149,[149] from Fabricius' edition, and with some conjectures of Paul de Lagarde.[150] Hilgenfeld argued that Greek, not Hebrew, was the original language of the PssSol. In 1871 there appeared two editions of the PssSol published a few months apart: by Otto

---

[146] From scattered references in the literature, one learns of other texts and translations that have appeared through the years: a German translation, reported by Viteau (*Psaumes de Salomon*, p. 242, n.1) to have been described by Fabricius (*Bibl. Graeca*. vol. XIV, 162ff) to have appeared in Leipzig in 1716, was also noticed by E. Geiger (*Psalter Salomo's*, 6). There have been at least two other French translations, one by E. Jacquier, "Les Psaumes de Salomon," in *L'Université catholique* (Lyon: n.p., 1893), Vol. XII, and another by A. Peyrollaz, "Le Psautier de Salomon" in *RTP*, Lausanne: G. Bridel, 1899), XXXII, pp. 493–511. Other German translations include one by a Dr Richard Akibon (pen name of Ludwig Noack) appeared in *Achtzehn Psalmen Salomo's welch sich in unserer Bibel nicht finden: aus einer gehaimgehaltenen Schrist in's Deutsche übertragen* (Cassel: J. C. J. Raabe, 1850), mentioned by E. Geiger (*Psalter Salomo's*, p. 6), and Viteau (*Psaumes de Salomon*, p. 242). Another allusion to a translation by S. G. Neumann in a 1687 "dissertation spéciale" is found in Migne's *Dictionaire des Apocryphes, ou Collection de tous les Livres Apocryphes relatifs à l'Ancient et au Nouveau Testament*, I, col. 940 (Paris: Barrière d'Enfer, 1856). J. Winter and A. Wünsche, *Geschichte der jüdisch-hellenistischen und talmudischen Litteratur*, first volume in the series, *Die jüdische Litteratur seit Abschluß des Kanons*, pp. 687–696 (Trèves: Mayer, 1894), published a translation of PssSol 1, 9, and 17, based on de la Cerda, Fabricius and Hilgenfeld. In this same publication Winter and Wünsche, citing Fabricius (*Codex Pseudepigraphus*), claim that the Vienna MS (149) came to Europe in 1615, a date that appears in no other source. All these, apparently, were based on de la Cerda's text. A Russian translation appeared in 1896, by A. Smirnoff: "Psalmy Solomona ö prilozenijem od Solomona.," ("The Psalms of Solomon, with an Appendix Containing the Odes of Solomon"), appeared in *Pravoslavnyj sobesjednik*. (Kazan: The Ecclesiastical/Church Academy) 1896, that, again, was based on von Gebhardt's edition.

[147] Hilgenfeld, "Himmelfahrt," pp. 133–168.

[148] Hilgenfeld, *Messias Iudaeorum*.

[149] J. Haupt, custodian at the Royal Library in Vienna, provided him with a collation of MS 149, quite inaccurate, as it appears (Hilgenfeld, "Himmelfahrt," p. 136; von Gebhardt, *Psalmen Salomo's,* p. 9).

[150] A number of the conjectural emendations made earlier by Hilgenfeld and de Lagarde were later confirmed by a comparison with MS 149 (von Gebhardt, *Psalmen Salomo's*, p. 9).

Fritzsche,[151] and by E. Geiger,[152] neither of whom had access to new manuscript material. Hilgenfeld published a German translation with notes in 1871.[153]

Julius Wellhausen added a German translation of the PssSol, with notations, as an appendix to his great *Die Pharisäer und die Sadducäer* of 1874.[154] Although he offered no new text, he did make several conjectural emendations based on his own reconstruction of what he believed to be the original Hebrew words behind the Greek text.

In 1883, Bernhard Pick produced the first widely-available edition in English.[155] His introduction and text were wholly dependent upon Hilgenfeld, E. Geiger, and Wellhausen, and the translation suffers from an imprecise knowledge of English and occasionally translates a text that is different from the one that is printed.

The first edition to use more than one manuscript was that of Ryle and James, published in 1891. They used three additional MSS: those from Copenhagen (MS 260), from Moscow (MS 471), and from Paris (MS 606). Although at first they used a copy of Haupt's faulty collation as the basis for MS 149, they later obtained a new collation.[156] The editors repeatedly made comparisons between readings of MS 149

and of what they called MS "A" (de la Cerda's text), revealing their belief in the separate identity of the so–called "Augsburg" manuscript. Their copy of MS 471 was in places defective and as von Gebhardt observed, "they rarely accepted readings not

---

[151] O.F. Fritzsche published *Libri Apocryphi Veteris Testamenti–Graece, recensuit et cum commentario critico edidit Otto Fridolinus Fritzsche. Accedunt libri veteris testamenti pseudepigraphi selecti* (Leipzig: Brockhaus, 1871). His edition of the PssSol, in an appendix (pp. 569–589), consisted of a Greek text with a short preface (p. xxv) and included readings from de la Cerda, Fabricius, Hilgenfeld, and Haupt (see p. xxv and, e.g., p. 571). He attempted to improve the Greek text by extensive conjecture.

[152] E. Geiger, *Der Psalter Salomo's*. This edition was based on de la Cerda's text and Haupt's collation of MS 149. He attempted to explain the difficulties in the extant Greek manuscripts by allusion to a presumptive Hebrew original.

[153] A. Hilgenfeld, "Die Psalmen Salomo's, deutsch übersetzt und aufs Neue untersucht," *ZWT* 14 (1871) pp. 383–418. This article, a translation with critical notes, apparently appeared as a refutation to E. Geiger's arguments in favor of a Hebrew original.

[154] Wellhausen, *Die Pharisäer und die Sadducäer*. Wellhausen prepared and intended to publish a Hebrew version that never appeared (see above). Shortly afterwards, Hilgenfeld responded with an appreciation of Wellhausen's translation and a defense of his own assertion of a Greek original, *ZWT* 17 (1874), pp. 140–142.

[155] B. Pick, "The Psalter of Solomon," *Presbyterian Review* (Oct. 1883, pp. 775–813). Whiston's was the first English translation, but it was not widely known.

[156] Ryle and James, *The Psalms of the Pharisees*, Preface, p. xcii.

based on a manuscript."[157] Ryle and James were the first to attempt to construct a *stemma*, a graphic representation of their judgments as to the relationships of the manuscripts.[158] Like E. Geiger and Wellhausen before them, Ryle and James made conjectures as to the text of a Hebrew archetype and made some comments on how certain terms would have been translated into Greek.[159] Ryle and James surmised, based on their examination of PsSol 18, that at one time the psalm may have been divided into two, forming a nineteenth psalm. Their deduction was at least partially confirmed with the discovery some decades later of MS 3004 that does, in fact, create an additional psalm by dividing PsSol 18.[160] Otto Zöckler prepared a brief introduction and a translation for his volume on the Apocrypha and Pseudepigrapha in 1891.[161]

In 1894, H. B. Swete, besides using MSS 149, 260, 471, and 606, was the first to use MS 253 from the Vatican Library, that he made the basis of his edition.[162]

The landmark edition of the PssSol by Oscar von Gebhardt that appeared in 1895 has served as the standard critical edition for more than a century. His work reduced prior editions to historical curiosities, and his text has been the basic text of reference for virtually all subsequent analyses of the PssSol. A major contribution by von Gebhardt to the study of the PssSol was the first recognition that certain manuscripts could be organized into text groups. He could do this because, first, he had access to more manuscripts than any of his predecessors. Then, having finally thrown off the weight of the *textus receptus* status accorded de la Cerda's *editio princeps* by so many prior editors, von Gebhardt was free to consider the relationships of the manuscripts themselves. Beyond the discovery of the virtual identity of MSS 149 and 260,[163] his comparative study of the MSS readings revealed a discrete and identifiable text group

---

[157] Von Gebhardt, *Psalmen Salomo's*, p. 10.

[158] Ryle and James, *Psalms of the Pharisees,* p. xxiv.

[159] Ryle and James, *Psalms of the Pharisees,* pp. lxxvii–lxxxvii.

[160] Ryle and James, *Psalms of the Pharisees*, pp. 174 f. See Baars, "A New Fragment" pp. 441–444. As no other MS divides the eighteenth psalm, and as the fifth-century citation in the index of the Codex Alexandrinus describes them as "18 Psalms of Solomon," it is more likely that this division is the result of later editorial creativity than original authorial intent.

[161] Zöckler, "Die pseudepigraphische Lyrik," I.9, pp. 405–420.

[162] H.B. Swete, *The Old Testament in Greek according to the Septuagint*, Greek text: III, pp. xvi–xvii, 765–787; "Introduction": IV, pp. 225, 282–283 (Cambridge, England: Cambridge University Press, 1894). Swete was disinclined toward conjectural emendation and, according to von Gebhardt's count, employs it on only three occasions (von Gebhardt, *Psalmen Salomo's,* p. 12).

[163] These two MSS are word-for-word identical, except for the difference at 16.13 where each has been revised, then corrected back. See Hann's useful analysis (*Manuscript History*, pp. 63f). Von Gebhardt determined that the two MSS were made by the same scribe, one after the other, but that MS 260 was slightly the older of the two (*Psalmen Solomo's*, p. 23).

composed of MSS 149, 260, 471 and 606.[164] Further, von Gebhardt concluded that MS 253 has preserved the greatest proportion of the earliest readings, as that text exhibits grammatical peculiarities characteristic of the oldest and best biblical manuscripts.[165] From these analyses he produced a *stemma* that displayed the relationships between the manuscripts and their relative chronology. So convinced was von Gebhardt of the coherence of these text groups that in his collation he allowed MS 260, for example, to represent the readings of the group 149–260–471–606, and, unfortunately, often omitted unique readings of what were, for him, dependent manuscripts.

In 1896 W. Frankenberg prepared a reconstruction of what aHebrew text might have looked like.[166] Swete's second English edition in 1899 added the new MSS included by von Gebhardt: MS 336, 629, and 769.[167] Emil Kautzsch published a translation by R. Kittel with introduction and notes in 1900.[168] A brief (56-page) study by Felix Perles appeared in 1902 that compared some verses in the back-translations of Delitzsch and Frankenberg.[169] Jacob Ecker published a Greek text, with translation and notes in 1903.[170] Johannes Lindblom published his doctoral thesis in 1909[171] that included a Swedish translation. All these were dependent to some degree upon von Gebhardt.

In 1909 J. Rendel Harris brought out the first Syriac edition, one based on a single MS (a second edition, with a photographic reproduction of the Syriac MS, appeared n 1911).[172] In 1916 (volume two in 1920), with Alphonse Mingana, he published a

---

[164] Von Gebhardt, *Psalmen Salomo's,* pp. 14–15, 20–25.

[165] Von Gebhardt, *Psalmen Salomo's*, pp. 30–32.

[166] Frankenberg, *Datierung*.

[167] H.B. Swete, *"The Psalms of Solomon with the Greek Fragments of the Book of Enoch* (Cambridge, England: Cambridge University Press, 1899).

[168] R. Kittel, "Die Psalmen Salomos," in E.F. Kautzsch, *Die Apocryphen und Pseudepigraphen des Alten Testaments*, II, pp. 127–148 (Tübingen: J. C. B. Mohr, 1900).

[169] F. Perles, *Zur Erklärung der Psalmen Salomos*, Sonderabzug aus der Orientalistischen Literatur-Zeitung, no. 5 (Berlin: Wolf Peiser, 1902).

[170] J. Ecker, *Porta Sion: Lexikon zum lateinischen Psalter (Psalterium Gallicanum) unter genauer Vergleichung der Septuaginta und des hebräischen Textes: mit einer Einleitung über die hebr.-griech.-latein. Psalmen und dem Anhang der apokryphe Psalter Salomons* (Trier/Treves: Paulinus-Druckerei, 1903). The PssSol is in cols. 1874–1931. , (Christian) B.

[171] (Christian) Johannes B. Lindblom, *Senjudiskt Fromhetslif Enligt Salomos Psaltare* , p. 206 (Uppsala: Almqvist & Wiksells, 1909). He reproduced von Gebhardt's Greek text, without critical notes, and it was accompanied by a translation and a theological analysis of the psalms within the context of Jewish messianic expectation.

[172] Harris, *The Odes and Psalms of Solomon*.

Syriac edition based on three MSS.[173]

J. Viteau published an edition in 1911. which besides a Greek text and a French translation, included significant variants from a Syriac edition.[174] He constructed a detailed chronology of all references to the PssSol in scholarly literature to that time.

In the 1912 publication of R. H. Charles' monumental *Apocrypha and Pseudepigrapha of the Old Testament*, one can find G. B. Gray's introduction, translation and notes to the PssSol. This has remained for nearly a century the standard English resource for the PssSol.[175]

Paul Reißler published a German translation in *Altjüdisches Schriftum außerhalb der Bibel* (Augsburg, 1928) 881–902, 1323–1324.

The PssSol are found in Rahlfs' *Septuaginta* in Vol. II, 471–489, edited in 1935. In 1937 K. G. Kuhn, in his *Die älteste Textgestalt der Psalmen Salomos*, argued that the Syriac version of the PssSol is a direct translation from a Hebrew original, not dependent on any Greek text.[176] J. Begrich attempted to counter Kuhn in 1939 when he argued that the Syriac version and Greek MS 253 are both derived from a common Greek textual source.[177]

In 1955, W. Pesch compared PsSol 11 with Baruch 5 and concluded that the PssSol was dependent upon exilic motifs found in Baruch.[178] W. Baars published in 1961 his collation of MS 3004 that contains PssSol 17.2–18.12.[179]

In 1965, Marinus de Jonge prepared an examination of the eschatology of the PssSol that included notes on several variant readings.[180]

In 1975, Robert Wright and Robert Hann published in a critical note a collation of a newly recognized fragment of the Greek text of Sirach that follows PsSol 18.5 in

---

[173] J.R. Harris and and A. Mingana. *The Odes and Psalms of Solomon, re-edited for the Governors of the John Rylands Library. Vol. I, The Text with Facsimile Reproductions* (Manchester: University Press; London; New York: Longmans, Green & Co., 1916); Vol. II, *Translation with Introduction and Notes* (Manchester, England: Manchester University Press; London/New York: Longmans, Green & Co., 1920).

[174] Viteau, *Psaumes de Salomon.*

[175] Gray, George Buchanan, "The Psalms of Solomon," *APOT*, ed. R. A. Charles II pp. 625–652 (Oxford: Clarendon, 1912).

[176] Kuhn, *Die älteste Textgestalt* .

[177] Begrich, "Der Text der Psalmen Salomos." This study included a *stemma* of the relationship between the Greek and the Syriac text traditions (p. 139).

[178] Pesch, "Die Abhängigkeit ," pp. 251–263.

[179] Baars, "A New Fragment."

[180] M. de Jonge, *De Toekomstverwachting in de Psalmen van Salomo* (Leiden: Brill, 1965). Reappeared as "The Expectation of the Future in the Psalms of Solomon," in *Neotestamentica* 23.1 (1989), pp. 93–117; and in *Jewish Eschatology, Early Christology and the Testaments of the Twelve Patriarchs: Collected Essays of Marinus de Jonge* (Leiden: E. J. Brill, 1991).

MS 336.[181] Svend Holm-Nielsen published a German translation of the PssSol with notes in 1977,[182] and in the same year J. Schüpphaus issued a revision of his doctoral dissertation on the theology of the PssSol.[183] An extensive general introduction in Polish appeared in 1979 in *Studia Theologica Varsaviensia* by Andrzej Suski[184] M. de Goeij translated Gray's English text into Dutch in 1980.[185]

In 1982, Robert Hann published *The Manuscript History of the Psalms of Solomon*, an exhaustive analysis of the Greek texts and their relationships.[186] Antonio Piñero Sáenz,[187] prepared a Spanish translation in the same year.

Sebastian P. Brock published an English translation in 1984,[188] and P. Prigent did a French rendering in 1987.[189] Joseph Trafton prepared a comparative study of the Syriac and Greek versions in 1985. He suggested that if the Syriac cannot yet be shown to preserve an independent and prior witness to the text of the PssSol, at least in many places the Syriac provides readings that are more suggesting of a Hebrew *Vorlage* than is the Greek text. Therefore, he concluded, the Syriac is an important witness to the text history of the PssSol.[190] In 1985, Robert B. Wright contributed an introduction, translation, and notes of the PssSol to the second volume of James H. Charlesworth's *The Old Testament Pseudepigrapha*.[191] During the same year, M. de Jonge brought out an introduction and translation in the Cambridge (England) Commentaries series.[192] Joseph Trafton contributed the article on "Psalms of Solomon" to the *Anchor Bible Dictionary*, ed. David Noel Freedman. VI, pp. 115–117 (New York: Doubleday, 1992). An article by Robert B. Wright on "Solomon, Psalms

---

[181] Wright and Hann, "A New Fragment."

[182] S.Holm-Nielsen, "Die Psalmen Salomos," *Poetische Schriften,* in *JSHRZ,* vol. IV, pt. 2 (Gütersloh: Mohn, 1977), pp. 51–112.

[183] J. Schüpphaus, *Die Psalmen Salomons.*

[184] Andrsej Suski, "Wprowadzenie do psalmów Salomona," *Studia Theologica Varsaviensia,* Vol. 17, No. 1 (1979), pp. 187–244.

[185] M. de Goeij, "Psalmen van Salomo," *De Pseudepigrafen,* pp. 16–42. (Kampen: J. H. Kok, 1980).

[186] Hann, *The Manuscript History.*

[187] A.P. Sáenz, "Salmos de Salomón." in A.D. Macho, M. Angeles Navarro, and A. de la Fuente. *Apoócrifos del Antiguo Testamento,*Vol. 3 (1982), pp. 9–57 (Madrid: Cristiandad, 1982–1987).

[188] S.P. Brock, "The Psalms of Solomon.," in *The Apocryphal Old Testament,* ed. H. F. D. Sparks,649–682 (Oxford: Clarendon, 1984).

[189] P. Prigent, "Psaumes de Salomon," in A. Dupont-Sommer & M. Philonenco, *La Bible: Écrits Intertestamentaires,* pp. 945–952 (Paris: Gallimard, 1987).

[190] Trafton, *The Syriac Version,* p. 218.

[191] Wright, "The Psalms of Solomon," pp. 639–670.

[192] M. de Jonge, "The Psalms of Solomon" in *Outside the Old Testament,* pp. 159–177 (Cambridge (England) University Press: Cambridge Commentaries on Writings of the Jewish and Christian World 200 BC to AD 200, 1985).

of" appeared in *Eerdmans Dictionary of the Bible.*[193].

Kenneth Atkinson has published several books and articles on the Psalms of Solomon:

"Herod the Great, Sosius, and the Siege of Jerusalem (37 B.C.E.) In Psalm of Solomon 17," *NovT* 38 (1996): pp. 313-322.

"Toward a Redating of the Psalms of Solomon: Implications for Understanding the *Sitz im Leben* of an Unknown Jewish Sect." JSOP 17 (1998); 95-112.

"On the Herodian Origin of Militant Davidic Messianism at Qumran: New Light from Psalm of Solomon 17." *JBL* 118 (1999): 435-460

"On the use of Scripture in the Development of Militant Davidic Messianism at Qumran: New Light from *Psalm of Solomon* 17," in Craig A. Evans, ed. *The Interpretation of Scripture in Early Judaism and Christianity.*(Studies in Scripture in Early Judaism and Christianity 7, 106-123. Sheffield, England: Sheffield Academic Press Ltd., 2000.)

An Intertextual Study of the Psalms of Solomon Pseudepigrapha Lewiston, NY: The Edwin Mellen Press, 2001

I Cried to the Lord: A Study of the Psalms of Solomon's Historical Background and Social Setting. (Leiden: Brill, 2003)

"Theodicy in the Psalms of Solomon." In Handbook of Theodicy in the World of the Bible, A. Laato and J.C. de Moor, eds. (Leiden: E. J. Brill, 2003)

"4QMMT and Psalms of Solomon 8: Two Anti-Sadducean Documents?" *The Qumran Chronicle 11* (2003).

---

[193] *Eerdmans Dictionary of the Bible*, ed. David Noel Freeman, pp. 1239-1240 (Grand Rapics: Eerdmans, 2000).

DOCTORAL DISSERTATIONS IN RECENT YEARS
CONCERNING THE PSALMS OF SOLOMON:

Hann, Robert. "A Prologomenon to a Critical Edition of the Psalms of Solomon." Temple University, 1980.

Trafton, Joseph, "A Critical Evaluation of the Syriac Version of the Psalms of Solomon," Duke University, 1981.

Donald L. Scott, "The Role of Remembrance in The Psalms of Solomon." Chicago Theological Seminary, 1995 (R.B.Wright, External Examiner).

Ward, Grant. "A Philological Analysis of the Greek and Syriac Texts of the Psalms of Solomon." Temple University, 1995.

Blackburn, Rollin J. "Hebrew Poetic Devices in the Greek Text of the Psalms of Solomon." Temple University, 1998.

Atkinson, Kenneth. "Toward a Redating of the Psalms of Solomon: Implications for Understanding the Sitz im Leben of an Unknown Jewish Sect." Philadelphia: Temple University, 1999.

Deborah J. Spink, "A City-Lament Genre in the Psalms of Solomon." Philadelphia: Temple University, 2001.

DIFFERENCES BETWEEN THIS EDITION
AND PREVIOUS EDITIONS

To prepare an edition of the Psalms of Solomon presents a major difficulty in contrast to a standard critical edition of an ancient text. If the original Hebrew text, and its translation into Greek, were composed and edited at the end of the last century BCE (with the Syriac at some later date), and if eleven of the extant Greek manuscripts of the text date from the tenth to the sixteenth centuries C.E., then there is a millennium and two translations between the composition of the PssSol and the available manuscripts. Undoubtedly there are many intermediate manuscripts missing from the chain of transmission. This makes one very cautious about claiming that one can reconstruct the text as it came from the pen of the Greek translator about the turn-of-the-era, much less from the Hebrew writer(s).

What appears to be a more reasonable goal, is not to attempt the usual "critical edition" of a supposed Greek translational autograph, but to work as far back as one can from the text of the extant Greek manuscripts to an intermediary state of the text that best explains the readings contained in our manuscripts. This means that conjectural emendations are not as valuable at this stage, and that it is vital that all readings, even those that we can know with some assurance to be scribal errors, need to be included. Therefore, the goal of this project is a reconstruction of this intermediate, if presumptive, stage of the text transmission, a transcript of yet unknown date and provenance. With later publications of commentary, analysis, and essays, scholars then will be able to compile the evidence from the Syriac and Greek texts, make reasoned conjectures as to how the earliest Greek text might have appeared and to analyze their implications for a Hebrew *Vorlage*.

This edition differs from those preceding it in five respects: availability of new MSS, completeness of the collation by including all variant readings from all of the MSS (and removing all previous conjectural emendations and introducing no new ones),[194] inclusion of significant variants from the Syriac MSS, improved accuracy of the collation by employing technological advances in the editing process, and the simple fact that this editor has personally compared this collation with all twelve of the extant Greek manuscripts.

Von Gebhardt had access to eight MSS, only four of them that he had examined himself (149, 253, 471, and 606). In these four texts the editing is of high quality with few transcriptional errors. Where von Gebhardt was supplied collations by others (MSS 260, 336, 629, and 769), transcriptional irregularities are much more numerous. Since von Gebhardt's edition in 1895, three new manuscripts have appeared that were not available to him: two MSS, 655 and 659, indeed, appear in Rahlfs' 1914 *Verzeichni+s* that were found concealed under the title Σοφία Σολομῶντος.[195] In

---

[194] For information, important conjectural emendations of the major editions are included in bracketed notes.

[195] Rahlfs, *Verzeichnis*, pp. 240, 241. A formula of the ratio of the relative lengths of *Wisdom of Solomon* and *Psalms of Solomon* was used to search for other possible mistitled texts. None further were located.

1961, W. Baars announced the discovery of MS 3004.[196] These have all been included in this edition.

Von Gebhardt, as was observed above, employed the practice of using what he judged to be the senior member of a manuscript group to represent the entire group. For example, in using the text of 260 to represent the readings of MSS 149, 471, and 606, he included references to these latter manuscripts only occasionally, and not even where the variants departed from MS 260. Von Gebhardt was probably correct in concluding that MS 260 (or its near twin, 149) is the direct ancestor of the other members of its group. However, if one needed the manuscript evidence to test the *stemma* or to propose a new one, or if new analytical techniques were developed to study the text and its variants, such an incomplete collation would then be deficient. To use an analog from archaeology, today excavators preserve as much of the primary data as possible, even if they are uncertain of its interpretation, so that subsequent scholars may prepare their own historical reconstructions. With the exceptions noted below, this edition is the first to include the full readings of all twelve known extant manuscripts.

The methods employed in the editing of this edition follow established text-critical principles. The *stemma* proposed by Hann[197] is based on a new analysis of the relationships of all the readings of the twelve known Greek manuscripts. This analysis was supported by an application of the so-called "Claremont Profile Method" for the classification of minuscule manuscripts.[198] Using the Claremont method to confirm the basic manuscript groups, Hann analyzed the textual characteristics of the individual witnesses and of their text types and then examined the relationships among the manuscripts and between the groups.[199] From this the history of the textual transmission was reconstructed. The result is a *stemma* reassuringly similar to that of von Gebhardt,[200] but with the additional MSS included.

In the preparation of this edition, the method began with external criteria and moved to internal, and only readings that satisfied the requirements of both were considered closest to the intermediate "original" that we are seeking. Readings that were genealogically blocked in their path to our archetype could not be original. External criteria were always considered superior to internal, and the latter were governed by the principle of giving weight to the reading that best explains the origin of the other readings. Both Intrinsic Probability and Transcriptional Probability were considered in each case, along with Internal Evidence of Documents, of Groups, and of Readings. In a few cases, a reading that is today considered lexically impossible is

---

[196] Baars, "A New Fragment," pp. 441–444.

[197] Hann, *The Manuscript History.* See chap 6, pp. 97–114.

[198] The latest detailed expositions of the Claremont Profile Method are found in F.W. Wisse, *The Profile Method for the Classification and Evaluation of Manuscript Evidence as Applied to the Continuous Greek Text of the Gospel of Luke*, Studies and Documents, no. 44 (Grand Rapids: Eerdmans, 1982), and in E.J. Epp, "The Claremont Profile Method," pp. 211–220.

[199] Hann, *The Manuscript History*, chaps. 4 and 5, pp 53–95.

[200] *Die Psalmen Salomo's*, p. 39.

included in the base text, because it is the reading that best explains the origin of the other MSS readings.[201] None of the other readings, if adopted as the base text, could explain the readings of the remaining manuscripts. One cannot assume the inerrancy of an original extrabiblical text (no matter what one's theology) nor can one assume a form is impossible because it cannot be found in modern lexica. What results is a reconstruction that displays the characteristics of what a text closer to the original translational autograph might have looked like. With this reconstruction comes the caveat that none of our complete extant manuscripts is nearer than nine hundred years to what the psalmist(s) penned or to what the Greek translator rendered, and most are more than a millennium away. Given this situation, resort was never made to conjectural emendations, tempting though they are.

This present edition includes comparisons with the Syriac MSS at places where there are significant differences from the Greek readings or where the Syriac agrees with one or more of the Greek text families, against others. As there is an excellent critical edition of the Syriac MSS available,[202] there is no attempt here to judge between variant readings of the Syriac witnesses. The Syriac evidence normally appears at the end of a line of variants, except where it is close to one of the Greek readings, in which case it follows that Greek variant, linked with an equal sign (=).

From what can be determined, von Gebhardt did not use photographic reproductions of MSS but relied on hand collations from the manuscripts obtained from colleagues or made by himself. Without the possibility of cross-checking against photographs, he was dependent upon the skill of the collator and would have had difficulty corroborating even his own work. Von Gebhard saw only four manuscripts himself.

This edition initially worked from microfilm photographs generously supplied by the archives that preserve the manuscripts. At the final stage, this editor, during a seven-week research trip during the summer of 1999, personally visited each of the libraries, museums, and monasteries, and compared every variant of this collation with the manuscripts themselves. The editor also re-measured the manuscripts, and took

---

[201] See, for example, 15.5, where the base text reads, ἐλογήσωμαι, a form that is lexically impossible. Clearly, this was of considerable difficulty to the scribes, as the MSS offer five different readings to correct the perceived problem. As none of the other MS readings, if adopted as the base text, could easily produce the other readings, this "impossible" reading is adopted as the reading "that best explains the origin of the other readings." See also, διηρπάζωσαν, at 8.11 and κληρονομίσαισαν, at 8.6. Bruce Metzger, discussing Karl Lachmann's 1842-50 critical edition of the Greek New Testament, observes: "It was not always appreciated that Lachmann did not pretend to print the original text of the New Testament, but only a provisional one, namely that current in the fourth century, including even palpable scribal errors if sufficiently well attested." (*The Text of the New Testament*, 1963, p. 125). Likewise, Metzger observes: "It must not be overlooked, however, that though some anomalies are the result of corruption in the transmission of the text, other anomalies may have been either intended or tolerated by the author himself." (Text..., p. 182). See also "The Critic Correcting the Author," *Philologus*, 99 (1955), pp. 295-303).

[202] Baars, "Psalms of Solomon."

color readings of the parchment or paper and the inks against the Pantone® Professional Color System,[203] the color standard in the graphic arts. New color photographs were obtained or made by this editor and edited into a CD ROM containing all 350 leaves of the Greek and Syriac MSS. Copies of the CD are available. See the notice at the end of this volume.

Computer technology certainly introduces the possibility of its own errors, but it does allow the rapid manipulation and reproduction of text while reducing the opportunity for the insidious introduction of new errors at each occasion of transcription.

This collation was begun with the electronic text of Rahlfs' *Septuaginta*, as provided by the CCAT[204] archive, from which were removed von Gebhardt's and Rahlfs' conjectural emendations. The variants from all twelve manuscripts were added, maintaining the CCAT "Word Variant" data file serial format. To proofread the edited text, a program was run against the master data file that created an electronic reconstruction of what the text of each manuscript should contain.[205] These reconstructions were then proofread using a speech synthesizer to read the electronically reconstructed texts in Greek, character-by-character, against photographs of each manuscript. With a unique program,[206] the serial data files, still in the CCAT format, were then configured into pages and the variants into footnotes. The pages were then ported into a word processing program that arranged the text and footnotes into the appropriate margins and headings. The footnote numbers, both in the text and in the footnotes, that normally appear in word-processing programs, were hidden as part of the formatting to conform to the standard page layout for a critical text. The pages were again twice proofread against the manuscript photographs. Finally, as mentioned above, all variants were personally verified by this editor against each of the original manuscripts.

Thus, this edition differs from previous ones by the inclusion of all twelve known extant manuscripts, and of all of the variants from these MSS, by the addition of significant variants from the Syriac witnesses, and by what is hoped to be a greater reliability in the manipulation of the text in its preparation. The Greek punctuation follows MS 253.

---

[203] Copyright by Pantone, Inc., 1990. L. Eiseman and L. Herbert, *The Pantone Book of Color* (New York: Harry N. Abrams, 1990).

[204] The Center for Computer Assisted Texts at the University of Pennsylvania, Robert A. Kraft, Director. The CCAT text originated at the *Thesaurus Linguae Graecae* electronic archive of ancient Greek texts housed at the University of California at Irvine. This text of the LXX was taken from the *Septuagint* edited by Alfred Rahlfs that, for the Psalms of Solomon, was based in turn on von Gebhardt's edition (see Rahlfs' *Septuagint,* II, p. 471, note) and included his conjectural emendations, that were subsequently removed. Important conjectural emendations are mentioned in the notes, but never appear in the base text.

[205] An adaptation of the CCAT program "RECON," prepared by Lester Dean, a graduate student in Temple University's Religion Department.

[206] Written by Dean.

To facilitate the final comparison of the collated text with the extant manuscripts, several of the graduate students acknowledged in the "Preface" above, assisted in the preparation of twelve booklets, each representing the text of one of the manuscripts. These booklets matched the MS folios, page-for-page and line-for-line. With them any word in any manuscript photograph could be located quickly in the printed text. These booklets are included in the CD containing the photographs.

The translation, found on the pages opposite to the Greek text, presents a rendering of the psalms into contemporary English that attempts to preserve an accurate representation of the meaning of the Greek: The English is intended be no more, but also, no less, ambiguous than the Greek. Where the author appears to be ambiguous, the attempt was made to preserve these sometimes enigmatic ideas. Likewise, care was taken not to use terms that would introduce later, often anachronistic concepts, and to assure that the terms used were at home in the ethos at the Turn of the Era.

This is a translation of the extant Greek text. There have been recent studies demonstrating that in many places the Greek has misunderstood or mistranslated a Semitic term that may have underlaid our text. Or, that the Syriac may have preserved a clearer or even preferable rendering of that Hebrew *vorlage*.[207] In many places these arguments are cogent and even persuasive. In further studies, many of these arguments could be developed to give us a better understanding what transpired before the Greek text appeared. But this is an edition of the extant Greek texts, not a reconstruction of a presumed Hebrew *Urtext*.

A word about the translation of "Lord Messiah."[208] The phrase, a rendering of the Greek χριστὸς κύριος, is a title for the expected messianic king first appearing in PsSol 17.32.[209] Most commentators have emended the text to read: Χριστὸς Κύριου, "The Lord's Messiah," regarding it as a mistranslation (with the LXX of Lam 4.20) of an original, common Hebrew expression, "Yahweh's Anointed."[210] However, there is evidence for retaining the readings of the text:

The Greek and Syriac MSS are uniform in reading "Lord Messiah." There is no manuscript evidence for a reading of χριστὸς κύριου a common expression in the LXX. The arguments that χριστὸς κύριος cannot represent the original text rest on the assumptions that: (1) the Semitic original was a form of מְשִׁיחַ יְהוָה and, (2) that

---

[205] Ward, Grant, *A Philological Analysis of the Greek and Syriac Texts of the Psalms of Solomon* (Philadelphia: Temple University Department of Religion doctoral dissertation, 1995. See also, Joseph L. Trafton, *The Syriac Version of the Psalms of Solomon: A Critical Evaluation,* ABLSCS no. 11, (Atlanta, GA: Scholars Press/Society of Biblical Literature, 1985).

[208] On Messianism in the Psalms of Solomon, see Atkinson, *I Cried to the Lord,* chapter 4, p. 129ff and also, "On the Herodian Origin of Militant Davidic Messianism at Qumran: New Light from Psalm of Solomon 17." *JBL* 118 (1999): 435-460.

[209] A different form, Χριστοῦ Κύριου, not the emendation often suggested , appears in 18.sup., and 18.7. Here, with two genitives together, it could indeed be rendered: "of the Lord's Anointed." But this is a grammatically different construction.

[210] See: K. Atkinson, *I Cried to the Lord,* p. 131-132, fn 2 where he defends the emmendation., and provides an extensive bibliographic survey of the question.

phrase, in the mouth (or from the pen) of a Judean Jew, could only have meant "the Lord's Messiah."

Against these assumptions are the following: (1) Lk 2.11 demonstrates that χριστὸς κύριος was available for use as a messianic title by the first century C.E. (2) Luke brings the two titles in proximity in Peter's sermon in Acts 2.36 where he declares that "God has made him (Jesus) both Lord and Messiah." (3) There are references in which κύριος is not a translation of יהוה but part of a royal title: Herod the Great and Herod Agrippa were both called βασιλεύς κύριος, "Lord King."[211]

As the adjectival use of κύριος also could have had the connotation "legitimate," it is not inconceivable that a group of religious and political dissidents, such as those behind the PssSol, would have described the anticipated righteous messiah-king by that adjective and with the phrase χριστὸς κύριος, so to deny legitimacy to the present corrupt rulers.[212]

The assumption that χριστὸς κύριος was an impossible combination to flow from the pen of a devout Judean Jew is to read χριστὸς in terms of its meaning for later Christology and not in terms of its use as a political title in its own time. Certainly the related title "King Messiah" was known to the later Jewish tradition. It is attested in GenR 2:4 and applied in LamR 2:4 to Simon bar Kokhba. When Rabbi Akiba saw Simon bar Kokhba, it is reported that he said: "This is the King Messiah!"[213]

CRITICAL MARKS

x^n	numbered occurrence of a word in a verse.
abrv	judged to be an abbreviation, not a variant.
om	omitted.
+	added.
ditt	dittography.
~	transposition in word order or Greek ellipsis mark.
pr	preceded by....

---

[211] See R.R. Hann, "Christos Kyrios in PsSOL 17.32: 'The Lord's Anointed' Reconsidered," NTS, 31 (1985), pp. 620-627.

[212] See: "legitimate, regular, proper," in Aeschylus. Ed. A. Sidgwick, Oxford (OCT). Scholia, Ed. W. Dindorf in Editione Aeschyli, Oxford 1851. Scholia in Aeschyli Persas, Ed. O. Dähnhardt, Leipzig (T.) 1894; the Oxford Greek Lexicon, H. G. Liddell, 1888.

[213] J. Taanit 4:68d. See also Y. Yadin, Bar-Kokhba (London: Weidenfeld and Nicholson, 1971) and J.A. Fitzmyer and D.J. Harrington, A Manual of Palestinian Aramaic Texts, pp. 158-163 (Rome: Biblical Institute Press, 1978). Other Talmudic references include: Gen 3.15 (Pseudo-Jonathan): "They are destined to make peace at the end, in the days of King Messiah;" Gen 35.21 (Ps.-J): "And Jacob moved on, and pitched his tent onward to the tower of Eder, the place whence the King Messiah is destined to reveal himself at the end of days;" Gen 49.1 (Ps.-J): "As soon as the date of the End when the King Messiah would arrive was revealed to him..." S.H. Levey, The Messiah: An Aramaic Interpretation, Monograph of the Hebrew Union College 2: Cincinnati: 1974.--cited with chart at NWNTI:108.]

inc	incomplete production omission.
m	marked by a later scribe usually with two or three dots indicating he suspected an error in the text.
c	correction by a scribe, original or later, differing from base text.
c^n	numbered occurrence of a correction.
c=Cerda	correction to de la Cerda by Fr. Junius in MS 3004. See p. 25.
e or eee	erasure by an editor, apparently as a correction.
marg	marginal correction or note, either in margin, or between lines.
sup	superscription.
*	original reading, a variant, corrected to our base text by scribe or a later editor.
...	lacuna: MS damaged and text not now present.
?	text present, but uncertain.
[ ]	text omitted or missing, usually the end of a word.
~~xxx~~	text stricken out or lined out.
=Syr	a Syriac reading matches a Greek variant.
{Ra}	conjectural emendation from Rahlfs' *LXX* edition.
{vG}	conjectural emendation from von Gebhardt's edition.
{Hilg}	conjectural emendation from Hilgenfeld's edition.

MSS groups are shown within parentheses, e.g: 260 (149 471 606). Variants are not normally accented. Thus, MSS readings differing only in diacriticals are not regarded as variants, and do not appear in the apparatus. However, where the accents appear to be of some significance in a MS reading, they are included.

Manuscripts often display "corrections," letters added above or below the text, especially at the ends of lines. In most cases it is difficult to determine if this was an intentional notation by the original scribe, an error that he[214] noticed and immediately corrected, a rectification by his overseer, or an emendation by a later scribe. Unless the modification is clearly made with a different ink, a distinguishable hand, or other unmistakable marker of a subsequent scribal amendment, these "corrections" are regarded as part of the original scribe's work, and not considered as subsequent critical variants.

List of Abbreviations of Periodicals, Reference Works and Serials

ABD	*Anchor Bible Dictionary*
ALGHJ	*Arbeiten zur Literatur und Geschichte des hellenistischen Judentums*
APOT	*The Apocrypha and Pseudepigrapha of the Old Testment. Ed. R. H. Charles. 2 vols. Oxford, 1913.*
APOT	*Apocrypha and Pseudepigrapha of the Old Testament*
BWANT	*Beiträte zur Wissenschaft vom Alten und Neuen Testament*

---

[214] As far as can be determined, there is no evidence that any of the scribes who labored over these manuscripts was a woman.

BWANT	*Beiträge zur Wissenschaft vom Alten und Neuen Testament*
BZAW	*Beihefte zur Zeitschrift für neutestamentliche Wissenschaft*
BZAW	*Beihefte zur Zeitschrift für die altestamentliche Wissenschaft*
CBQ	*Catholic Biblical Quarterly*
CBQ	*Catholic Biblical Quarterly*
CRINT	*Compendia rerum iudaicarum ad Novum Testamentum*
DBSup	*Dictionaire de la Bible: Supplément. Ed L. Pirot and A. Robert. Paris, 1928-.*
DBSup	*Dictionnaire de la Bible, Supplément*
IDB	*Interpreter's Dictionary of the Bible*
IDB	*Interpreters Dictionary of the Bible*
JBL	*Journal of Biblical Literature*
JBL	*Journal of Biblical Literature*
JJS	*Journal of Jewish Studies*
JQR	*Jewish Quarterly Review*
JSHRZ	*Jüdische Schriften aus hellenistisch-römischer Zeit*
JSHRZ	*Jüdische Schriften aus hellenistisch-römischer Zeit*
JSJ	*Journal for the Study of Judaism in the Persian, Hellenistic, and Roman Periods*
JSOP	*Journal for the Study of the Pseudepigrapha*
JSOPSS	*Journal for the Study of the Pseudepigrapha Supplement Series*
JSS	*Journal of Semitic Studies*
NovT	*Novum Testamentum*
NovT	*Novum Testamentum*
NTS	*New Testament Studies*
NWNTI	*Noncanonical writings and New Testamentinterpretation. by Craig A. Evans*
OTP	*Old Testament Pseudepigrapha. Ed. J. H. Charlesworth, 2 vols. New York, 1983.*
PG	*Patrologia graeca=Patrologiae cursus completus: Series graeca. Ed. J.-P. Migne. 162 vols. Paris. 1857-1886.*
RC	*Revue Critique*
RE	*Realencyklopädie für protestantische Theologie und Kirche*
RE	*Realencyklopädie für protestantische Theologie und Kirche*
RevQ	*Revue de Qumran*
RevQ	*Revue de Qumran*
SBLEJL	*SBL Early Judaism and Its Literature*
SBLEJL	*Society of Biblical Literature Early Judaism and its Literature*
SBLSCS	*Society of Biblical Literature Sources for Biblical Study*
SBLSCS	*SBL Septuagint and Cognate Studies*
SJLA	*Studies in Judaism in Late Antiquity*
SNT	*Studien zum Neuen Testament*
SR	*Studies in Religion/Sciences religieuses*
SR	*Studies in Religion*
SVTP	*Studia in Veteris Testamenti pseudepigrapha*
VD	*Verbum domini*

List of Abbreviations

VT	*Vetus Testamentum*
WMANT	*Wissenschaftliche Monographien zum Alten und Neuen Testament*
WMANT	*Wissenschaftliche Monographien zum Alten und Neuen Testament*
ZAW	*Zeitschrift für die alttestamentliche Wissenschaft.*
ZNW	*Zeitschrift für die neutestamentliche Wissenschaft*
ZWT	*Zeitschrift für wissenschaftliche Theologie*
ZWT	*Zeitschrift für wissenschaftlice Theologie*

MS 260-83v

King Solomon on his throne, with Sophia (Wisdom) behind and Ben Sira below

1. Ψαλμοὶ Σολομῶντος Α

1. Ἐβόησα πρὸς κύριον ἐν τῷ θλίβεσθαί με εἰς τέλος·
   πρὸς τὸν θεὸν ἐν τῷ ἐπιθέσθαι ἁμαρτωλούς·
2. ἐξάπινα ἠκούσθη κραυγὴ πολέμου ἐνώπιόν μου·
   ἐπακούσεταί μου ὅτι ἐπλήσθην δικαιοσύνης·
3. ἐλογισάμην ἐν καρδίᾳ μου ὅτι ἐπλήσθην δικαιοσύνης·
   ἐν τῷ εὐθηνῆσαί με
   καὶ πολλὴν γενέσθαι ἐν τέκνοις·
4. Ὁ πλοῦτος αὐτῶν διεδόθη εἰς πᾶσαν τὴν γῆν·
   καὶ ἡ δόξα αὐτῶν· ἕως ἐσχάτου τῆς γῆς·

Α] om 253 629 336

Ψαλμοὶ Σολομῶντος] om 471 (NB: MS 471 has a title only for PsSol 3). Ψαλμὸς τῶ Σαλομών πρῶτος 336 [N.B: The base text of the superscription/title (without the "Α") is the reading of the listing in the Codex Alexandrinus, the oldest extant reference to the PssSol.]
Σοφία Σολομῶνος 253 (655 659)

1. Ἐβόησα] βόησα 471 inc (Initial letter absent, here and elsewhere, because of an incomplete production defect. These omissions are not regarded as textual variants.) 769: The inside of "Ε" eaten away, probably by corrosive ink, leaving only a faint outline.

   εἰς τέλος] ܕܠܥܠܡ

   τὸν] om 253 (655 659)

2. ἐπακούσεται] ἐπακούσετε 659*

   ἐπλήσθην] ἐπλήσθη (655 659)

   δικαιοσύνης] δικαιοσσύνης 769
   ὅτι] ܡܛܠ

3. ἐπλήσθην] ἐπλήσθη (655 659)

   εὐθηνῆσαί] εὐθυνῆσαί (655 659)

   πολλὴν] πολὺν 260 (149 471 606) 336

   γενέσθαι] γηνέσθαι (655* 659*)

4. διεδόθη] διέλθοι 260 (149 471 606)

   ἡ] + ἡ 769

   αὐτῶν²] αὐτοῦ 769

   ἐσχάτου] +τὴν γῆν καὶ ἡ δόξα αὐτῶν ἕως ἐσχάτου 253m

1. The Psalms of Solomon[1]

1. I[2] cried[3] to the Lord[4] when I was overwhelmed,[5]
   to God when sinners attacked.
2. Suddenly I heard cries of the battle right in front of me.[6]
   "He will hear me because I am righteous."[7]
3. I reminded myself[8] that I was indeed righteous;
   hadn't I prospered and given birth to many children?[9]

4. Their[10] influence[11] spread over the whole earth,[12]
   and their reputation extended to the far reaches of the earth.

---

[1] "Dedicated to Solomon;" "to" or "for" Solomon. The singular is assumed to be the older title, before the collection was assembled. This collation attempts to reconstruct an intermediate version of the text, after the collecting. This plural title, used in our oldest extant reference, in the index list of Codex Alexandrinus, is employed here, as we attempt to create an intermediate version of these psalms.

[2] The speaker is Jerusalem personified as a woman. See vs. 3.

[3] "Cried out," "Screamed out;" an anguished shout.

[4] There is no article before "Lord," but there is before "God" in the next line. The Hebrew antecedent, as in the LXX, was probably YHWH. The convention in English Bibles to print "LORD" in large and small capital letters to represent the Sacred Name. However, we are translating the Greek text, and we have no Hebrew antecedent. Therefore, we transliterate the word as "Lord" as in LXX translations and in the NT.

[5] Gk: "squeezed to the end." It may be durative ("continually/endlessly/ completely"), or intensive ("severely."), or refer to the author's endurance ("to the limit"); here and in 2:5.

[6] Gk: "was heard right in front of my face."

[7] Gk: "filled with righteousness."

[8] Gk: "considered in my heart."

[9] Two of the covenantal markers of God's blessing and of the people's righteousness.

[10] "Their:" the ruling class and citizenry of Jerusalem; see vss. 1.1 and 1.8.

[11] Gk: "wealth," the source of their influence.

[12] See 2 Macc 4.18ff; 1 Macc 10.4; Josephus, Ant 13.10ff

5. ὑψώθησαν ἕως τῶν ἄστρων·
   εἶπαν οὐ μὴ πέσωσιν·
6. καὶ ἐξύβρισαν ἐν τοῖς ἀγαθοῖς αὐτῶν,
   καὶ οὐκ ἤνεγκαν·
7. αἱ ἁμαρτίαι αὐτῶν ἐν ἀποκρύφοις,
   καὶ ἐγὼ οὐκ ᾔδειν·
8. αἱ ἀνομίαι αὐτῶν ὑπὲρ τὰ πρὸ αὐτῶν ἔθνη·
   ἐβεβήλωσαν τὰ ἅγια κυρίου ἐν βεβηλώσει:

---

5. ἕως] om (655 659)

   εἶπαν] εἶπον 769

   πέσωσιν] πέσωσι (471ₘ 606) 336 769 + μεν 769

6. ἐξύβρισαν] ܥܠܝ

   ἤνεγκαν] ܐܝܬܝ

7. καὶ ἐγὼ] κἀγὼ 260 (149 471 606) 769

   ᾔδειν] ᾔδες 655*

8. τὰ ἅγια] ܩܘܕܫܐ 16h1 ܩܕܫ 10h1

5. They soared[13] as high as the stars;
   they never expected they would ever fall.[14]
6. Their wealth made them too proud,
   and they did not acknowledge God.[15]
7. Their sins were in secret;
   I knew nothing about them.
8. Their crimes were worse than the Gentiles before them;
   they repeatedly profaned the Lord's Sanctuary.[16]

---

[13] Gk: "They were lifted up."

[14] Intensively emphatic.

[15] See Psalms 28 (29). 1,2; 95 (96). 7,8. "Ascribe glory and thanks to God for His blessings." Alternatively: "bring offerings," (to God), as in Ps 67 (68). 29 and 75 (76). 11. Sy: "they did not understand."

[16] Gk: "the holy things of the Lord," as in Ez 5.11; 23.38; 25.3; Mal 2.11; or: "the sanctuary," as in Ez 23.38; 25.3; Mal 2.11; or: "(our) Holy Place," as in 1 Macc 1.12. See also Ex 36.1. The phrase may also refer to the services and sacrifices of the sanctuary as in Lev 19.8, or inclusive of both the buildings and the rites. Syriac: "the sanctuary." See, Devorah. Dimant, "A Cultic Term."

2. Ψαλμὸς τῷ Σαλομών περὶ Ἰερουσαλήμ:

1. Ἐν τῷ ὑπερηφανεύεσθαι τὸν ἁμαρτωλόν· ἐν κριῷ
   κατέβαλε τείχη ὀχυρά, καὶ οὐκ ἐκώλυσας·
2. ἀνέβησαν ἐπὶ τὸ θυσιαστήριόν σου ἔθνη ἀλλότρια,
   κατεπατοῦσαν ἐν ὑποδήμασιν αὐτῶν ἐν ὑπερηφανίᾳ·

3. Ἀνθ' ὧν οἱ υἱοὶ Ἰερουσαλὴμ ἐμίαναν τὰ ἅγια κυρίου,
   ἐβεβηλοῦσαν τὰ δῶρα τοῦ θεοῦ ἐν ἀνομίαις·
4. ἕνεκεν τούτων εἶπεν·
   ἀπορρίψατε αὐτὰ μακρὰν ἀπ' ἐμοῦ·
   οὐκ εὐόδωκεν αὐτοῖς.

Σαλομων] σαλωμων 253 σολομων 655m c

περὶ Ἰερουσαλήμ] om 769*
  + B 606 629 (769) 336

1. Ἐν] Initial letter missing: inc.
   ἐν κριῷ] ܟܐܟܝܪܝ

   κατέβαλε] κατέβαλλε 253 336 κατάβαλλε (655 659)

2. κατεπατοῦσαν] κατεπάτουν 260 (149 471 606) 769
   336 καταπατοῦσαν 655 659

   ὑποδήμασιν] ὑπο ποδήμασιν (655 659)

3. ἀνθ' ὧν] ἀνθὼν m 655
   οἱ] om 336

   τὰ ἅγια] ܡܟܬܘܢ ܕܝܢ 16h1 ܡܟܬܘܢ 10h1

   ἐβεβηλοῦσαν] ἐβεβήλουν 260 (149 471 606) 769 336

4. ἀπορρίψατε] ἀπορίψατε 253 (655 659) ἀπερρίψατε
   336

   εὐόδωκεν] εὐώδωκεν 260 (149 471 606) ἐνέδωκεν (655 659)
     +τούτων εἶπεν 655m ditt ܩܘܕ
     εὐδοκῶ ἐν {Ra=vG=Hilgenfeld [1869]=Fabricius=de la Cerda}

2. A Psalm of Solomon: About Jerusalem

1. When the sinner contemptuously used his battering-ram[17]
    to smash down the fortified walls, you did not interfere.
2. Gentiles who worship other gods[18] went up to your altar;
    they brazenly trampled around with their sandals on.
3. For their part, the people of Jerusalem
    desecrated the Lord's sanctuary.
    Their crimes[19] profaned the offerings to God.
4. Because of all this he said:
    "Get these things far away from me! They are repugnant!"[20]

---

[17] Syr: "on a feast day." See Atkinson, *I Cried to the Lord,* p. 23.

[18] Gk: "nations belonging to another/foreign (god)."

[19] Gk: ἀνομίαις "lawless," here and elsewhere.

[20] Gk: "do not give them a pleasant path." Other MSS read: "there is no sweet odor in them ;" "not fit (to be offered);" Some editors emend: "I am not pleased with them.."

5. τὸ κάλλος τῆς δόξης αὐτοῦ·
  ἐξουθενώθη ἐνώπιον τοῦ θεοῦ·
  ἠτιμώθη ἕως εἰς τέλος·
6. Οἱ υἱοὶ καὶ αἱ θυγατέρες ἐν αἰχμαλωσίᾳ πονηρᾷ,
  ἐν σφραγίδι· ὁ τράχηλος αὐτῶν,
  ἐν ἐπισήμῳ ἐν τοῖς ἔθνεσιν·
7. Κατὰ τὰς ἁμαρτίας αὐτῶν ἐποίησεν αὐτοῖς·
  ὅτι ἐγκατέλιπεν αὐτοὺς εἰς χεῖρας κατισχυόντων·
8. ἀπέστρεψεν γὰρ τὸ πρόσωπον αὐτοῦ
  ἀπὸ ἐλέους αὐτῶν·
  νέον καὶ πρεσβύτην καὶ τέκνα αὐτῶν εἰς ἅπαξ·

---

5. κάλλος] κάλλο 769

  τῆς δόξης αὐτοῦ] ܡܕܡ ܫܘܒܚܗ 16h1 τῆς δόξης αυτῆς
    471 = ܡܕܡ ܫܘܒܚܗ 10h1

  ἐξουθενώθη] ἐξουθενήθη 260 (149 471 606)

  του θεοῦ] ܐܠܗܐ

  ἠτιμώθη] εἰτιμώττη (655m 659)

  ἕως] om 260 (149 471 606)

6. οἱ] om 253 (655 659)

  αἱ] om 253 (655 659)

  ἐν σφραγῖδι...ἔθνεσιν]
    ܒܚܬܡܐ܂ ܨܘܪܗܘܢ ܚܝ܂ ܘܝܕܝܥ ܡܢ ܥܡܡܐ

  ἔθνεσιν] ἔθνεσι 260 (149 471 606) 336

7. Κατὰ] κατ 606

  ἐγκατέλιπεν] ἐγκατέλειπεν 253
    ἐνκατέλειπεν (655 659)

  κατισχυόντων] κατεσχιόντων (655 659)

8. ἀπέστρεψεν] ἀπέστρεψε 260 (149 471 606) 336

  ἐλέους αὐτῶν] ἐλέου αὐτοῦ 336 ܡܢܗܘܢ τὸ] om 260
    (149 471 606) 769 336

  ἐλέους] ἐλέου 260 (149 471 606) 769 336

  πρεσβύτην] πρεσβήτην 655

5.   His beautiful and glorious sanctuary[21]
         was despised before God,[22]
         it was completely dishonored.
6. The sons and daughters[23] (of Jerusalem) were held prisoner
         in terrible conditions:
         a seal on their necks, a Gentile mark.[24]
7. He dealt with them according to their sins;
         he abandoned them to the hands of their oppressors.
8. For he turned[25] away and showed them no mercy —
         young and old and their children — all alike,

---

[21] The phrase "beauty of His glory" may refer to the Temple (as in Isa 60:7), or to the Temple draperies and tapestries (as in Isa 6:1), or to a theophany in the Temple (as in Ezek 1:28; 10:18).

[22] Gk: "in God's eyes."

[23] Syr: "her sons and daughters." See Atkinson, *I Cried to the Lord,* p. 37.

[24] Or: "a spectacle among the Gentiles." See 3 Mac 2:29; SibOr 8.244. Syr: "the people's sealed yoke is put around their neck."

[25] Gk: "he turned his face away."

      ὅτι πονηρὰ ἐποίησαν εἰς ἅπαξ τοῦ μὴ ἀκούειν·
9.   καὶ ὁ οὐρανὸς ἐβαρυθύμησεν,
          καὶ ἡ γῆ ἐβδελύξατο αὐτούς·
        ὅτι οὐκ ἐποίησε πᾶς ἄνθρωπος ἐπ' αὐτῆς
          ὅσα ἐποίησαν·
10. Καὶ γνώσεται ἡ γῆ τὰ κρίματά σου
       πάντα τὰ δίκαια, ὁ θεός·

11. Ἔστησαν τοὺς υἱοὺς Ἰερουσαλὴμ εἰς ἐμπαιγμὸν
       ἀντὶ πορνῶν ἐν αὐτῇ·
      πᾶς ὁ παραπορευόμενος
      εἰσεπορεύετο κατέναντι τοῦ ἡλίου·
12. ἐνέπαιζον ταῖς ἀνομίαις αὐτῶν
       καθὰ ἐποίουν αὐτοί,
     ἀπέναντι τοῦ ἡλίου παρεδειγμάτισαν
     ἀδικίας αὐτῶν·

   ἐποίησαν] ἐποίησεν 655*

   ἀκούειν] ἀκούον (655 659)

   εἰς ἅπαξ[1,2]] (vG= εἰσάπαξ)

 9. ἐβαρυθύμησεν] ἐβαρυθύμησε 253 260 (149 471 606)
    ἐβαρύθμησε (655 659)

   ἐβδελύξατο] βδελύξατο (655 659)

   ἐποίησε] ἐποίησεν (655 659)

   ἐπ'] 655m

10. πάντατὰ τὰ δίκαια] τὰ δίκαια πάντα 336

11. ἔστησαν] ἔστησεν 260 (149) ἔστησε (471 606)
   Ἰερουσαλὴμ] ἠδὴμ (655m 659)

   ἐμπαιγμὸν] ἐμπεγμὸν 253 ἐμπαγμὸν 655m ἐμπαγμ
    659 ἐμπαγὸν 659c
   πορῶν] 655m
   παραπορευόμενος] πορευόμενος 253 (655 659)
   εἰσεπορεύετο] ܘܥܠ

12. ἐνέπαιζον] ἐνέπεζον (655 659)

   ταῖς ἀνομίαις] τὰς ἀνομίας (655 659)

because they all sinned alike, for they would not listen.

9. The heavens were appalled, and the earth loathed them.
    Because no one had ever acted as they.

10. The world will know all your judgments; they are just, O God.

11. The Gentiles[27] maligned [28] the men[29] of Jerusalem,
        because of the prostitutes among her.
    Everyone who passed by
        went in to them in broad daylight.

12. Even the Gentiles[30] ridiculed such crimes,
        compared to how they themselves acted.
    They made a public[31] display of their evil deeds.

---

[26] Gk: "They." Some MSS read: "He," i.e.: God.

[27] Gk: "held up for ridicule."

[28] In contrast to the "women" in vs. 13.

[29] Gk: "They."

[30] Gk: "in the eyes of the sun."

13. καὶ θυγατέρες Ἰερουσαλὴμ βέβηλοι κατὰ τὸ κρίμα σου·
    ἀνθ᾽ ὧν αὐταὶ ἐμιαίωσαν αὑτὰς
      ἐν φυρμῷ ἀναμίξεως·
14. τὴν κοιλίαν μου καὶ τὰ σπλάγχνα μου
    πονῶ ἐπὶ τούτοις·

15. Ἐγὼ δικαιώσω σε, ὁ θεός, ἐν εὐθύτητι καρδίας·
    ὅτι ἐν τοῖς κρίμασίν σου ἡ δικαιοσύνη σου ὁ θεός·
16. ὅτι ἀπέδωκας τοῖς ἁμαρτωλοῖς κατὰ τὰ ἔργα αὐτῶν·
    καὶ κατὰ τὰς ἁμαρτίας αὐτῶν τὰς πονηρὰς σφόδρα
17. ἀνεκάλυψας τὰς ἁμαρτίας αὐτῶν
      ἵνα φανῇ τὸ κρίμα σου·
    ἐξήλειψας τὸ μνημόσυνον αὐτῶν ἀπὸ τῆς γῆς·
18. ὁ θεὸς κριτὴς δίκαιος, καὶ οὐ θαυμάσει πρόσωπον·

---

13. θυγατέρες] θυγατέρας (655 659)
    ἀνθ᾽ ὧν] ἀνθὼν 655
    αὐταὶ] αὗται 655

    ἐμιαίωσαν] = ‏ܐܛܡܐ‎ ἐμίαινον 260 (149 471 606) 769
      336
    αὑτὰς] ἑαυτὰς 260 (149 471 606) 769 336
    ἀναμίξεως] ‏ܪܚܠܡܝܬ‎
14. σπλάγχνα] σπλάχνα 769 336
    τούτοις] τούτους 659
15. ὁ θεός[1]] ‏ܐܠܗ‎
    κρίμασίν] κρίμασί 659* 260 (149 471 606) 769
    κρίμασί 336
    σου[1]] om 659*
16. αὐτῶν[1]] αὐτῷ 769
    καὶ] om 260 (149 471 606) 769
    σφόδρα] σφόδρον 253 σφόδραν (655 659)
17. ἀνεκάλυψας] ἔναμψας 655 ἔκαμψας 659
    ἐξήλειψας] ἐξήλιψας 253 (655 659) ἐξηύλιψας 659c
18. θαυμάσει] θαυμάσε (655m 659)

13. And you have judged the women of Jerusalem poluted,
    For they defiled themselves with sexual promiscuity.[31]
14. Thinking about these things makes me sick to my stomach.[32]

15. I will defend[33] your justice, O God, with integrity,[34]
    because your judgments are just, O God.
16. because you have repaid sinners according to their deeds
    and according to their exceedingly wicked sins.
17. You uncovered their sins that your judgment might be evident;
    you wiped out their memory from the earth.
18. God is an impartial[35] judge, and is not impressed by appearances[36]

---

[31] Gk: "mingling of intermixing."

[32] Gk: "I strain my belly and my inward parts are pained...;" "my stomach churns..." (See Lam 1.20, NRSV)

[33] Gk: "...show you to be just," "...affirm you justice."

[34] Gk: "in straightness of heart."

[35] Gk: "just," here and elsewhere.

[36] Or: "God will not put up with deceptive disguises." Gk: "God will not stare at a (false) mask."

19. 'Ωνείδισαν γὰρ ἔθνη Ἰερουσαλὴμ ἐν καταπατήσει·
    κατέσπασεν τὸ κάλλος αὐτῆς ἀπὸ θρόνου δόξης·
20. περιεζώσατο σάκκον ἀντὶ ἐνδύματος εὐπρεπείας·
    σχοινίον περὶ τὴν κεφαλὴν αὐτῆς ἀντὶ στεφάνου·
21. περιείλατο μίτραν δόξης ἣν περιέθηκεν αὐτῇ ὁ θεός·
    ἐν ἀτιμίᾳ τὸ κάλλος αὐτῆς, ἀπερρίφη ἐπὶ τὴν γῆν·

22. Καὶ ἐγὼ εἶδον καὶ ἐδεήθην τοῦ προσώπου κυρίου·
    καὶ εἶπον
    Ἱκάνωσον, κύριε τοῦ βαρύνεσθαι
    χεῖρά σου ἐπὶ Ἰερουσαλήμ· ἐν ἐπαγωγῇ ἐθνῶν·

---

19. ὠνείδισαν] ὠνίδησαν 253 (655 659) ὠνείδισας 471
    ὀνείδισαν 336

    ἐν] om 336

    καταπατήσει] καταπατῆσαι 336 ܀ܡܒ ܟܐܝ

    κατέσπασεν] κατέσπασε 260 (149 471 606) 336
    κατέπαισεν 655 659 ܐܡܒܕܝܪ {κατεσπάσθη Ra= vG}

21. περιείλατο] περιείλετο (655 659) 260 (149 471 606) 769 336
    μίτραν] μήτραν 769 336 ܟܐܘܝ
    τὸ κάλλος] ܡܬܒܘ
    ἀπερρίφη] ἀπε᾽ ῤρίφει (655 659)

22. κυρίου] + τοῦ θεοῦ 336

    καὶ²] κἀγὼ 336

    κύριε] om 336

    τοῦ βαρύνεσθαι χεῖρά σου] χεῖρά σου τοῦ βαρύνεσθαι
    336

    χεῖρά] χεῖρας 253 (655 659)

    Ἰερουσαλήμ] Ἰσραὴλ 253 ܠ ܐܝܣ

    ἐν] om (655 659)

    ἐπαγωγῇ] ἐπ᾽ἀγωνή (655m 659) ἀπαγωγή 260 (149)

19. The Gentiles humiliated Jerusalem when she was trampled down;
        He[37] dragged her beauty from her once magnificent throne.
20. She was wrapped in sackcloth instead of beautiful clothes;
        a rope was around her head instead of a wreath.
21. He snatched the crown of glory that God had put on her.
        Her beauty lies in disgrace; it was flung down upon the earth.

22. And I saw all this and pleaded in the Lord's presence:
        I said: "Make it stop, Lord!
    By bringing in the Gentiles
        you have laid your hand heavily upon Jerusalem."

---

[37] The allusion appears to be to the Gentile Pompey and his soldiers. Syr: "was dragged down."

23. ὅτι ἐνέπαιξαν καὶ οὐκ ἐφείσαντο·
　　 ἐν ὀργῇ καὶ θυμῷ μετὰ μηνίσεως
　　 καὶ συντελεσθήσονται· ἐὰν μὴ σύ, κύριε
　　 ἐπιτιμήσῃς αὐτοῖς ἐν ὀργῇ σου·
24. Ὅτι οὐκ ἐν ζήλει ἐποίησαν ἀλλ᾿ ἐν ἐπιθυμίᾳ ψυχῆς·
　　 ἐκχέαι τὴν ὀργὴν αὐτῶν εἰς ἡμᾶς ἐν ἁρπάγματι·
25. Μὴ χρονίσῃς ὁ θεός τοῦ ἀποδοῦναι αὐτοῖς
　　 εἰς κεφαλάς·
　　 τοῦ εἰπεῖν τὴν ὑπερηφανίαν τοῦ δράκοντος ἐν ἀτιμίᾳ·

---

23. ἐνέπαιξαν] ἐνέπαιζαν (655, 659)

　　 καὶ θυμῷ] om Syr

　　 μηνίσεως] μανίασεως 655 659 μηνήσεως 260 (149 471 606)

　　 ܟܚܒܘ

　　 συντελεσθήσονται] συντελεσθήσοντ 769 (ποσσιβλε υνμαρκεδ

　　 αβρέιατιον) ܢܝܠܟܘ

　　 ἐπιτιμήσῃς] ἐπιτιμήσεις 253 (655 659)

　　 αὐτοῖς] αυτοὺς 769 336

24. ζήλει] ζήλῳ 260 (149 471 606) 336

　　 ἀλλ᾿] ἀλλὰ (655 659) 260 (149 471 606)

　　 ἐκχέαι] ἔκχαιε (655 659) ἐκχέας 336

25. μὴ] pr καὶ 253 (655 659)

　　 χρονίσῃς] χρονήσῃς 253 λεγονήσεις (655m 659m) ~ γεγο 659c marg
　　 ὁ θεός] ܟܠܝܗ

　　 εἰπεῖν] ܠܝܬܘܣ

　　 δράκοντος] 769: Insertion marker for a marginal note, now mostly
torn away. Text preserved by von Gebhardt (ΥΑΛΜΟΙ
ΣΟΛΟΜΩΝΤΟΣ, p. 96, n.25): "δράκοντα λέγει τὸν
ἀποστάτην διάβολον. πολλαχοῦ γὰρ ἡ θεία γραφὴ δράκοντα
τοῦτον ἐπονομάζει, διὰ τὸ ἄπληστον τῆς ὑπερηφανίας.
ὑπερήφανον γὰρ ὁ δράκων καὶ ἴταμον τὸ πάθος τῆς
ὑπερηφανίας ὡς προείπομεν."

　　 ἀτιμίᾳ] αἱ τίαμία 253 αἰτία μία (655,659) ἀτιμία μιᾶ
336

23.   They have humiliated[38] them,[39]
         and their frenzied passion did not let up,
         nor did their angry violence.
      And they will be destroyed[40]
         unless you, O Lord, angrily denounce them,
24.   because they did not act out of zeal,
         but out of an obsession,[41]
         venting their thieving anger against us.
25.   Don't delay, O God, in retaliating against their leaders
         by disgracing the dragon's[42] arrogance .

---

[38] Gk: "made child's play."

[39] In this impassioned tirade syntax and pronouns are somewhat convoluted .

[40] Gk: "bring to an end," i.e: the people of Jerusalem.

[41] Gk: "Lust of soul."

[42] A marginal note in MS 769, folio 295r, now torn away, but preserved by von Gebhardt (P. 96, n 25) reads: "He calls the rebellious devil 'dragon'. For often the sacred scripture names this one 'dragon,' on account of the excessiveness of his arrogance. For the dragon is an arrogant and headstrong thing, as regards the experience of arrogance, as we said before." See Atkinson, *I Cried to the Lord* (p. 36) for a discussion of the biblical allusions here.

26. Καὶ οὐκ ἐχρόνισα ἕως ἔδειξέν μοι ὁ θεὸς
τὴν ὕβριν αὐτοῦ·
ἐκκεκεντημένον ἐπὶ τῶν ὀρέων Αἰγύπτου·
ὑπὲρ ἐλαχίστου ἐξουδενωμένον
ἐπὶ γῆς καὶ θαλάσσης·
27. τὸ σῶμα αὐτοῦ διαφερόμενον ἐπὶ κυμάτων
ἐν ὕβρει πολλῇ·
καὶ οὐκ ἦν ὁ θάπτων, ὅτι ἐξουθένωσεν
αὐτὸν ἐν ἀτιμίᾳ·

28. Οὐκ ἐλογίσατο ὅτι ἄνθρωπός ἐστιν·
καὶ τὸ ὕστερον οὐκ ἐλογίσατο·
κραταιὸς ἐν ἰσχύι αὐτοῦ τῇ μεγάλῃ·

---

26. ἐχρόνισα] ἐχρόνησα 253 (655 659)

ἕως] + οὗ 336

ἔδειξέν] ἔδωξέ (655 659) ἔδειξέ 260 (149 471 606) 336
θεὸς] ܐܠܗܐ
τὴν ὕβριν αὐτοῦ] ܡܚܣܕ
ἐκκεκεντημένον] ܡܕܩܪ
ὑπὲρ ἐλαχίστου] ܡܢ ܕܩܕܡ ܙܥܘܪ {ὑπὲρ ἐλάχιστον Ra=vG}
ἐξουδενωμένον] ἐξουδενωμένος 471 ἐξ οὐδενωμένον 769

27. διαφερόμενον] διαφερόμιενον 253 διεφθαρμένον 260 (149
471 606) διὰ φερόμιενον 769

ἐν ὕβρει] ܒܨܥܪ

πολλῇ] πολληῖα 769

ἦν] ἢν 659 471
θάπτων] MS 629 begins here.

ἐξουθένωσεν]= ܫܛܗ 16h1 10h1 ἐξουδένωσεν 260 (149 471 606)
629 (769) ἐξούδένωσεν 336 ܐܫܛܗ 16h1*

28. ἐλογίσατο] ἐλ[...]ίσατο 629
ἐστιν] ἐστί 260 (149 471 606) 629

κραταιὸς] + ܟܕ 471
κραταιὸς...μεγάλη] ܗܘ ܒܥܘܫܢܐ ܪܒܐ
ἰσχύι] ἰσχύει 253 (655 659) [...]χύει 629

26. I did not have long to wait until God showed me his arrogance.
    Stabbed[59] on the sand dunes[60] of Egypt,
    he was more despised than anything in the whole world.[61]
27. His body was violently carried over the waves
    and there was no one to bury him,
    because God contemptuously despised him.

28. He did not realize that he was merely mortal,
    and he didn't think about the future.

---

[43] Gk: "pierced through."

[44] Gk: "hills, mountains" "deserts."

[45] Gk: "worthless and disdained on earth and sea."

29. Εἶπεν ἐγὼ κύριος γῆς καὶ θαλάσσης ἔσομαι
    καὶ οὐκ ἐπέγνω· ὅτι ὁ θεὸς μέγας,
30. Αὐτὸς βασιλεὺς ἐπὶ τῶν οὐρανῶν
    καὶ κρίνων βασιλεῖς καὶ ἀρχάς·
31. ὁ ἀνιστῶν ἐμὲ εἰς δόξαν
    καὶ κοιμίζων ὑπερηφάνους
    εἰς ἀπώλειαν αἰῶνος ἐν ἀτιμίᾳ
    ὅτι οὐκ ἔγνωσαν αὐτόν·
32. Καὶ νῦν ἴδετε, οἱ μεγιστᾶνες τῆς γῆς τὸ κρίμα
    τοῦ κυρίου· ὅτι μέγας βασιλεὺς καὶ δίκαιος κρίνων τὴν ὑπ᾽
    οὐρανόν·
33. εὐλογεῖτε τὸν θεόν οἱ φοβούμενοι τὸν κύριον
    ἐν ἐπιστήμῃ·
    ὅτι τὸ ἔλεος κυρίου ἐπὶ τοὺς φοβουμένους αὐτόν·
    μετὰ κρίματος

---

29. εἶπεν] εἶπεῖν 629? (769)
    ὁ θεὸς μέγας] ‎ܐܠܗܐ ܗܘ ܪܒ
30. οὐρανῶν] οὐρανὸν 655m c marg + ‎ܪܘܡܐ ܠܐ
    βασιλεῖς] βασιλεὺς (655 659) ‎ܪܚܫܠܝܢ
31. ὁ] om 260 (149 471 606) 336
    ἀπώλειαν] ἀπώλιαν 253 ἀπόλιαν (655 659)
    αἰῶνος] αἰώνιον 260 (149 471 606) 629 (769) 336
    ἀτιμίᾳ] ἀτομία (655* 659*)
    αὐτόν] αὐτῶν (655 769) αὐτοίς 471
32. τοῦ] om 260 (149 471 606) 629 (769) 336
    μέγας] om Syr
23. ἐνέπαιξαν] ἐνέπαιζαν (655, 659)
33. τὸν θεόν] ‎ܠܐܠܗܐ
    ἐπιστήμῃ] ἐπιστίμη 253 ‎ܒܝܘܕܥܐ
    κυρίου] αὐτοῦ 629*marg 769*marg
    αὐτὸν] αὐτοῦ (655 659)

29.   He said: "I will be lord of the whole world;" [46]
        he failed to recognize that it is God who is great,[47]
        who is mighty in his great strength.
30.   He himself is king over the heavens,
        he who judges kings and rulers.
31.   He is the one who raises me up into glory,
           and who brings down the arrogant to sleep,[48]
        to their dishonorable destruction forever,
          because they did not know him.
32.   And now, you rulers of the earth, see the judgment of the Lord,
        because he is a great and righteous king,
          judging what is under heaven.
33.   Praise God, those of you who know enough to fear the Lord,
          because his mercy will be with those
          who have good reason to fear him,[49]

---

[46] Gk: "...of the earth and of the sea."

[47] Syr: "the Lord is God."

[48] Or: "the sleep of death."

[49] Gk: "with (good) judgment."

34. τοῦ διαστεῖλαι ἀνὰ μέσον δικαίου καὶ ἁμαρτωλοῦ·
    ἀποδοῦναι ἁμαρτωλοῖς εἰς τὸν αἰῶνα
        κατὰ τὰ ἔργα αὐτῶν·
35. καὶ ἐλεῆσαι δίκαιον ἀπὸ ταπεινώσεως ἁμαρτωλοῦ·
    καὶ ἀποδοῦναι ἁμαρτωλῷ ἀνθ' ὧν ἐποίησεν δικαίῳ·
36. Ὅτι χρηστὸς ὁ κύριος τοῖς ἐπικαλουμένοις αὐτὸν
    ἐν ὑπομονῇ·
    ποιῆσαι κατὰ τὸ ἔλεος αὐτοῦ τοῖς ὁσίοις αὐτοῦ·
    παρεστάναι διὰ παντὸς ἐνώπιον αὐτοῦ ἐν ἰσχύι·
37. εὐλογητὸς κύριος εἰς τὸν αἰῶνα ἐνώπιον δούλων αὐτοῦ·

---

34. μέσον] μέσων 253 (655 659)

35. ἐλεῆσαι] ἐλεῆσας (655 659)

    ταπεινώσεως] ταπηνώσεως (655 659)

    ἁμαρτωλοῦ] +ἀποδοῦναι ἁμαρτωλοῖς εἰς τὸν αἰῶνα
        κατὰ τὰ ἔργα αὐτῶν 336

    ἐποίησεν] ἐποίησε 260 (149 471 606) 629 336

36. τοῖς] τούς (655 659)

    ἐπικαλουμένοις] ἐπικαλουμένους (655 659)

    ὑπομονῇ] ὑπὸ μονῆς 769

    ποιῆσαι] ποιῆσας (655 659)

    ὁσίοις] μετ' 260 (149 471 606) 629

    παρεστάναι] παραστάναι 336 ܪܡܠ

    ἰσχύι] ἰσχύει 253 (655 659) 336

37. ἐνώπιον] ܥ

34.   for he will separate the righteous from the sinner,
       because he will always retaliate against sinners
       according to their deeds.
35.   He will have mercy on the righteous,
       keeping them from the humiliation of sinners,
   and he will retaliate against the sinner
       for what he has done to the righteous.
36.   The Lord is kind to those who persistently appeal to him;
       he treats his devout in accordance with his mercy,
   to keep them constantly before him in strength.
37.   Praised be the Lord forever in the eyes of his servants.

3. Ψαλμὸς τῷ Σαλωμὼν περὶ δικαίων·

1. Ἵνα τί ὑπνοῖς ψυχή, καὶ οὐκ εὐλογεῖς τὸν κύριον·
   ὕμνον καινὸν ψάλατε τῷ θεῷ τῷ αἰνετῷ·
2. ψάλλε καὶ γρηγόρησον ἐπὶ τὴν γρηγόρησιν αὐτοῦ·
   ὅτι ἀγαθὸς ψαλμὸς τῷ θεῷ ἐξ ἀγαθῆς καρδίας·

3. Δίκαιοι μνημονεύουσιν διὰ παντὸς τοῦ κυρίου·
   ἐν ἐξομολογήσει καὶ δικαιώσει τὰ κρίματα κυρίου·
4. οὐκ ὀλιγωρήσει δίκαιος παιδευόμενος ὑπὸ κυρίου·
   ἡ εὐδοκία αὐτοῦ διὰ παντὸς ἔναντι κυρίου·

3=Γ] *om* 260 (149 606)

τῷ] τοῦ (655 659)

Σαλωμὼν] σολομῶντος 655 σαλομῶντος 659c σαλομῶν
659 260 (149 471 606) 629 (769) 336
NB: This is the only superscription that MS 471 preserves.

1. οὐκ εὐλογεῖς] οὐλογεῖς 253*

   καινὸν] καὶ αἶνον 253 (655 659) 629 (769)

   ψάλατε] ψάλλετε 253 (655 659) ψάλλατε 471
   ψάλατε...αἰνετῷ *om* Syr

2. ψάλλε] ψάλαι 336
   καὶ] *om* 336

   γρηγόρησον] ⲙⲇⲁⲓ̈ⲉ, ⲓ̈ⲉⲇⲇⲓⲉ

   θεῷ] κυρίῳ 336

   ἀγαθῆς] ὅλης 260 (149 471 606) 629 (769)
      ἀγαω...ς 655

3. μνημονεύουσιν] μνημονεύουσι 260 (149 471 606)
      629 (769) 336

   ἐν] 769* marg

   κυρίου²] τοῦ κυρίου 253 (655 659)

4. ὀλιγωρήσει] ὀλιγορήσει 253 (655 659)

   κυρίου¹] τοῦ κυρίου 253 (655 659)

   ἔναντι] ἐναντίον 260 (149 471 606) 629 (769) 336

3. A Psalm of Solomon about the Righteous[51]

1. Why am I sleeping,[52] and not praising the Lord?
    Strum a new song[53] to God who is worthy to be praised.
2. Keep on strumming[54] and keep awake for he is awake.[55]
    For a good psalm to God comes from a good heart.[56]

3. The Lord is on the mind of the righteous through everything.
    by recognizing[57] and proving that the Lord'S judgments are right.[58]
4. The righteous will not be ashamed[59] to be taught[60] by the Lord,
    their desire is to be always in the Lord'S presence.

---

[50] Gk: "Just." The substantive use of the adjective; could also mean "things that are just," or "People who are Fair and Equitable."

[51] Gk: "Why do you sleep, O soul." Syr: "Why sleep, my soul..."

[52] "Pluck a new song...." The phrase describes singing with the accompaniment of a stringed instrument. Some MSS read: "song and praise," or "a song and a hymn." See Ps LXX 143.9; 148.1.

[53] This may reflect a Hebrew infinite absolute intensifying the verbal form.

[54] Gk: "keep watching for his watching," or "stay awake because of his wakefulness" or "be aware of his being aware of you." Both the Gk and Syr are obscure.

[55] Other MSS read: "from a whole heart." See Deut 6.5.

[56] The implication of the Hebrew that may lie behind the Greek is a ritual confession of gratitude and thanksgiving.

[57] Gk: "just," here and elsewhere.

[58] "Belittle," "be embarrassed by," "make light of."

[59] Or "corrected." The word invokes the image of the training of a child.

5. Προσέκοψεν ὁ δίκαιος καὶ ἐδικαίωσεν τὸν κύριον·
      ἔπεσεν, καὶ ἀποβλέπει τί ποιήσει αὐτῷ ὁ θεός·
      ἀποσκοπεύει ὅθεν ἥξει σωτηρία αὐτοῦ·

6. ἀλήθεια τῶν δικαίων παρὰ θεοῦ σωτῆρος αὐτῶν·
      οὐκ αὐλίζεται ἐν οἴκῳ δικαίου ἁμαρτία ἐφ' ἁμαρτίαν·

7. Ἐπισκέπτεται διὰ παντὸς τὸν οἶκον αὐτοῦ ὁ δίκαιος·
      τοῦ ἐξᾶραι ἀδικίαν ἐν παραπτώματι αὐτοῦ.

8. ἐξιλάσατο περὶ ἀγνοίας ἐν νηστείᾳ
      καὶ ταπεινώσει ψυχὴν αὐτοῦ·
      καὶ ὁ κύριος καθαρίζει πᾶν ἄνδρα ὅσιον
      καὶ τὸν οἶκον αὐτοῦ.

---

5. προσέκοψεν] προσέκιψεν (655 659)

   ἐδικαίωσεν] ἐδικαίοσεν (655 659) ἐδικαίωσε 260
      (149 471 606) 629 (769) 336

   κύριον] ܟ̈ܝܪܝܐ S ܐܠܗܐ 16h1 10h1

   ἔπεσεν] ἔπεσε 260 (149 471 606) 629 336

   ἀποβλέπει] ܢܚܘܪ

   ὁ θεός] = ܐܠܗܐ S ܟܝܪܝܐ 16h1

   ἀποσκοπεύει] ἀποσκόπευε (655m 659)

   σωτηρία] ἡ σωτηρία 606 336

   αὐτοῦ] αὐτῷ 253 (655 659) 629*

6. ἀλήθεια] ἀλήθια 253 (655 659) ܩܘܫܬܐ

   αὐλίζεται] εὐλίζεται (655m 659)

   οἴκῳ]· τοῦ 471

   δικαίου] τοῦ δικαίου 260 (149 471) 629 (769) 336

7. ὁ δίκαιος] ܟܐܢܐ

8. ἐξιλάσατο] ἐξηλάσατο (655 659) ܚܣܝ ܘܕܟܝ

   ταπεινώσει] ܘܒܡܘܟܟܐ

   ψυχὴν] om Syr {ψυχῆς Ra=vG}

   αὐτοῦ[1]] om 253 (655m 659m)

   πᾶν] πάντα 260 (149 471 606) 629 (769) 336

   ὅσιον] θεῖον 629 (769)

5.   The righteous stumble and still prove the Lord is right;
         if they fall, they expect God[60] to help them;[61]
         they look to the source of their salvation..
6.   The confidence[62] of the righteous comes from God their savior.
         Repeated sin[63] is not found in the home of the righteous.
7.   The righteous thoroughly examine their homes[64] to remove their unintentional
         offences.
8.   They atone for sins of ignorance by fasting and humility[65]
         and the Lord will cleanse every devout person and their household.[66]

---

[60] "Lord...God;" Syr: "God...Lord."

[61] Gk: "they look for what God will do for them."

[62] Gk: "Truth," "faithfulness," or "dependability."

[63] Gk: "Sin after sin."

[64] Syr: "he (God) searches the house of the righteous."

[65] Gk: "humbling their soul."

[66] Gk: "every devout man." Although the heads of the household are usually described
in biblical and post-biblical literature as male, there are passages that seem to indicate
females with that designation. See Mt 13.52; Jn 4.53; Acts 16.15: "she and her
household;" Acts 17.34.

9.   Προσέκοψεν ἁμαρτωλός· καὶ καταρᾶται ζωὴν αὐτοῦ·
     τὴν ἡμέραν γενέσεως αὐτοῦ καὶ ὠδῖνας μητρός.
10. προσέθηκεν ἁμαρτίας ἐφ' ἁμαρτίας τῇ ζωῇ αὐτοῦ·
     ἔπεσεν, ὅτι πονηρὸν τὸ πτῶμα αὐτοῦ·
     καὶ οὐκ ἀναστήσεται.
11. ἡ ἀπώλεια τοῦ ἁμαρτωλοῦ εἰς τὸν αἰῶνα·
     καὶ οὐ μνησθήσεται ὅταν ἐπισκέπτηται δικαίους.
12. αὕτη ἡ μερὶς τῶν ἁμαρτωλῶν εἰς τὸν αἰῶνα·
     οἱ δὲ φοβούμενοι τὸν κύριον ἀναστήσονται
     εἰς ζωὴν αἰώνιον·
     καὶ ἡ ζωὴ αὐτῶν ἐν φωτὶ κυρίου καὶ οὐκ ἐκλείψει ἔτι.

---

9. ἁμαρτωλός] ὁ ἁμαρτωλός 336

    ζωὴν] ζωῆς (655 659) τὴν ζωὴν 336

10. προσέθηκεν] προσέθηκαν 260 (149 471 606) 629?
    προσέ...] MS 629 ends here.

    ἁμαρτίας²] ἁμαρτίαις 253 (655 659) 629 (769)

    πτῶμα] σπέρμα 336

    ἀναστήσεται] ἀνεστήσεται 655*

    NB: MS 606 has running headers on every page. Here, at folio 228r, the original
    header begins: "σοφια," in red, and is written over in black: "ψαλμος," in a
    different hand.

11. οὐ] οὐ μὴ 253 (655 659)

    μνησθήσετα] μνυσθήσεται (655m 659m)

    ἐπισκέπτηται] ἐπισκόπτηται (655 659) ἐπισκέπτεται 336

12. ἡ¹] om 260 (149 471 606) 629 (769) 336

    τὸν²] om 260 (149 471 606) 629 (769)

    αἰώνιον] αἰώνιος 769

    καὶ²] om 253 (655 659)

    ἐκλείψει] ἐκλείψη 253 (655 659)

    ἔτι] + ܪܚܠܡܗ

9.   The sinners[67] stumble and curse their life,
        the day of their birth and their mother's labor pain.
10. They sin repeatedly[68] in their life:
        They fall, and are seriously hurt,[69]
        they will never get up again.
11. The destruction of sinners is forever,
        and they will not be remembered
        when God looks after the righteous.
12. This is the fate[70]of sinners forever;
        but those who fear the Lord
            shall rise up to eternal life,[71]
        and their life shall be in the Lord's light
            and it shall never end[72]

---

[67] Here and elsewhere, the gnomic singular is best translated by plural in English.
[68] See fn. 63.

[69] Gk:"his fall was evil."

[70] Gk: "portion," "share," "doom," or "what is reserved for." See 4.14; 5.4; 14.9;
also Ps 49.13 NRSV; 81.15.

[71] See Dan 12.2; 2 Mac 7.9; Job 33.29f.

[72] "...be in eclipse." See Thucydides, *History of the Peloponnesian War*, 1.23; 2.28;
Plutarch, *Aemilius Panlus* 17.

4. Διαλογὴ τοῦ Σαλωμὼν τοῖς ἀνθρωπαρέσκοις:

1. Ἵνα τί σύ, βέβηλε· κάθησαι ἐν συνεδρίῳ ὁσίων·
    καὶ ἡ καρδία σου μακρὰν ἀφέστηκεν ἀπὸ τοῦ κυρίου·
    ἐν παρανομίαις παροργίζων τὸν θεὸν Ἰσραήλ·
2. περισσὸς ἐν λόγοις· περισσὸς ἐν σημειώσει ὑπὲρ πάντας·
    ὁ σκληρὸς ἐν λόγοις κατακρῖναι ἁμαρτωλοὺς ἐν κρίσει·

4=Δ] 253 629 (769) Γ 260 (149) + τέτρατος Δ 336
Διαλογὴ] σοφία (orig text in red) ψαλμὸς (overwritten in black)
   606 Ψαλμὸς 149

τοῦ] *om* 336* τῷ 260 (149 606)

Σαλωμὼν] σολομωντος (655 659 *) σαλομὼν 659c 260 (149 606)
   629 (769) 336

τοῖς] *om* (655 659)

ἀνθρωπαρέσκοις] ἀνθρωπευρεσκην 655m 659
   + τεταρτος Δ 336

1. βέβηλε κάθησαι] = ܕܘܪ ܨܠ ܪܐܬܝ κάθησαι βέβηλε 260 (149 471
   606) 629 (κάθησε βέβηλε 769) 336

   κάθησαι] κάθησε 769

   ὁσίων] *om* 260 (149 471 606) ὁσίῳ 253 (655 659) 629 (769)
     ܟܐܘܝ

   τοῦ] *om* 336
   κυρίου] ܪܡܠܪ

2. περισσὸς[1]] περισὸς 769*

   σημειώσει] σειμειώσει (655 659*)

   ὁ] *om* 336 οἱ (655 659m)
   σκληρὸς] Σσκληρὸς 336

   κατακρῖναι] κατακρίνας 655 659m κατακρίνων 260 (149 471
     606) κατακρίνει 629 (769)

4. A Dialogue[72] of Solomon with Hypocrites [73]

1.Why are you sitting in the Holy Sanhedrin,[74] you foul[75] person?
   When your heart is far from the Lord,
   provoking the God of Israel with your rotten behavior?
2. Verbose and flamboyant more than anyone,
   harshly condemning defendants[76] in court.[77]

---

[72] "Debate." Other MSS read: "Psalm.."

[73] Gk: "those who flatter people," "those trying to impress people," "opportunists," "demagogues," "Tartuffes," or even "politicians." "Those who attempt to win public approval and applause at the sacrifice of principle."

[74] Gk: "assembly of the holy ones/devout." Some MSS omit "of the devout." In Jerusalem, in the first century B.C.E., the "assembly of the holy ones" (or "holy assembly") it most probably refers to the supreme council, the Great Sanhedrin, rather than to a local sanhedrin.

[75] "Desecrator," profainer."

[76] Gk: "sinners," "criminals."

[77] Gk: "in judgment."

3. Καὶ ἡ χεὶρ αὐτοῦ ἐν πρώτοις ἐπ' αὐτὸν ὡς ἐν ζήλει.
     καὶ αὐτὸς ἔνοχος ἐν ποικιλίᾳ ἁμαρτιῶν
     καὶ ἐν ἀκρασίαις·
4. Οἱ ὀφθαλμοὶ αὐτοῦ ἐπὶ πᾶσαν γυναῖκα ἄνευ διαστολῆς·
     ἡ γλῶσσα αὐτοῦ ψευδὴς ἐν συναλλάγματι μεθ' ὅρκου·
5. ἐν νυκτὶ καὶ ἐν ἀποκρύφοις ἁμαρτάνει ὡς οὐχ ὁρώμενος·
     ἐν ὀφθαλμοῖς αὐτοῦ λαλεῖ πάσῃ γυναικὶ
     ἐν συνταγῇ κακίας·
     ταχὺς εἰσόδῳ εἰς πᾶσαν οἰκίαν
     ἐν ἱλαρότητι ὡς ἄκακος·
6. Ἐξάραι ὁ θεὸς τοὺς ἐν ὑποκρίσει ζῶντας μετὰ ὁσίων·
     ἐν φθορᾷ σαρκὸς αὐτοῦ καὶ πενίᾳ τὴν ζωὴν αὐτοῦ·

---

3. πρώτοις] η ρώτοις 655m 659m
     αὐτὸν] α[...]τὸν
     ζήλει] ζήλῳ 260 (149 471 606) 629 (769) 336
     ἁμαρτιῶν] ἁμαρτωλῶν 253 (655 659) ܢܚܒܠ
     ἁμαρτιῶν καὶ ἐν ἀκρασίαις] ܪܬܝܡܘܐܚ ܕܚܒܪ
     καὶ³] om 253 (655 659)
     ἀκρασίαις] εὐκρασίαις 336
4. διαστολῆς] ܒܚܘܚ
     αὐτοῦ²] om 253 (655 659)
     συναλλάγματι] συναλάγματι 659
5. ἀποκρύφοις] ܢܣܬܪ
     ἁμαρτάνει] om Syr
     οὐχ] ὀχ' 253 (655 659)
     πάσῃ] πασα 659*
     συνταγῇ] ܣܝܚܠ
     εἰσόδῳ] εἰσώδω (655 659)
     οἰκίαν] οἰκεῖαν 253
     ἐν ⁵] om 253 (655 659)
     ἱλαρότητι] ἱλαρότι 253 (655 659)
     ὡς ἄκακος] σάκκος 655 ὡσάκκος 253 (655 659)
     ܡܗ ܒܡ ܕܢܬܚ ܡܗ
6. τοὺς...ὁσίων] ܪܒܡܚܕ ܟܐܕ ܩܕܐܟ ܕܚ ܝܢܠ ܚ ܚ ܒܡ ܚܕ ܬܕ ܪ
     πενίᾳ] πεμά (655m πολεμά 655c marg 659) ܪܚܡܘܚ

3. His hand is among the first to be lifted against the defendant,[78]
        as if he were motivated by a virtuous zeal,
        but he himself is guilty of a whole hoard of sins
        with no self-control.[79]
4. His eyes are on every woman promiscuously,[80]
        he lies when making contracts under oath.[81]
5. He sins secretly and at night, as if no one saw him.
        With his eyes he propositions every woman for illicit affairs.[82]
    However, he is quick to enter cheerfully into every house,
        as if he were innocent.
6. May God snatch away[83] these hypocrites
        from among his devout;
    May he live his life in sickness and in poverty.[84]

---

[78] The courtroom defendants.

[79] One MS reads: "appears content."

[80] Syr: "immodestly."

[81] Gk: "his tongue is false in making a contract under oath."

[82] Gk: "with his eyes he speaks...of evil arrangements."

[83] Gk: "lift off" (the earth.); "banish."

[84] Gk: "May their flesh be decayed and their life be impoverished."

7. ἀνακαλύψαι ὁ θεὸς τὰ ἔργα ἀνθρώπων ἀνθρωπαρέσκων·
   ἐν καταγέλωτι καὶ μυκτηρισμῷ τὰ ἔργα αὐτοῦ·
8. καὶ δικαιώσαισαν ὅσιοι τὸ κρίμα τοῦ θεοῦ αὐτῶν·
   ἐν τῷ ἐξαίρεσθαι ἁμαρτωλοὺς ἀπὸ προσώπου δικαίου·
   ἀνθρωπάρεσκον λαλοῦντα νόμον μετὰ δόλου·
9. Καὶ οἱ ὀφθαλμοὶ αὐτῶν ἐπ' οἶκον ἀνδρὸς ἐν εὐσταθείᾳ·
   ὡς ὄφις διαλῦσαι σοφίαν ἀλλήλων
   ἐν λόγοις παρανόμων·
10. Οἱ λόγοι αὐτοῦ παραλογισμοὶ
    εἰς πρᾶξιν ἐπιθυμίας ἀδίκου·
    οὐκ ἀπέστη ἕως ἐνίκησεν· σκορπίσαι ὡς ἐν ὀρφανίᾳ·

---

7. ἀνακαλύψαι] ἀνακαλύψας (655* ἀνακαλύψαι 655c)

8. δικαιώσαισαν] δικαιώσασαν 655* 659 δικαιώσαιεν 260 (149 471
      606) δικαίωσαιαν 629 δικαίωσαειαν 769
   ὅσιοι] οἱ ὅσιοι 260 (149 471 606) 336 ܪܫܝܐ
   δικαίου] τοῦ δικαίου 336
   νόμον] μόνον 253 (655 659)
   δόλου] δούλου 253 (655 659)

9. αὐτῶν] αὐτοῦ 336 ܥܝܢܘܗܝ
   ἐπ'] ἐν 260 (149 471 606)
   οἶκον] οἴκῳ 260 (149 471 606)
   ἀνδρὸς] om Syr
   εὐσταθείᾳ] εὐσταθία 253 (655 659) (471 606) 336
   ἀλλήλων] ܚܕ ܚܕܒ
   παρανόμων] ܕܥܘܠܐ

10. Οἱ] [...] I 629
    παραλογισμοὶ] ܚܘܫܒܐ ܘܥܘܠܐ
    ἀδίκου] ἀδίκων 253 (655 659)
    ἀπέστη] ἀνέστη 260 (149 471 606) ܩܡ
    ἐνίκησεν] ἐνίκησε 260 (149 471 606) 336 om Syr
    ἐν ὀρφανίᾳ] ܚܝܬ ܝܬܡܐ

7.   May God unmask the deeds of those hypocrites.
      and expose their deeds with ridicule and derision.
8.   And may the devout prove their God's judgment to be right,
      by the removal of the sinners from the presence of the righteous.
      even that hypocrite who deceitfully quotes the Torah.
9.   And then their eyes are on another person's peaceful home
      like a serpent.
   Their arguments[85] destroy with distorted words.
10.   He speaks deceitfully, so that he may carry out his evil desires.
   He does not give up until he succeeds
   in scattering them as orphans.

---

[86] "Specious arguments intending to deceive," "casuistry." Gk: " the wisdom of one another."

11. Καὶ ἠρήμωσεν οἶκον ἕνεκεν ἐπιθυμίας παρανόμου·
παρελογίσατο ἐν λόγοις·
ὅτι οὐκ ἔστιν ὁρῶν καὶ κρίνων·

12. Ἐπλήσθη ἐν παρανομίᾳ ἐν ταύτῃ·
καὶ οἱ ὀφθαλμοὶ αὐτοῦ ἐπ᾽ οἶκον ἕτερον·
ὀλεθρεῦσαι ἐν λόγοις ἀναπτερώσεως·

13. Οὐκ ἐμπίπλαται ἡ ψυχὴ αὐτοῦ·
ὡς ᾅδης· ἐν πᾶσι τούτοις·

14. Γένοιτο· κύριε· ἡ μερὶς αὐτοῦ ἐν ἀτιμίᾳ ἐνώπιόν σου·
ἡ ἔξοδος αὐτοῦ ἐν στεναγμοῖς
καὶ ἡ εἴσοδος αὐτοῦ ἐν ἀρᾷ·

15. ἐν ὀδύναις καὶ πενίᾳ καὶ ἀπορίᾳ ἡ ζωὴ αὐτοῦ· κύριε
ὁ ὕπνος αὐτοῦ ἐν λύπαις
καὶ ἡ ἐξέγερσις αὐτοῦ ἐν ἀπορίαις·

---

11. οἶκον] om 260 (149 471 606)

12. ἐν παρανομίᾳ ἐν ταύτῃ] ܪ‌ܠܐܬ ܪܝܡܐ
ὀλεθρεῦσαι] ὀλοθρεῦσαι 260 (149 471 606) 629? (769) 336

13. ἐμπίπλαται] ἐμπέπλαται 655 ἐμπέλαται 659 ἐμπίμπλαται 769
ὡς] om 260 (149 471 606)
ᾅδης] om 260 (149 471 606) ὁ ᾅδης 336 ܠܐܬ

14. ἀτιμίᾳ] ἀτιμί 659*

15. ὀδύναις] ὀδώναις 655*
πενίᾳ] ἐν πενίᾳ 260 (149 471 606)
καὶ²] om 253 (655 659)
λύπαις] ὀδύναις 260 (149 471 606)
ἐξέγερσις] ἔγερσις 336
ἀπορίαις] ἀπορίας (655 659) ἀπορίᾳ (471 606)

11. He devastates a home with his twisted desire.
     He deceives with words, for he thinks:
       "There is no one who sees or judges."
12. He gorges himself with these kinds of crooked acts at one place,
       and then his eyes focus on another house,
       to destroy it with seductive words[1]
13. With all this his appetite,[2] like Death,[3] is not satisfied.

14. Lord, may his destiny be disgrace.[4]
       May he go out groaning and come back cursing.
15. Lord, may his life be lived in agony, poverty, and distress;
       may he have trouble sleeping and difficulty getting up.

---

[87] Gk: "words that give wings," "agitating words."

[88] Gk: "soul."

[89] Gk: "Hades."

[90] Gk: "May his portion be in dishonor before you."

16. ἀφαιρεθείη ὕπνος ἀπὸ κροτάφων αὐτοῦ ἐν νυκτί·
  ἀποπέσοι ἀπὸ παντὸς ἔργου χειρῶν αὐτοῦ
  ἐν ἀτιμίᾳ.
17. Κενὸς χερσὶν αὐτοῦ εἰσέλθοι εἰς τὸν οἶκον αὐτοῦ·
  καὶ ἐλλιπὴς ὁ οἶκος αὐτοῦ ἀπὸ παντὸς
  οὗ ἐμπλήσει ψυχὴν αὐτοῦ·
18. ἐν μονώσει ἀτεκνίας τὸ γῆρας αὐτοῦ
  εἰς ἀνάλημψιν·

19. Σκορπισθείησαν σάρκες ἀνθρωπαρέσκων ὑπὸ θηρίων·
  καὶ ὀστᾶ παρανόμων κατέναντι τοῦ ἡλίου ἐν ἀτιμίᾳ·
20. Ὀφθαλμοὺς ἐκκόψαισαν κόρακες ὑποκρινομένων·
  ὅτι ἠρήμωσαν οἴκους πολλοὺς ἀνθρώπων ἐν ἀτιμίᾳ·
  καὶ ἐσκόρπισαν ἐν ἐπιθυμίᾳ·

---

16. ἀφαιρεθείη] ἀφαιρευθείη (655 659)

  νυκτί] υκτὶ 659

  ἀποπέσοι] ἀποπέσοιεν 253 ἀποπάσοιεν (655 659m)
    ἀποπέσει (471 606)

  χειρῶν] χειρῶς 655m 659 χειρὸς (471 606)

  ἐν ἀτιμίᾳ...αὐτου² (verse 17)] om 253 (655 659)
  ἀτιμίᾳ] ἀτιμίον 629

17. ἐλλιπὴς] ἐλλειπὴς 253 (655 659) 769

18. μονώσει] μονία 253 (655 659)

  ἀνάλημψιν] ἀνάληψιν (655 659) 260 (149 471 606) 629
    (769) 336

  ἐν...ἀνάλημψιν] ‎ܐܩܠ ܪܘ ܡܪܠ ܐܠܩ

19. σκορπισθείησαν] οὐ σκορπισθείησαν (655 659)

20. ὀφθαλμοὺς] om Syr
  ἐκκόψαισαν] ἐκκόωειαν 260(149 471 606) 629 (769) 336

  ὀφθαλμοὺς...κόρακες]~ ἐκκόψειαν κόρακες ὀφθαλμοὺς ἀνθρώπων
    260 (149 471 606) 629 (769) 336

  ὑποκρινομένων] ὑποκρινιμένων (655 659)

  ἠρήμωσαν] ἠρήμωσεν 253 (655 659)

  πολλοὺς ἀνθρώπων] ἀνθρώπων πολλῶν 629 (769)

  ἐσκόρπισαν] ἐσκόρπισεν 253 (655 659)

  ἐν²] om 253 (655 659)

16. May he be unable to sleep at night,[1]
    May he fail disgracefully in everything he does.[2]

17. May he return to his house empty-handed,
    may his house lack everything
    with which he would satisfy himself;[3]

18. May his old age be spent alone and childless,
    until he passes away.[4]

19. Let wild animals tear apart the flesh of the hypocrites,
    and may the bones of the criminals[5]
    disgracefully bleach out in the sun.[6]

20. May crows peck out the eyes of these hypocrites,
    because they disgracefully seized so many people's homes,
    and greedily evicted[7] them.

---

[91] Gk: "May sleep be taken away from his temples at night."

[92] Gk: "to which he sets his hand."

[93] Gk: "fill his soul."

[94] Gk: "his being taken up." The term is not found in the LXX and only in Lk 9.51. Syr: "and may none of his children come near to him."

[95] Gk: "Those who twist the law." ("Lawyers"?)

[96] See Dt 28.26; Ez 6.5; 29.5; 39.17.

[97] Gk: "scatter."

21. Καὶ οὐκ ἐμνήσθησαν θεοῦ·
      καὶ οὐκ ἐφοβήθησαν τὸν θεὸν ἐν ἅπασι τούτοις·
      καὶ παρώργισαν τὸν θεὸν καὶ παρώξυναν.
22. ἐξάραι αὐτοὺς ἀπὸ τῆς γῆς·
      ὅτι ψυχὰς ἀκάκων παραλογισμῷ ὑπεκρίνοντο·
23. Μακάριοι οἱ φοβούμενοι τὸν κύριον ἐν ἀκακίᾳ αὐτῶν·
      ὁ κύριος ῥύσεται αὐτοὺς ἀπὸ ἀνθρώπων δολίων
      καὶ ἁμαρτωλῶν·
      καὶ ῥύσεται ἡμᾶς ἀπὸ παντὸς σκανδάλου παρανόμου.
24. Ἐξάραι ὁ θεὸς τοὺς ποιοῦντας
      ἐν ὑπερηφανίᾳ πᾶσαν ἀδικίαν·
      ὅτι κριτὴς μέγας καὶ κραταιὸς κύριος ὁ θεὸς ἡμῶν
      ἐν δικαιοσύνῃ·
25. Γένοιτο· κύριε· τὸ ἔλεός σου
      ἐπὶ πάντας τοὺς ἀγαπῶντάς σε:

---

21. ἐμνήσθησαν] ἐμνήσθης 253 (655 659)

   θεοῦ] ἀνθρώπου 253 (655 659)

   οὐκ²] οὐ καὶ 769

   ἐφοβήθησαν] φοβήθησαν 769

   θεὸν] κύριον (655 659)

   ἅπασι] πᾶσι 260 (149 471 606) 336

   παρώργισαν] παρόργησαν 253χ (655 659)

   παρώξυναν] παρώξυνεν 253 659 ܐܬܘܙܚ παρώξηνεν 655

22. ἐξάραι] ἐξάρας (655 659) ܢܘܣܬ

   ὑπεκρίνοντο] ὑπεκρίνετο 659 ὑπεκρύνοντο 336

     ܘܣܗ ܐܟܖܚܡ

23. αὐτῶν] +καὶ 253 (655 659) 336

   ῥύσεται²] ῥήσεται 655

   ἡμᾶς] ὑμᾶς (655 659)

24. ἐξάραι] ξάραι 253 (655 659) ܐܖܣܬ

   ὑπερηφανίᾳ] ὑπεριφανία (655 659) ὑπσρηφανία 769

   μέγας] om Syr

21.   In all these things they have not remembered God,
     nor have they feared God in all these things;
     but they have angered and aggravated God..
22.   May he banish them from the earth,
     because they betrayed these poor souls[1] with their lies.
23.   Happy are those who are innocent and fear the Lord.
     The Lord will rescue them from deceitful and sinful people,
     and will rescue us from every legal trap.[2]
24.   May God banish those arrogantly doing every injustice,
     because our God is a powerful Lord
     and a great and just judge.
25.   Lord, may your mercy be upon all those who love you.

---

[98] Gk: "souls of the innocent ones."

[99] Gk: "from the snare of one who twists the law."

5. Ψαλμὸς τῷ Σαλωμών:

1. Κύριε ὁ θεός· αἰνέσω τῷ ὀνόματί σου ἐν ἀγαλλιάσει·
   ἐν μέσῳ ἐπισταμένων τὰ κρίματά σου τὰ δίκαια·
2. ὅτι σὺ χρηστὸς καὶ ἐλεήμων· ἡ καταφυγὴ τοῦ πτωχοῦ·
   ἐν τῷ κεκραγέναι με πρὸς σὲ
   μὴ παρασιωπήσῃς ἀπ' ἐμοῦ·
3. οὐ γὰρ λήψεταί σκῦλα παρὰ ἀνδρὸς δυνατοῦ·
   καὶ τίς λήψεται ἀπὸ πάντων ὧν ἐποίησας
   ἐὰν μὴ σὺ δῷς·
4. ὅτι ἄνθρωπος καὶ ἡ μερὶς αὐτοῦ παρὰ σοῦ ἐν σταθμῷ·
   οὐ προσθήσει τοῦ πλεονάσαι
   παρὰ τὸ κρίμα σου: ὁ θεός·

---

5 = Δ] 260 (149) Ε 253 629 (769) 336

Ψαλμὸς τῷ Σαλωμών] ~ τῷ σαλομών ψαλμὸς πέμπτος Ε 336

τῷ] *om* 149 τοῦ 655 το 659

Σαλωμών] σαλομών 260 (149 606) 336 σολομών 629 (769)
   σολομῶντος 655 σαλομῶντος 659

1. αἰνέσω] ἐναίσω (655 659)

   τῷ] τὸ (471 606) 336

   ὀνόματί] ὄνομά (471 606) 336 ὄνομά 606

2. σὺ] *om* 253 (655 659)

   χρηστὸς] εὔχρηστος 253 (655 659)

   ἡ] εἶ 260 (149 471 606)

3. οὐ] +τὰς (655m 659)
   ου...δυνατοῦ] *om* 629 (769)

   γὰρ] *om* (655m 659)

   σκῦλα] + ἄνθρωπος 260 (149 471) 606 {pr τις vG}
   ⲕⲑⲩⲥⲝ ⲕⲩⲓⲟ

   παρὰ] ἀπὸ 336

   ὧν] ὧν 769

4. σοῦ¹] σοὶ 260 (149 471 606)

5. A Psalm of Solomon

1. O Lord God, I will joyfully praise your name
      among those who know your equitable judgments.
2. Because you are kind and merciful, the refuge of the destitute.[1]
      When I cry out in anguish[2] to you, do not ignore me.
3. For if no one can rob[3] a strong man,
      who can take anything from all you have made,
      unless you give it away?
4. Because a person and their destiny are on the scales before you;
      no one can add anything that goes against your decisions, O God.

---

[101] Gk: "beggar."

[102] Gk: "scream,""croak." See 1.1.

[103] Gk: "take loot from...."

5. Ἐν τῷ θλίβεσθαι ἡμᾶς ἐπικαλεσόμεθά σε εἰς βοήθειαν
    καὶ σὺ οὐκ ἀποστρέψῃ τὴν δέησιν ἡμῶν·
    ὅτι σὺ ὁ θεὸς ἡμῶν εἶ·

6. μὴ βαρύνῃς τὴν χεῖρά σου ἐφ' ἡμᾶς·
    ἵνα μὴ δι' ἀνάγκην ἁμάρτωμεν·

7. καὶ ἐὰν μὴ ἐπιστρέψῃς ἡμᾶς· οὐκ ἀφεξόμεθα·
    ἀλλ' ἐπὶ σὲ ἥξομεν.

8. Ἐὰν γὰρ πεινάσω· πρὸς σὲ κεκράξομαι· ὁ θεός·
    καὶ σὺ δώσεις μοι·

9. Τὰ πετεινὰ καὶ τοὺς ἰχθύας σὺ τρέφεις·
    ἐν τῷ διδόναι σε ὑετὸν ἐρήμοις εἰς ἀνατολὴν χλόης·

---

5. σε] om 253 (655) καὶ (659)
    ἀποστρέψῃ] ἀποστρέψεις 260 (149 471 606) ἀποστρέψῃς 336
    ὅτι σὺ ὁ θεὸς ἡμῶν] om (655 659)
    ὁ θεὸς ἡμῶν εἶ] ~ εἶ ὁ θεὸς ἡμῶν 260 (149 471 606) 629 (769) 336

6. βαρύνῃς] βαρύνεις 336 ,ܪܘܐܝܟܝ

    δι'] δ' (655 659)
    δι' ἀνάγκην] ܩܘܝܝ

7. ἐὰν μὴ ἐπιστρέψῃς ἡμᾶς] ܠܐ ܢܗܦܟ ܐܪܝܢ ܝܢ ܠܡ
    ἀφεξόμεθα] ἀφεσόμεθα (655 659) ܢܘܚ ܝܢ

8. πεινάσω] πινάσω 253 (655 659) 336 πεινάς 769 * + ܒܝܐ
    σὺ] σοὶ 336

9. τρέφεις] lat to end of verse 629
    ὑετὸν] εἰς τὸν 655 659 υἱετὸν 769 + ἐν 260 (149 471 606) 629
    (769) 336

5.   When we are persecuted, we call on you for help
        and you will not turn away from our prayer,
        because you are our God.
6.   Don't be too demanding of us,[104] lest we sin in desperation.
7.   And even if you don't turn us back,
        we will not keep away, but we will come to you.[105]
8.   For if I am hungry, I will cry out to you, O God,
        and you will give me something.
9.   You feed the young birds and the fish,
        when you send rain to the wilderness[106] that the grass may grow;

---

[104] Gk: "make your hand heavy against us." See Job 2.5.

[105] Syr: "...and do not turn your face from us lest we go far from you."

[106] Gk: "savannahs," "empty grasslands."

10. ἑτοιμάσαι χορτάσματα ἐν ἐρήμῳ παντὶ ζῶντι·
	καὶ ἐὰν πινάσωσιν· πρὸς σὲ ἀροῦσιν πρόσωπον αὐτῶν·
11. τοὺς βασιλεῖς καὶ ἄρχοντας
	καὶ λαοὺς σὺ τρέφεις· ὁ θεός·
	καὶ πτωχοῦ καὶ πένητος ἡ ἐλπὶς τίς ἐστιν
	εἰ μὴ σύ· κύριε·
12. καὶ σὺ ἐπακούσῃ· ὅτι τίς χρηστὸς
	καὶ ἐπιεικὴς ἀλλ' ἢ σύ·
	εὐφρᾶναι ψυχὴν ταπεινοῦ
	ἐν τῷ ἀνοῖξαι χεῖρά σου ἐν ἐλέει·
13. Ἡ χρηστότης ἀνθρώπου ἐν φειδῷ καὶ ἡ αὔριον·
	καὶ ἐὰν δευτερώσῃ ἄνευ γογγυσμοῦ
	καὶ τοῦτο θαυμάσειας·

---

10. ἑτοιμάσαι {ἡτοίμασας Ra=vG}

χορτάσματα] χοράσματα (655 659) χορτάσμα 769* χορτάσματ 769c

ἐρήμῳ] ἐρημίω (655 659)

πινάσωσιν] πεινάσωσι 260 (149 471 606) 336 πεινήσωσι 769 (629)

ἀροῦσιν] ἀροῦσι 260 (149 471 606) 629 (769) 336

πρόσωπον] πρόσωπα 260 (149 471 606) πρόσωπ 769c

11. ἄρχοντας] τοὺς ἄρχοντας 260 (149 471 606)

τρέφεις] στρέφεις 253 (655 659)

πένητος] πένητο 769c

ἐλπὶς] ελπὴς (655 659)

12. ἐπακούσῃ] ἐπακούσῃς 253 (655 659)

τίς] ܐܝܢ ܗܘ

εὐφρᾶναι] ܚܕܘܠ 16h1° ܚܕܘܠ 16h1*

ψυχὴν] τὴν ψυχὴν (655 659)

ταπεινοῦ] om Syr

ἐλέει] ἐλέω 26 (149 471 606) 629 336 ἐλέη (655 659) ἐλαίώ 769

13. φειδῷ] φίλω 260 (149 606 471) φειδοῖ 336

αὔριον] ܘܡܚܪ ܝܘܡܐ

ἐὰν] +καὶ 260 (149 471 606) 336

δευτερώσῃ] δευτερώσει (655 659) ܗܘ ܕܬܪܝܢ ܙܒܬܐ

θαυμάσειας] θαυμ(---)ς erased 253 θαυμάσιάσω 629 (769) θαυμάσας 655 659

10. So to provide pasture in the wilderness;
    for every living thing; when they are hungry, will turn to you.[107]
11. You feed kings and rulers and their subjects,[108] O God,
    and who is the hope of the poor and the needy, if not you, O Lord?
12. And you will listen, because who is kind and generous but you,
    cheering the humble,[109] by reaching out in mercy? [110]
13. Human kindness comes meagerly, and delayed [111]
    and if it is repeated without grumbling this is remarkable.

---

[107] Gk: "they will lift up their faces to you."

[108] Gk: "(common) people."

[109] Gk: "at cheering [the] soul of [the] lowly man." Syr: "...satisfied."

[110] Gk: "opening your hand in mercy?"

[111] Gk: "tomorrow." The sense is that human help is always "too little and too late,"
     in contrast to God's help that is generous and prompt. For "meagerly" one MS
     reads: "to a friend."

14. Τὸ δὲ δόμα σου πολὺ μετὰ χρηστότητος καὶ πλούσιον·
    καὶ οὗ ἐστιν ἡ ἐλπὶς ἐπὶ σέ οὐ φείσεται ἐν δόματι·
15. Ἐπὶ πᾶσαν τὴν γῆν τὸ ἔλεός σου· κύριε· ἐν χρηστότητι·
16. Μακάριος οὗ μνημονεύει ὁ θεὸς
    ἐν συμμετρίᾳ αὐταρκείας·
    ἐὰν ὑπερπλεονάσῃ ὁ ἄνθρωπος· ἐξαμαρτάνει·
17. ἱκανὸν τὸ μέτριον ἐν δικαιοσύνῃ·
    καὶ ἐν τούτῳ ἡ εὐλογία κυρίου
    εἰς πλησμονὴν ἐν δικαιοσύνῃ·

---

14. χρηστότητος] χρηστότη 336* (the last word of text of ms 336
    before the lacuna extending to 8.12a)

και πλούσιον...ἀκαθαρσίας (8.12)] *om* 336

πλούσιον] ܪܕܡܐ

οὗ¹] οὐκ 253 (655 659) ܪܕܘܠܐ

ἐστιν] ἔστη (655 659)

ἡ ἐλπὶς ἐπὶ σέ] = ܢܕܠܝܗ ܪܝܣܡ
    ~ ἐπὶ σέ κύριε ἡ ἐλπίς 260 (149 471 606) 629 (769)

ἐν] ἐὰν (655 659)

16. οὗ] οὐ (655 659)

θεὸς] ܪܝܬ

ἐν συμμετρίᾳ αὐταρκείας] ܡܬܘܡܢܬ .ܪܕܘܒܪܐܚܣ

αὐταρκείας] αὐταρκεσίας 260 (149 471 606) αὐταρκίας 253
    (655 659)

17. ἱκανὸν] ܪܣܦܩ

μέτριον] ܪܕܡܣܘܚ

καὶ...δικαιοσύνῃ] *om* Syr

πλησμονὴν] πλεισμονὴν 253

14. But your gift is abundantly kind and generous,
    and those who hope in you will have everything they need.
15. O Lord, your kind mercy[112] extends over all the earth.
16. Happy is the one whom God[113] remembers
    　　　with only what is necessary.[114]
    If people are[115] excessively rich, they easily sin.
17. Moderate wealth with righteousness is enough,
    　　for this comes with the Lord's blessing:
    　　to be satisfied with righteousness.

---

[112] Gk also: "May your mercy..."

[113] Syr: "Lord."

[114] Gk: "with a proportionate sufficiency."

[115] Gk: "If a man is. . . ."

18. Εὐφράνθησαν οἱ φοβούμενοι κύριον ἐν ἀγαθοῖς·

    καὶ ἡ χρηστότης σου ἐπὶ Ἰσραὴλ ἐν τῇ βασιλείᾳ σου·
19. Εὐλογημένη ἡ δόξα κυρίου ὅτι αὐτὸς βασιλεὺς ἡμῶν:

---

18. εὐφράνθησαν] ηὐφράνθησαν 253 (655 659)
    {εὐφρανθείησαν Ra=vG}

  ἐν²] om 253 (655 659)

19. εὐλογημένη] εὐλογιμένη 655 769

18.   Those who fear the Lord are content with their possessions.

      May your kindness be upon Israel as you rule.
19.   Praised be the glory of the Lord because he himself is our king.

6. Ἐν ἐλπίδι τῷ Σαλωμών·

1. Μακάριος ἀνὴρ οὗ ἡ καρδία αὐτοῦ ἑτοίμη
   ἐπικαλέσασθαι τὸ ὄνομα κυρίου·
   ἐν τῷ μνημονεύειν αὐτὸν τὸ ὄνομα κυρίου σωθήσεται·
2. αἱ ὁδοὶ αὐτοῦ κατευθύνονται ὑπὸ κυρίου·
   καὶ πεφυλαγμένα ἔργα χειρῶν αὐτοῦ
      ὑπὸ κυρίου θεοῦ αὐτοῦ·
3. Ἀπὸ ὁράσεως πονηρῶν ἐνυπνίων αὐτοῦ
   οὐ ταραχθήσεται ἡ ψυχὴ αὐτοῦ·
   ἐν διαβάσει ποταμῶν καὶ σάλον θαλασσῶν
   οὐ πτοηθήσεται.

6=Ϛ] 769 *om* 253 606 629 336

  ἐλπίδι] ἐλπίς (655m 659m)

  τῷ] τοῦ (655 659)

  Σαλωμών] σαλομῶν 260 (149 606) 629 (769) σολομῶν 253
    σολομῶντος 655 σαλομῶντος 659

1. ἐπικαλέσασθαι] ἐπικαλεῖσθαι 260 (149 471 606)
   κυρίου[1]] θέου 629

   μνημονεύειν] μνημόνεύεσθαι 655m ~νευεν c marg 655 (659)
   ὄνομα] pr τὸ 629

2. ὑπὸ] ܣܩܠ ܩܝ

   κυρίου[2]] *om* Syr

3. ὁράσεως] ὁράσεων 260 (149 606) 629 (769)

   πονηρῶν] πονηρον 659*

   ἐνυπνίων] ܪܠܠܝ

   οὐ[1]...αὐτοῦ] ܣܐܘܩ .ܐܡ ܩܠ.ܬ ܕܠܒ . ܕܐܒܕ ܐܠ

   διαβάσει] διαβάσετε (655 659) ܪܬܐܪ

   ποταμῶν] πομῶν 769 ποτμῶν 769c

   σάλον] 655m σάων 655c marg σάλων 260 (149 471 606) ܪܝܠܩܣ
      σάλῳ {Legarde, vG}

   πτοηθήσεται] πτωηθήσεται 253

6. With Hope. Of Solomon

1. Happy is the person whose heart is ready
      to call upon the name of the Lord for help.
   When they remember the name of the Lord they will be saved.
2. Their ways are directed by the Lord,
      and the works of their hands are guarded
      by the Lord [116] their God.
3. Their spirit will not be troubled by nightmares;[117]
      they will not be frightened when crossing rivers or rough seas.

---

[116] Syr omits "the Lord."

[117] Gk: "the vision of evil dreams."

4. Ἐξανέστη ἐξ ὕπνου αὐτοῦ
     καὶ ηὐλόγησεν τῷ ὀνόματι κυρίου·
   ἐπ᾽ εὐσταθείᾳ καρδίας αὐτοῦ ἐξύμνησεν
     τῷ ὀνόματι τοῦ θεοῦ αὐτοῦ·
5. καὶ ἐδεήθη τοῦ προσώπου κυρίου
     περὶ παντὸς τοῦ οἴκου αὐτοῦ·
   καὶ κύριος εἰσήκουσεν προσευχὴν παντὸς
     ἐν φόβῳ θεοῦ·
6. καὶ πᾶν αἴτημα ψυχῆς ἐλπιζούσης πρὸς αὐτὸν
     ἐπιτελεῖ ὁ κύριος·
   εὐλογητὸς κύριος ὁ ποιῶν ἔλεος
     τοῖς ἀγαπῶσιν αὐτὸν ἐν ἀληθείᾳ·

---

4. ηὐλόγησεν] εὐλόγησεν (655 659) εὐλόγησε 260 (149 471) 606)
     629

   τῷ ὀνόματι¹] τὸ ὄνομα 260 (149 471 606)

   κυρίου...ὀνόματι] om (655 659)

   εὐσταθείᾳ] εὐσταθίᾳ 253 (471 606)

   ἐξύμνησεν] ἐξύμνησε 260 (149 471 606) 629

   τῷ²] τὸ 260 (149 471 606)

   ὀνόματι¹] ὄνομα 260 (471 606)

   τοῦ θεοῦ αὐτοῦ] ܪܝܫ

   αὐτοῦ³] om 253 (655 659)

5. κύριος] om (655 659)

   εἰσήκουσεν] εἰσήκουσε 260 (149 471 606) 629 (769)

   ἐν φόβῳ θεοῦ] ܐܡ ܡܕܠܘܬܗ

6. αὐτὸν] α᾽ τὸν {νG}

   ὁ¹] om 260 (149 471 606) 629 (769)

   κύριος²] om Syr

   ἔλεος] ἔλεον 260 (149 471 606)

PsSol 6

4. They rise out of sleep and give praise to the name of the Lord,
   when their hearts are strong,[118]
      they sing out to the name of their God.[119]
5. They seek the Lord for everyone in their household,
      and the Lord hears the prayers of all who fear God.[120]
6. The Lord fulfills every request from all those who hope in him.
   Praised be the Lord who shows mercy
      to those who truly love him.

---

[118] Gk: "in good health; well-equipped; in good form."

[119] Syr: "the Lord."

[120] Syr: "Him."

7. Τῷ Σαλωμών· ἐπιστροφῆς:

1. Μὴ ἀποσκηνώσῃς ἀφ᾽ ἡμῶν· ὁ θεός·
   ἵνα μὴ ἐπιθῶνται ἡμῖν οἳ ἐμίσησαν ἡμᾶς δωρεάν·
2. ὅτι ἀπώσω αὐτούς· ὁ θεός
   μὴ πατησάτω ὁ πούς αὐτῶν
   κληρονομίαν ἁγιάσματός σου·
3. σὺ ἐν θελήματί σου παίδευσον ἡμᾶς·
   καὶ μὴ δῷς ἔθνεσιν·
4. ἐὰν γὰρ ἀποστείλῃς θάνατον·
   σὺ ἐντελῇ αὐτῷ περὶ ἡμῶν·
5. ὅτι σὺ ἐλεήμων·
   καὶ οὐκ ὀργισθήσῃ τοῦ συντελέσαι ἡμᾶς·

6. Ἐν τῷ κατασκηνοῦν τὸ ὄνομά σου ἐν μέσῳ ἡμῶν
   ἐλεηθησόμεθα·
   καὶ οὐκ ἰσχύσει πρὸς ἡμᾶς ἔθνος·

7=Z] 253 629 (769) Ϛ 260 (149)

Τῷ] τοῦ (655 659)

Σαλωμών] σαλομών (655 659) 260 (149 606) 629 (769) σολομών 253

1. ἡ] pr Ϛ 253*

   πιθῶνται] = ܘܣܡ ἀπιθῶνται (655 659)

   ἡμῖν] ἡμή (655 659)

   ἐμίσησαν] μισήσαντες 260 (149 471 606) 629 (769) ܘܣܩܝܘܬ

2. ἀπώσω] ἀπόσω 659

   πατησάτω] πατισάντω 253

   ἁγιάσματός] ἀγαιάσματος 769

3. θελήματί] ἐθελήματί (655 659)

   ἔθνεσιν] ἔθυεαν (655m 659)

4. γὰρ] om (655 659)

   ἀποστείλῃς] ἀποστέλῃς (655 659)

   ἐντελῇ] ܗܣ

7. Of Solomon: Restoring.

1. Don't leave us[121] O God,
    > so those who hate us without cause might not attack us,
2. > because you have pushed them away, O God.
    May their feet not trample your holy inheritance.[122]
3. Discipline us as you wish,
    > but don't turn us over to the Gentiles;[123]
4. for if you send Death away, it will be because
    > you, yourself, have told him what to do about us.[124]
5. Because you are kind,
    > and you would not be angry enough to destroy us.

6. While your name lives among us, we will receive mercy;
    > and the Gentiles will not defeat us.

---

[121] Gk: "Don't pitch your tent away, far away from us."

[122] The Temple; see 2.2, 19.

[123] Or: "You, yourself, instruct us about what you desire
    and don't give (such instruction) to the Gentiles..."

[124] Or: "For if ever you dispatch Death, you give him orders about (avoiding) us."A
possible allusion to the Exodus (12.23).

7. ὅτι σὺ ὑπερασπιστὴς ἡμῶν·
       καὶ ἡμεῖς ἐπικαλεσόμεθά σε·
       καὶ σὺ ἐπακούσῃ ἡμῶν·
8. ὅτι σὺ οἰκτιρήσεις τὸ γένος Ἰσραὴλ εἰς τὸν αἰῶνα·
       καὶ οὐκ ἀπώσῃ·
9. καὶ ἡμεῖς ὑπὸ ζυγόν σου τὸν αἰῶνα
       καὶ μάστιγα παιδείας σου·
10. κατευθυνεῖς ἡμᾶς ἐν καιρῷ ἀντιλήψεώς σου·
       τοῦ ἐλεῆσαι τὸν οἶκον Ἰακὼβ
         εἰς ἡμέραν ἐν ᾗ ἐπηγγείλω αὐτοῖς·

---

7. ὑπερασπιστὴς ἡμῶν] ܡܥܕܪ

   σὺ²] om 629 (769)

   ἐπακούσῃ] ἐπακούσεις 629 (769)

8. οἰκτιρήσεις] οἰκτειρήσεις 253 260 (149 471 606)
   ὁ ἰκτηρμων 655 ὁ ἰκτηρήσας (655c 659) οἰκτηρήσεις 769
   γένος] ܙܪܥܐ
   ἀπώσῃ] ἀπώσει 253 ἀπόσει (655 659) ܬܫܒܘܩ,

9. καὶ¹...σου² (vs 9)] om Syr
   παιδείας] παιδίας 253 παιδιάσε (655m 659) παιδείᾳ 629? (769)

10. κατευθυνεῖς] κατευθύνεις 260
   καιρῷ] κερῷ 655 καερῷ 655χ
   ᾗ] ᾧ 253 (655 659)
   ἐπηγγείλω] ἐπειγγείλω 769* ܡܠܟ

7.   Because you are our protector,[125]
          we will call to you
          and you will hear us.
8.   Because you yourself will have compassion
          on the family of Israel forever,
              and will not reject them.[126]
 9.   But we are forever under your yoke
          and the whip of your discipline.
10.   For your help will direct us at the right time,
          to show mercy to the house of Jacob
          for the day when you promised it to them.

---

[125] Gk: "...holder of a shield above us."

[126] Gk: "push them away."

8. Τῷ Σαλωμών· εἰς νῖκος:

1. Θλῖψιν καὶ φωνὴν πολέμου ἤκουσεν τὸ οὖς μου·
   φωνὴν σάλπιγγος ἠχούσης σφαγὴν καὶ ὄλεθρον·
2. φωνὴ λαοῦ πολλοῦ ὡς ἀνέμου πολλοῦ σφόδρα·
   ὡς καταιγὶς πυρὸς πολλοῦ φερομένου δι᾽ ἐρήμου·
3. Καὶ εἶπα τῇ καρδίᾳ μου· ποῦ ἄρακρινεῖ
   αὐτὸν ὁ θεός;
4. φωνὴν ἤκουσα εἰς Ἱερουσαλὴμ πόλιν ἁγιάσματος·
   συνετρίβη ἡ ὀσφῦς μου ἀπὸ ἀκοῆς·
5. παρελύθη γόνατά μου:
   ἐφοβήθη ἡ καρδία μου·
   ἐταράχθη τὰ ὀστᾶ μου ὡς λίνον·

8= H] 629 (769) Θ 53* Ζ 260 (149)

Σαλωμών] σολομών 253 (655) σαλομών 659 260 (149 606) 629
  (769)

1. ἤκουσεν] ἤκουσε 260 (149 471 606) 629 (769)

   τὸ οὖς μου] ἡ ψυχή μου 629 marg [=vG only]

   σάλπιγγος] ܩܪܢܐ

   ἠχούσης] ܪܥܡܐ

   ὄλεθρον] + φωνὴν σάλπιγγος ἠχούσης σφαγὴν καὶ ὄλεθρον
     769 ditt.

2. φωνὴ] φωνὴν (655 659)

   πολλοῦ² ... πολλου³] om 655 659 +ὡς ἀνέμου πολλοῦ 629 (769)

   πολλοῦ³] om Syr

   ἐρήμου] ἐρήμου 659

3. εἶπα] εἶπον 260 (149 471 606) 629 (769)
     + ἐν {Hilgenfeld, vG}

   κρινεῖ] κρονεῖ (655m 659m)

   αὐτὸν] αὐτὴν 629 (769)

   θεός] om Syr

4. εἰς] ἐν 260 (149 471 606)

   ἡ ὀσφῦς μου] ܥܘܫܡܐ, ܣܝ

   ἁγιάσματος] ἁγιά σ...ματος... σματος (repeated as marker for folio
     assembly) 655

5. εφοβηθη...μου] om Syr

8. Of Solomon: On to Victory

1. I heard[127] sounds of suffering and battle,
   the blast of a trumpet sounding slaughter and destruction:
2. the sound of a huge mob, like a violent, raging wind,
   like a roaring fire storm sweeping down through the wilderness.
3. Then I said to myself:[128] "Is this God's judgment?" [129]
4. I heard these sounds in Jerusalem,[130] the holy city;
5. my stomach was sick at what I heard;[131]
   my knees buckled, my heart was terrified,
   my bones shook like reeds.[132]

---

[127] Gk: "My ear heard...."

[128] Gk: "in my heart."

[129] Gk: "Where then will God judge him?"

[130] See Jer 4.5.

[131] Gk: "My loins were crushed..."

[132] Gk: "flax reeds," or "linen cloth" or "(linen) sails."

6. εἶπα· κατευθύνουσιν ὁδοὺς αὐτῶν ἐν δικαιοσύνη·

7. Ἀνελογισάμην τὰ κρίματα τοῦ θεοῦ
   ἀπὸ κτίσεως οὐρανοῦ καὶ γῆς·
   ἐδικαίωσα τὸν θεὸν ἐν τοῖς κρίμασιν αὐτοῦ
   τοῖς ἀπ' αἰῶνος·

8. ἀνεκάλυψεν ὁ θεὸς τὰς ἁμαρτίας αὐτῶν
   ἐναντίον τοῦ ἡλίου·
   ἔγνω πᾶσα ἡ γῆ τὰ κρίματα τοῦ θεοῦ τὰ δίκαια·

9. ἐν καταγαίοις κρυφίοις αἱ παρανομίαι αὐτῶν
   ἐν παροργισμῷ·
   υἱὸς μετὰ μητρὸς καὶ πατὴρ μετὰ θυγατρὸς
   συνεφύροντο·

10. ἐμοιχῶντο ἕκαστος τὴν γυναῖκα τοῦ πλησίον αὐτοῦ·
    συνέθεντο αὐτοῖς συνθήκας μετὰ ὅρκου περὶ τούτων·

---

6. εἶπα] εἶτα (655 659) εἶπον 260 (149 471 606) 629 (769)
   ὁδοὺς] δοὺς 253 (655 659)
   αὐτῶν] αὐτόν (655 659)

7. Ἀνελογισάμην] Ἀνελογησάμην 253 ܐܬܚܫܒܬ
   θεου] ܐܠܗܐ
   κτίσεως] κρίσεως (655 659)
   ἐδικαίωσα] ἐδικαίωσαν (655 659)

8. ἀνεκάλυψεν] ἀνακάλυψεν 253 (659) ἀνακάληψεν (655)
   τὰς ἁμαρτίας αὐτῶν] ܚܛܗܝܗܘܢ
   ἐναντίον] ἐναντίων (655 659)
   ἔγνω] ἔγνωσαν 629 (769)
   θεοῦ] ܐܠܗܐ

9. ἐν¹] εἰς (655 659)
   καταγαίοις] καταγαίους (655m 659) καταγαίης 769 ܒܐܪܥܐ
   κρυφίοις] κρυφίους (655 659) κρυφοῖς 629 (769)
   αἱ...παροργισμῷ] ܒܢܟܠܐ ܗܘܘ
   παροργισμῷ] 769c
   θυγατρὸς] θυτρὸς 629 (769)

10. τὴν] om 260 (471 606) 629 (769)
    συνέθεντο] συνένθεντο 769

6. I said: "Are not these people righteous?"[133]

7. I considered[134] God's judgments
        since the creation of Heaven and Earth,
    I believed God to be right in his judgments,
        those from the beginning of time.[135]
8. God exposed their sins to the light of the sun;
        all the earth recognized the righteous judgments of God.
9. But their offenses were in secret hiding-places,
        provoking him to anger:
    son with mother, and father with daughter—
        they were incestuously involved[136]
10. They all were committing adultery with their neighbor's wives,
    they made agreements with each other about these things, under oath.

---

[133] Gk: "Are they directing their ways in righteousness?" (An ironic rhetorical question.)

[134] Gk: "calculated," "added up."

[135] Gk: "...from the ages."

[136] Gk: "mixed," "kneaded together (like dough)." See 2.13.

11. Τὰ ἅγια τοῦ θεοῦ διηρπάζωσαν·
         ὡς μὴ ὄντος κληρονόμου λυτρουμένου·
12. ἐπατοῦσαν τὸ θυσιαστήριον κυρίου
         ἀπὸ πάσης ἀκαθαρσίας
         καὶ ἐν ἀφέδρῳ αἵματος ἐμίαναν τὰς θυσίας
         ὡς κρέα βέβηλα·
13. οὐ παρέλιπον ἁμαρτίαν
         ἣν οὐκ ἐποίησαν ὑπὲρ τὰ ἔθνη·
14. Διὰ τοῦτο ἐκέρασεν αὐτοῖς ὁ θεὸς πνεῦμα πλανήσεως·
         ἐπότισεν αὐτοὺς ποτήριον οἴνου ἀκράτου εἰς μέθην·
15. ἤγαγεν τὸν ἀπ᾽ ἐσχάτου τῆς γῆς· τὸν παίοντα κραταιῶς·
         ἔκρινεν τὸν πόλεμον ἐπὶ Ἰερουσαλὴμ
         καὶ τὴν γῆν αὐτῆς·

---

11. Τὰ ἅγια] ܩܘܕܫܘܗܝ

     διηρπάζωσαν] διηρπάζουσαν (655 659) διήρπαζον 260 (149 471
         606) 629 (769) {διηρπάζωσαν =Ra}

     ὡς μὴ] οὐκ 260 (149 471 606) 629 (769)

12. ἐπατοῦσαν] ἐπάτουν 260 (149 471 606) 629 (769)

     θυσιαστήριον κυρίου] ܡܕܒܚܗ

     καὶ ἐν ἀφέδρῳ...] first words after end of lacuna in MS 336
         extending from 5.14b.

     ἀφέδρῳ] ἀφεδρῷ 243 ἀφαίδρων (655m 659m)

     αἵματος] pr δι᾽ (655m 659)

     ἐμίαναν] = ܘܛܘܫܘ ἐμίαινον 260 (149 471 606) 629 (769) 336

13. παρέλιπον] παρέλειπον 253 (655 659)

14. ἐκέρασεν] ἐκέρασαν (655 659)

     αὐτοὺς] αὐτοῖς 260 (149 471 606)

     ἀκράτου] ܚܝܐ

15. ἤγαγεν] ἤγαγε 260 (149 471 606) 629 336

     τὸν¹] το (655 659)

     ἀπ᾽ ἐσχάτου] ἀπαισχάτου 253 (655 659)

     τὸν²] om 336

     ἔκρινεν] ἔκρινε 659 260 (149 471 606) 629 (769) 336

11. They plundered God's sanctuary[137]
  as if there were no redeeming heir.
12. They trampled the Lord's altar[138]
  coming straight from every kind of impurity,
 and with menstrual blood on them they defiled the burnt-offerings as if they
  were ordinary meat.[139]
13. There was no sin that was not worse than the Gentiles.
14. On account of this God confused their minds;[140]
  he made them drink as if with undiluted wine.
15. He brought the one from the end of the earth,
   the mighty warrior,[141]
  he declared war against Jerusalem, and against her land.

---

[137] "The Temple , its furniture and offerings."

[138] Syr: "Temple."

[139] See Lev 18.19.

[140] Gk: "God mixed for them a spirit of confusion/wandering."

[141] Gk: "the one who strikes strongly."

16. ἀπήντησαν αὐτῷ οἱ ἄρχοντες τῆς γῆς μετὰ χαρᾶς·
    εἶπαν αὐτῷ ἐπευκτὴ ἡ ὁδός σου·
        δεῦτε εἰσέλθατε μετ᾽ εἰρήνης·
17. ὡμάλισαν ὁδοὺς τραχείας ἀπὸ εἰσόδου αὐτοῦ·
    ἤνοιξαν πύλας ἐπὶ Ἰερουσαλήμ·
        ἐστεφάνωσαν τείχη αὐτῆς·

18. Εἰσῆλθεν ὡς πατὴρ εἰς οἶκον υἱῶν αὐτοῦ μετ᾽ εἰρήνης·
    ἔστησεν τοὺς πόδας αὐτοῦ μετὰ ἀσφαλείας πολλῆς·
19. κατελάβετο τὰς πυργοβάρεις αὐτῆς
        καὶ τὸ τεῖχος Ἰερουσαλήμ·
    ὅτι ὁ θεὸς ἤγαγεν αὐτὸν μετὰ ἀσφαλείας
        ἐν τῇ πλανήσει αὐτῶν·
20. ἀπώλεσεν ἄρχοντας αὐτῶν καὶ πάντα σοφὸν ἐν βουλῇ·
    ἐξέχεεν τὸ αἷμα τῶν οἰκούντων Ἰερουσαλήμ
        ὡς ὕδωρ ἀκαθαρσίας·

---

16. ἀπήντησαν] ἠπάντησαν 253 ἐπάτησαν (655 659)
    οἱ ἄρχοντες] ܪ̈ܘܪܒܢܐ
    εἶπαν] εἶπον 260 (149 606) 629? (769) 336
    ἐπευκτὴ] ܡܚܒܒܐ
    εἰσέλθατε] εἰσέλθετε 260 (149 471 606) 629 (769) 336
17. ὡμάλισαν] ὁμάλισαν 336
    τραχείας] ταραχείας (655 659)
    αὐτοῦ] αὐτῶν 260 (149 471 606)
18. υἱῶν] υἱῷ (655 659)
    ἔστησεν] ἔστησε 260 (149 606) lat 629 336
    πόδας 253; NB: Several letters have been erased following this word,
        at the beginning of the next line, but no new text has been overwritten.
    μετὰ ἀσφαλείας] μετασφαλείας 336
19. πυργοβάρεις] πυργοβάστας (655 659)
    ὁ] om 260 (149 471 606) 629 (769) 336
    πλανήσει] πλάνη (655 659)
20. ἀπώλεσεν] ἐκάλεσεν (655 659)
    πάντα] πᾶν 253 (655 659)
    ἐξέχεεν] ἐξέχεε 260 (149 471 606) 629 336
    οἰκούντων] οἰκούν 336

16. The leaders of the country[142] met him[143] with joy.
    They said to him, "Welcome, "We have expected you.
       Come, all of you, enter in peace."[144]
17. They graded the rough roads for his coming;[145]
    they opened the gates to Jerusalem, they lined her walls.[146]

18. He entered peacefully, like a father into his sons' house;
    he secured a foothold.[147]
19. He pulled down her battlements and the wall of Jerusalem,
    for God led him in unscathed in their confusion.
20. He killed off their leaders and all the councilmen;[148]
    he poured out the blood of the people of Jerusalem
       as if it were so much dirty water.[149]

---

[142] See Atkinson, *I Cried to the Lord*, p. 59, who sees a second group of sinners here, separate from the Priests.

[143] Met the invader.

[144] Gk: plural. Perhaps referring to Pompey and his troops. "Peace be to you!"

[145] A parody on Isaiah 40.3 ?

[146] Gk: "...they crowned her walls."

[147] Gk: "he stood his feet firmly on the ground."

[148] Gk: "each wise man in the council." (As far as the evidence shows, there were no female members of the Sanhedren.)

[149] Gk: ἀκαθαρσίας, the same word as in 8.12 and 8.22.

21. ἀπήγαγεν τοὺς υἱοὺς καὶ τὰς θυγατέρας αὐτῶν·
    ἃ ἐγέννησαν ἐν βεβηλώσει·
22. Ἐποίησαν κατὰ τὰς ἀκαθαρσίας αὐτῶν·
    καθὼς οἱ πατέρες αὐτῶν· ἐμίαναν Ἰερουσαλὴμ
    καὶ τὰ ἡγιασμένα τῷ ὀνόματι τοῦ θεοῦ·

23. Ἐδικαιώθη ὁ θεὸς ἐν τοῖς κρίμασιν αὐτοῦ
    ἐν τοῖς ἔθνεσιν τῆς γῆς·
    καὶ οἱ ὅσιοι τοῦ θεοῦ ὡς ἀρνία ἐν ἀκακίᾳ
    ἐν μέσῳ αὐτῶν·
24. αἰνετὸς κύριος ὁ κρίνων πᾶσαν τὴν γῆν
    ἐν δικαιοσύνῃ αὐτοῦ·
25. Ἰδοὺ δή· ὁ θεός· ἔδειξας ἡμῖν
    τὸ κρίμα σου ἐν τῇ δικαιοσύνῃ σου·
    εἴδοσαν οἱ ὀφθαλμοὶ ἡμῶν τὰ κρίματά σου· ὁ θεός·

---

21. ἀπήγαγεν] ἀπήγαγε 260 (149 471 606) 629 lat 336

    ἃ] ἃς 260 (149 471 606) 629 (769) 336

    ἐγέννησαν] ἐγέννησεν 471] om Syr

22. ἀκαθαρσίας] ἀκαρθαρσίας 769

    ἐμίαναν] ἐμίανεν 253 655 659 ܐ‍ܚܣܒܐ

23. ἔθνεσιν] ἔθνεσι 253 (final "ν" erased and marked with two dots) (659)
    260 (149 471 606) 629 336

    αὐτῶν] αὐτὸν 659

24. αἰνετὸς] αὐτὸς (655* 659)

    κύριος] ܐܠܗܐ

    γῆν ἐν] om 336

25. δή] δε (655 659)

    τὸ κρίμα σου] om Syr

    εἴδοσαν] εἶδον 260 (149 471 606) 629 (769) 336

    ἡμῶν] αὐτῶν 260 (149 471 606)

21. He led off their sons and daughters, those born defiled.[1]
    They acted according to their defiled ways,
22.   just like their ancestors, they defiled Jerusalem
        and the things consecrated to the name of God.

23 God has been shown to be justified in his decisions
        among the world's Gentiles,
    and God's devout are like innocent lambs among them.
24. The Lord is worthy to be praised,
        who judges the whole earth in his righteousness.
25. See now, O God, you have shown us
        your righteousness in your judgments.[2]
    Our own eyes have seen[3] your judgments, O God.

---

[150] See 8.9-10.

[151] Gk: "your judgment is in your justice."

[152] Other MSS read: "their eyes have seen."

26. ἐδικαιώσαμεν τὸ ὄνομά σου τὸ ἔντιμον εἰς αἰῶνας·
    ὅτι σὺ ὁ θεὸς τῆς δικαιοσύνης·
    κρίνων τὸν Ἰσραὴλ ἐν παιδείᾳ·
27. ἐπίστρεψον· ὁ θεός· τὸ ἔλεός σου ἐφ᾽ ἡμᾶς
    καὶ οἰκτείρησον ἡμᾶς·
28. συνάγαγε τὴν διασπορὰν Ἰσραὴλ μετὰ ἐλέους
    καὶ χρηστότητος·
    ὅτι ἡ πίστις σου μετὰ ἡμῶν
29. καὶ ἡμεῖς ἐσκληρύναμεν τὸν τράχηλον ἡμῶν·
    καὶ σὺ παιδευτὴς ἡμῶν εἶ·
30. μὴ ὑπερίδῃς ἡμᾶς· ὁ θεὸς ἡμῶν·
    ἵνα μὴ καταπίωσιν ἡμᾶς ἔθνη·
    ὡς μὴ ὄντος λυτρουμένου·
31. καὶ σὺ ὁ θεὸς ἡμῶν· ἀπ᾽ ἀρχῆς·
    καὶ ἐπὶ σὲ ἡ ἐλπὶς ἡμῶν· κύριε·

---

26. τῆς] τὴν 253 (655 659)

    δικαιοσύνης] δικαιοσύνην 253 (655 659)

    παιδείᾳ] παιδία (655 659) παιδίας 769

27. ὁ θεός] om Syr

28. Ἰσραὴλ] Ἰερουσαλὴμ 629* αβόε

    μετὰ] μετ᾽ 149 629 + πα (lat) 629

    ἐλέους] ἐλέου 260 (149 471) 629 (769) 336 ἐλαίου 606

    ἡ] om 253

    πίστις] πιστῆς 655 659 ἡ πίστις 260 (149 471 606) 629 (769)
       336

29. ἡμεῖς] ἡμει' 659

    ἐσκληρύναμεν] εσκληρύνημεν (655 659)

    τὸν] om 253 (655 659)

30. ὑπερίδῃς] ὑπερίδες 659

    καταπίωσιν] καταπίῃ 260 (149 471 606) 629 (769) 336

    ὡς] = ܐܝܟ om 260 (149 471 606) 629 (769) 336

31. ἡ ἐλπὶς ἡμῶν] = ܣܒܪܢ ἠλπίσαμεν 260 (149 471 606)
       629 (769) 336

26. We have vindicated your name,[1] forever honored.
        because you are a God of justice, judging Israel with discipline.
27. O God, turn your mercy towards us,
        and be compassionate to us:
28. gather the scattered[2] of Israel with mercy and kindness,
        because your faithfulness is with us.
29. For we have stiffened our necks,
        but you are our teacher.
30. Don't neglect[3] us, our God,
        lest the Gentiles swallow us whole[4]
        as if there were no deliverer.[5]
31. You have been our God from the beginning,
        and our hope is in you, O Lord.

---

[153] Gk: "proven your name to be true."

[154] Gk: "the dispersed ones...," "the diaspora." The meaning is: "scatter, like sowing seed," from which comes the English "spore." Here, not "exile, punishment, and genocide," but "fruitfulness, new growth, and spring," reflective of Second Isaiah's saying that "Israel would be a light unto the Gentile nations."

[155] "Overlook us."

[156] Gk: "gulp us down."

[157] Gk: "avenging one," or "redeemer."

32. καὶ ἡμεῖς οὐκ ἀφεξόμεθά σου·
　　 ὅτι χρηστὰ τὰ κρίματά σου ἐφ' ἡμᾶς·
33. Ἡμῖν καὶ τοῖς τέκνοις ἡμῶν ἡ εὐδοκία εἰς τὸν αἰῶνα·
　　 κύριε· σωτὴρ ἡμῶν·
　　 οὐ σαλευθησόμεθα ἔτι τὸν αἰῶνα χρόνον·
34. αἰνετὸς κύριος ἐν τοῖς κρίμασιν αὐτοῦ ἐν στόματι ὁσίων·
　　 καὶ σὺ εὐλογημένος Ἰσραὴλ ὑπὸ κυρίου εἰς τὸν αἰῶνα:

---

32. ἡμεῖς] ἡμᾶς (655 659)
　　 ἐφ'] εἰς 253 (655 659)
33. Ἡμῖν καὶ τοῖς τέκνοις ἡμῶν] ܚܠ ܘܩܕܐ ܕܒܪ̈ܝܢ
　　 ἡ] om 629 (769)
　　 εὐδοκία] + αὐτῶν 336
　　 κύριε] κύριος 629 (769) 336 + ܐܠܗܐ
　　 σαλευθησόμεθα] σαλευθῇ 659
34. στόματι] στόμασιν 336
　　 σὺ] om 253 (655 659) 629 (769) 336

32. We distance ourselves,[1]
  because your judgments are kind towards us.
33. Be pleased with us and with our children forever,
  O Lord, our Savior; we won't be upset ever again.[2]
  but you are our teacher.
34. The Lord is worthy to be praised for his judgments
  by the voice of his devout people.
May Israel be blessed by the Lord forever.

---

[158] Gk: "...keep ourselves at a distance from you," "...depart from you," "leave you."

[159] Gk: "for all time."

9. Τῷ Σαλωμών·   εἰς ἔλεγχον:

1. Ἐν τῷ ἀπαχθῆναι Ἰσραὴλ ἐν ἀποικεσίᾳ
      εἰς γῆν ἀλλοτρίαν·
   ἐν τῷ ἀποστῆναι αὐτοὺς ἀπὸ κυρίου·
      τοῦ λυτρωσαμένου αὐτούς·
   ἀπερίφησαν ἀπὸ κληρονομίας ἧς ἔδωκεν αὐτοῖς κύριος·
2. ἐν παντὶ ἔθνειή διασπορὰ τοῦ Ἰσραὴλ
         κατὰ τὸ ῥῆμα τοῦ θεοῦ·
      ἵνα δικαιωθῇς· ὁ θεός· ἐν δικαιοσύνη σου
         ἐν ταῖς ἀνομίαις ἡμῶν·
      ὅτι σὺ κριτὴς δίκαιος ἐπὶ πάντας τοὺς λαοὺς τῆς γῆς·

9= Θ] NB: the title to PsSol 9 appears at the bottom of MS 253, folio 129r and
also at the top of folio 129v]
Σαλωμών σαλομών 253 (655 659) 260 (149 606) 769 336

   +εἰς νῖκος ψαλμὸς και 336

1. Ἐν¹] pr Θ 253

   ἀπαχθῆναι] ἀπελθῆναι (655m 659)

   Ἰσραὴλ] ἰλη⁻ 769 Ἰερουσαλὴμ 336

   αποικεσία] ἀποικησία 260 (149 471 606)

   κυρίου] θεοῦ (655 659)

   τοῦ λυτρωσαμένου αὐτούς] ܠܡܦܪܩ

   ἀπερίφησαν] ἀπερρίφησαν 260 (149 471 606) 629 (769) 336
   ἀπεριφείσαν (655 659)

   αὐτοῖς] αὐτῶν (655 659)

   κύριος] pr ὁ 336 ܪܡܝܐ

2. ἔθνει] ἔθνη 253 (655 659)

   ἡ] ἐπὶ 260 (149 471 606)

   ἵνα] ἵν' 253 (655 659)

   δικαιωθῇς] δικαιόσης 253 (655 659)

   ἐν²] + τῇ 253 (655 659) 260 (149 606) 769

   κριτὴς] κριτὶς (655 659)

9. Of Solomon: As Proof[1]

1. When Israel[2] was led away into exile in a foreign country,
       when they abandoned the Lord [3] who had redeemed them,
     they were expelled from the inheritance
       that the Lord gave to them.

2. Israel was scattered[4] in every Gentile nation,
       as God had spoken:
     that you may be proven right in this matter, O God:
       in your justice and in our lawlessness;
     because you are a righteous judge
       over all the peoples of the earth.

---

[160] "As proof," "in rebuttal," "as reproof." One MS adds: "A Psalm of Victory."

[161] One MS reads: "Jerusalem."

[162] Syr: "God."

[163] Gk: "the diaspora." See 8.28.

3. οὐ γὰρ κρυβήσεται ἀπὸ τῆς γνώσεώς σου
    πᾶς ποιῶν ἄδικα·
  καὶ αἱ δικαιοσύναι τῶν ὁσίων σου ἐνώπιόν σου· κύριε·
  καὶ ποῦ κρυβήσεται ἄνθρωπος ἀπὸ τῆς γνώσεώς σου·
    ὁ θεός;
4. Τὰ ἔργα ἡμῶν ἐν ἐκλογῇ καὶ ἐξουσίᾳ τῆς ψυχῆς ἡμῶν·
  τοῦ ποιῆσαι δικαιοσύνην καὶ ἀδικίαν
    ἐν ἔργοις χειρῶν ἡμῶν·
  καὶ ἐν τῇ δικαιοσύνῃ σου ἐπισκέπτῃ υἱοὺς ἀνθρώπων·
5. ὁ ποιῶν δικαιοσύνην θησαυρίζει ζωὴν αὑτῷ παρὰ κυρίῳ·
  καὶ ὁ ποιῶν ἀδικίαν· αὐτὸς αἴτιος τῆς ψυχῆς
    ἐν ἀπωλείᾳ·
  τὰ γὰρ κρίματα κυρίου ἐν δικαιοσύνῃ
    κατ᾽ ἄνδρα καὶ οἶκον.

---

3. γὰρ κρυβήσεταιἀπὸ τῆς] [...] 629
κρυβήσεται] κριβήσεται 336 κριβυβήσεται 655 κριβυθήσεται 659
ἀπὸ] erased and written over 655
γνώσεώς[1]] γνώσσεώς 769 ܩܕܝܫܝܢ
ἄδικα]= ܪܠܐܣ κακὰ 260 (149 471 606) 629 (769) 336
αἱ] om 629
δικαιοσύναι τῶν ὁσίων] [...] 629
κρυβήσεται] κριβήσεται 659
γνώσεώς[2]] ܩܕܝܫܝܢ

4. ἐξουσίᾳ] ܪܚܐܝܪܘ
δικαιοσύνην] ܪܕܩܠ
ἀδικίαν] ܪܕܚܣܐ
ἐν[2]] om 253 (655 659) 336
δικαιοσύνῃ] δικαιοσύνης 769
ἐπισκέπτῃ] ἐπισκέπη (655 659)

5. ζωὴν] τῷ ἐν (655 659)
αὑτῷ] ἑαυτῷ 260 (149 606) 629 (769) 336
ἀδικίαν] ἄδικα 260 (149 471 606)
αἴτιος] + ܪܠܝܢ
κρίματα] κρίμα 769 κρίματ 769c (abrv. for κρίματα ?)
κατ᾽] καὶ (655 659)

3. For none that do evil can be hidden from your knowledge,
    Lord, you know[164] of the righteous deeds of your devout;
    where will a person hide from your knowledge, O God?
4. We are free to choose and do what we will[165]
        to do right or wrong[166] in how we live our lives;[167]
    in your justice you watch mortals[168] closely.
5. Those who do what is right
    save up life for themselves with the Lord,
    and those doing what is wrong
        cause their own lives to be destroyed;
    for the Lord's righteous judgments
        come down on man and household.[169]

---

[164] Gk: "...are before you."

[165] Gk: "our works are in the choice and authority of our souls." Ryle and James reconstruct the sentence as: "Our deeds are by the choice (of God) and (at the same time) we have power to do ...." *Psalms of the Pharisees*, 95-96. Syr: "In freedom and in choosing."

[166] Gk: "to do righteousness and unrighteousness..."

[167] Gk: "in the actions of our hands."

[168] Gk: "the sons of men."

[169] Gk: "upon man (ἄνδρα) and household." See note at 3.8. Syr: "according to every person and their house."

6. Τίνι χρησιμεύσει· ὁ θεός·
   εἰ μὴ τοῖς ἐπικαλουμένοις τὸν κύριον·
   καθαρίσει ἐν ἁμαρτίαις ψυχὴν ἐν ἐξομολογήσει·
   ἐν ἐξαγορίαις·
   ὅτι αἰσχύνη ἡμῖν
   καὶ τοῖς προσώποις ἡμῶν περὶ πάντων·

7. καὶ τίνι ἀφέσει ἁμαρτίας· εἰ μὴ τοῖς ἡμαρτηκόσιν
   δικαίους εὐλογήσεις·
   καὶ οὐκ εὐθυνεῖς περὶ ὧν ἡμάρτοσαν
   καὶ ἡ χρηστότης σου περὶ ἁμαρτάνοντας
   ἐν μεταμελείᾳ·

8. Καὶ νῦν σὺ ὁ θεός καὶ ἡμεῖς λαὸς ὃν ἠγάπησας·
   ἴδε καὶ οἰκτείρησον· ὁ θεὸς Ἰσραήλ· ὅτι σοί ἐσμεν·
   καὶ μὴ ἀποστήσῃς ἔλεός σου ἀφ᾽ ἡμῶν·
   ἵνα μὴ ἐπιθῶνται ἡμῖν·

---

6. χρησιμεύσει] χρηστεύσῃ 253 (655 659) 260 (149 471 606)
   χρεστεύσει 769 χρηστεύσει 629 (769c)
   {καθαριεῖς= vG} ܐܪܠ

   μὴ] μει 655

   καθαρίσει] καθαριεῖς {Ra=vG}

   ἐν ἁμαρτίαις ψυχὴν] ܪܚܐܝܬ ܡܦܠܝ

   ἐξαγορίαις] ἐξηγορίαις 260 (149 471 606) 629 (769*) ἀξαγορίαις
      336 ἐξαγορίαν (655 659) *om* Syr

   πάντων] ἁπάντων 253 (655 659) 260 (149 471 606) 769

7. ἀφέσει] ἀφήσει 260 (149 471 606) 629 (769) 336 ἀφέσι (655
   659) {ἀφήσεις Ra=vG}

   εἰ] overwirtten: εἠ 655

   ἡμαρτηκόσι] ἡμαρτηκόσιν 769

   εὐθυνεῖς] εὐθυνει (655 659)

   ἡμάρτοσαν] ἡμαρτον 260 (149 471 606) 629 (769) 336

   μεταμελείᾳ] μεταμελία (655 659)

8. σύ¹] σοι 336

   ἡμεῖς] ἡμης 655

   λαὸς] + σου 253 (655 659) ܥܡܐ

   οἰκτείρησον] οἰκτείρον 260 (149 606) 629 (769) 336

   ἔλεός] ἔλεόν 260 (149 606) 629 (769) 336 pr τὸ 655 659 marg

   μὴ²] + ܪܚܬܐ

6. To whom will you be kind, O God,[170]
        except to those who appeal to the Lord?
    He will cleanse from sin the person[171]
        who both confesses
            and publically acknowledges[172] it,
    For all of these things we are ashamed, and we are embarrassed [173]
7. And whose sins will he forgive, except those who have sinned?
        You will bless the righteous, and not accuse them for their sin.
    Because your kindness is upon those that sin, when they repent.
8. Now, then, you are God and we are the people
        whom you have loved:
    Look, and be compassionate, O God of Israel,
            because we are yours,
        and don't take away your mercy from us,
            lest they[174] set upon us.

---

[170] Gk: "to whom will you be helpful?"or "for whom will they [the 'judgments' in 9.5] be helpful." Syr: "To whom is God kind?" Sir 13.4 (NRSV): "can be of use to him." Wis 4.3: "be of no use."

[171] Syr: "'he cleanses the sins of the soul.'"

[172] Gk: "confesses and proclaims it in the marketplace," also, "excantation for disease."

[173] Gk: "it shows on our faces."

[174] Syr: "the peoples..."

9. ὅτι σὺ ἡρετίσω τὸ σπέρμα Ἀβραὰμ παρὰ πάντα τὰ ἔθνη·
   καὶ ἔθου τὸ ὄνομά σου ἐφ' ἡμᾶς· κύριε·
   καὶ οὐ καταπαύσεις εἰς τὸν αἰῶνα·
10. ἐν διαθήκῃ διέθου τοῖς πατράσιν ἡμῶν περὶ ἡμῶν·
   καὶ ἡμεῖςἐλπιοῦμεν ἐπὶ σὲ
        ἐν ἐπιστροφῇ ψυχῆς ἡμῶν·
11. τοῦ κυρίου ἡ ἐλεημοσύνηἐπὶ οἶκονἸσραὴλ
   εἰς τὸν αἰῶνα καὶ ἔτι:

---

9. καταπαύσεις] = ܪ‌ܠ‌ܚ καταπαύσῃ 260 (149 471 606) 629 κατὰ
      παύσει 769) καταπαύσης 655 καταπαύσει 336 659 {οὐκ ἀπώσῃ
      Ra=vG}
   εἰς] om 253 (655 659) + εἰς τὸν 659 marg
10. ἡμεῖς] ἡμᾶς (655 659)
11. ἡ] om 253 (655 659) 629
   ἐλεημοσύνη] ἐλεμοσύνη 253 ἐλεημωσύνη 655
   ἐπὶ] ἐπ' 655 659
   οἶκον] οἴκου (655 659)
   ἔτι] om 659 εἰς τὸν αἰῶνα τοῦ αἰῶνος 655

9. Because you have chosen the descendants of Abraham
      over all other nations;
   you put your name upon us, O Lord,
     and that [175] will not cease for ever.
10. You made a covenant with our ancestors about us,
   and we will place our hope in you,
     when we turn ourselves towards you.[176]
11.   May the Lord's mercy be upon the house of Israel forever and ever.

---

[175] Other MSS read: "you."

[176] Gk: "when we turn our soul to you," "in the conversion of our soul."

10. Ἐν ὕμνοις· τῷ Σαλωμών

1. Μακάριος ἀνὴρ οὗ ὁ κύριος ἐμνήσθη ἐν ἐλεγμῷ·
   καὶ ἐκυκλώθη ἀπὸ ὁδοῦ πονηρᾶς ἐν μάστιγι·
     καθαρισθῆναι ἀπὸ ἁμαρτίας τοῦ μὴ πληθύναι·
2. ὁ ἑτοιμάζων νῶτον εἰς μάστιγας καθαρισθήσεται·
   χρηστὸς γὰρ ὁ κύριος τοῖς ὑπομένουσιν   παιδείαν.
3. ὀρθώσει γὰρ ὁδοὺς δικαίων
   καὶ οὐ διαστρέψει ἐν παιδείᾳ·
   καὶ τὸ ἔλεος κυρίου ἐπὶ τοὺς ἀγαπῶντας αὐτὸν
   ἐν ἀληθείᾳ·

10= I] om 253
Ἐν] om 260 (149 606) 629 (769) 336 [at this point MS 253 has a sketch of a
  bird in the left margin, drawn in red ink]
ὕμνοις] ὕμνος 260 (149 606) 629 (769) 336
Σαλωμών] σαλομών (655 659) 260 (149 606) 629 σαλομών ψαλμός
  336

1. κύριος] ܡܪܝܐ
   ἐν ἐλεγμω] ܒܡܟܣܢܘܬܐ
   ἐκυκλώθη] ἐκακλώθη 769 ܘܚܕܪ.
   μάστιγι] μάστιγε (655 659)
   καθαρισθῆναι] pr καὶ 260 (149 471 606) 629 (769)
   πληθύναι] πληθύναι 336
2. μάστιγας] + καὶ 253 (655 659) = ܐܦ
   χρηστὸς] χριστὸς (655 659)
   γὰρ] om 629 (769) καὶ (655 659)
   κύριος] om Syr
   ὑπομένουσιν] ὑπομένουσι (659) 260 (149 471 606) 629 (769) 336
   ܕܡܣܝܒܪܝܢ
   παιδείαν] 655m
3. ὀρθώσει] ܬܩܢ ܗܘ ܗ.
   διαστρέψει] διαπρέψει 253 (655) διατρέψει (659)
   ἐν] om Syr
   Παιδεία] 659m
   ἔλεος] ܚܢܢܗ
   ἀγαπῶντας] ἀγαπόντας 253

10. With Hymns.[1] Of Solomon

1. Happy is the person whom the Lord remembers with punishment,
    and who has been restrained[2] from going the wrong way
        with a whip,
    to be cleansed from sin so that it will not increase.
2. Those who prepare their backs for the whips will be cleansed,
    for the Lord is kind to those who endure discipline.
3. For he will set straight the ways of the righteous,
    and will not lead them astray by discipline.
    and the mercy of the Lord is upon those who truly love him.

---

[177] Other MSS read: "A Hymn."

[178] Gk: "encircled." Syr: "restrained."

4. καὶ μνησθήσεται κύριος τῶν δούλων αὐτοῦ ἐν ἐλέει·
   ἡ γὰρ μαρτυρία ἐν νόμῳ διαθήκης αἰωνίου·
   ἡ μαρτυρία κυρίου ἐπὶ ὁδοὺς ἀνθρώπων ἐν ἐπισκοπῇ.
5. Δίκαιος καὶ ὅσιος κύριος ἡμῶν κρίμασιν αὐτοῦ
   εἰς τὸν αἰῶνα·
   καὶ Ἰσραὴλ αἰ νέσει τῷ ὀνόματικυρίου ἐν εὐφροσύνῃ.
6. καὶ ὅσιοι ἐξομολογήσονται ἐν ἐκκλησίᾳ λαοῦ·
   καὶ πτωχοὺς ἐλεήσει ὁ θεὸς ἐν εὐφροσύνῃ Ἰσραήλ·
7. ὅτι χρηστὸς καὶ ἐλεήμων ὁ θεὸς εἰς τὸν αἰῶνα·
   καὶ συναγωγαὶ Ἰσραὴλ δοξάσουσιν τὸ ὄνομα κυρίου.
8. τοῦ κυρίου ἡ σωτηρία ἐπὶ οἶκον Ἰσραὴλ
   εἰς εὐφροσύνην αἰώνιον.

---

4. μνησθήσεται] μνήσεται 253 (655 659)
   τῶν δούλων] τοῦ δούλου (655 659)
   γὰρ] om 260 (149 471 606)
   νόμῳ] ὁμω (655 659)
5. κύριος] ܡܪܐ ὁ κύριος 260 (149 471 606) 629 (769) 336
   ἡμῶν] +ἐν 336
   εἰς τὸν αἰῶνα] om Syr
   αἰνέσει] ἐνεσει 769 αἰενεσει 769c
   τῷ] τὸ 260 (149 471 606)
   ὀνόματι] ὄνομα 260 (149 471 606)
   κυρίου]+ εἰς τὸν αἰῶνα 336
6. ὅσιοι] ὅτιοι 253* ὅσιος (659)
   ἐκκλησίᾳ] ἐκληστια 655
   θεὸς] ܐܠܗܐ
7. δοξάσουσιν] δοξάσουσι 260 (149 471 606) 629 (769)
      δοξάσωσι 336
8. ἡ] om (655 659)
   σωτηρία] om 655 659
   ἐπὶ] ἐπ' 260 (149) 629 (769) 336
   οἶκον] οἴκου (655 659)
   εἰς εὐφροσύνην] εἰσωφροσύνην 253 εἰς σωφροσύνην (655 659) 260
      (149 471 606) ܠܚܕܘܬܐ

4. The Lord will remember his servants with compassion,
    for the testimony is in the Torah of the eternal covenant,
    this testimony of the Lord is found in the lives of persons
        under his watchful care.
5. Our Lord [179] is just and holy in his judgments forever.[180]
    and Israel will joyfully praise the Lord's name,[181]
6. And the devout will celebrate in the assembly of the people,
    and God[182] will be merciful to the poor to the joy of Israel.,
7. because God always is kind and merciful,
    and the synagogues of Israel will glorify the Lord's name.
8. May the Lord's salvation cover the house of Israel
        to bring unending joy.

---

[179] Syr: "Our God."

[180] Syr: "...upright in all his judgments."

[181] MS336 adds: "...forever."

[182] Syr: "...the Lord."

11. Τῷ Σαλωμών· εἰς προσδοκίαν

1. Σαλπίσατε ἐν Σιὼν ἐν σάλπιγγι σημασίας ἁγίων·
κηρύξατε ἐν Ἰερουσαλὴμ φωνὴν εὐαγγελιζομένου·
ὅτι ἠλέησεν ὁ θεὸς Ἰσραὴλ ἐν τῇ ἐπισκοπῇ αὐτῶν.

2. Στῆθι· Ἰερουσαλήμ· ἐφ' ὑψηλοῦ
καὶ ἴδε τέκνα σου ἀπὸ ἀνατολῶν καὶ δυσμῶν
συνηγμένα εἰς ἅπαξ ὑπὸ κυρίου.

3. ἀπὸ βορρᾶ ἔρχονται τῇ εὐφροσύνῃ τοῦ θεοῦ αὐτῶν·
ἐκ νήσων μακρόθεν συνήγαγεν αὐτοὺς ὁ θεός.

4. ὄρη ὑψηλὰ ἐταπείνωσεν εἰς ὁμαλισμὸν αὐτοῖς·
οἱ βουνοὶ ἐφύγοσαν ἀπὸ εἰσόδου αὐτῶν·

5. οἱ δρυμοὶ ἐσκίασαν αὐτοῖς ἐν τῇ παρόδῳ αὐτῶν·
πᾶν ξύλον εὐωδίας ἀνέτειλεν αὐτοῖς ὁ θεός·

11= IA
τῷ] om 769
Σαλωμών] pr ψαλμὸς 336 σολομών 253 σαλομών (655 659) 260 (149
336 606)
προσδοκίαν] + ΣΗ marg 336

1. σημασίας] ‏ܪܚܫܝ‎
ἠλέησεν] ἐλεησεν 659 (769)
θεὸς] + ἐν 260 (149 471 606)
αὐτῶν] αὐτου 336

2. Ἰερουσαλὴμ] 655m
ἴδε] + τὰ 253 (655 τώ 659) 260 (149 471 606) 629 (769)
εἰς] om 336
ὑπὸ] ἀπὸ 253 (655 659)

3. αὐτῶν] 655m

4. ὄρη] ὄροι 336
ἐφύγοσαν] ἔφυγον 260 (149 471 606) 629 (769) 336

5. οἱ δρυμοὶ...αὐτῶν] om (655 659)
δρυμοὶ] βουνοὶ 629 δριμοὶ (769) ‏ܪܝܐܪ‎
ἐσκίασαν] ἐσκίρτησαν (471 606)
ξύλον] ξύλων 659
ἀνέτειλεν] ‏ܡܢܬ‎

11. Of Solomon: In Expectation[183]

1. Sound in Zion the trumpet that summons the holy ones.[184]
   Announce in Jerusalem the voice
      of one proclaiming good news:
   "God has been merciful to Israel
      by his watchful care over them."
2. Stand on a high place, O Jerusalem,
      and see your children from east to west
         finally brought together[185] by the Lord.
3. From the north they come with the joy of their God;
      from far distant islands God brings them together.
4. He flattened high mountains into level ground for them,
      The hills fled at their coming.
5. the woods[186] shaded them as they passed by;
      God made every fragrant tree to spring up for them:

---

[183] This psalm is related to 1 Bar 4.36-5.9, and both passages are linked to Isa 40-66. See Introduction.

[184] Or: "...signals holy events." See Joel 2.1,10.

[185] Or: "...brought all together...."

[186] Syr: "...the cedars."

6. ἵνα παρέλθῃ Ἰσραὴλ ἐν ἐπισκοπῇ δόξης θεοῦ αὐτῶν.

7. Ἔνδυσαι· Ἱερουσαλήμ· τὰ ἱμάτια τῆς δόξης σου·
   ἑτοίμασον τὴν στολὴν τοῦ ἁγιάσματός σου·
   ὅτι ὁ θεὸς ἐλάλησεν ἀγαθὰ Ἰσραὴλ εἰς τὸν αἰῶνα
   καὶ ἔτι.

8. ποιήσαι κύριος ἃ ἐλάλησεν ἐπὶ Ἰσραὴλ καὶ Ἱερουσαλήμ·
   ἀναστήσαι κύριος τὸν Ἰσραὴλ ἐν ὀνόματι δόξης αὐτοῦ·

9. τοῦ κυρίου τὸ ἔλεος ἐπὶ τὸν Ἰσραὴλ
   εἰς τὸν αἰῶνα καὶ ἔτι.

---

6. Ἰσραὴλ] pr ὁ (655 659) οιη 629*
   θεοῦ] om 336

7. ἔνδυσαι] ἔνδυσας (655 659)
   ἱμάτια] ἱματι 659
   Ἰσραὴλ] οιη 629* ~εἰς τὸν αἰῶνα καὶ ἔτι Ἰσραὴλ 629 (769)

8. καὶ] +ἐν 260 (149 471 606)

9. τὸ] om 629 (769)

6. that Israel might pass by in the watchful care
   of the glory of their God.

7. O Jerusalem, put on your glorious clothes, prepare your holy robes,
   because God has pronounced blessings on Israel
      forever and ever.
8. May the Lord do to Israel and Jerusalem the things that he has spoken;
   may the Lord lift up Israel by his glorious name.
9. May the mercy of the Lord be upon Israel forevermore.

12. Τῷ Σαλωμών· ἐν γλώσσῃ παρανόμων

1. Κύριε· ῥῦσαι τὴν ψυχήν μου
   ἀπὸ ἀνδρὸς παρανόμου καὶ πονηροῦ·
   ἀπὸ γλώσσης παρανόμου καὶ ψιθύρου
   καὶ λαλούσης ψευδῆ καὶ δόλια.
2. ἐν ποικιλίᾳ στροφῆς οἱ λόγοι
   τῆς γλώσσης ἀνδρὸς πονηροῦ·
   ὥσπερ ἐν λαῷ πῦρ ἀνάπτον καλλονὴν αὐτοῦ.

12=IB

Σαλωμών] Σαλομών (655 659) 260 (149 606 629) 336

1. ψιθύρου] ψυθύρου 655*m

δόλια] πονηρά 629* δολερά (769)

2. ἐν ποικιλίᾳ...γλώσσης] ܡܢܐܠ ܐܬܪ ܪܠܬܐ ܬܠ ܪܐܘܡܢܐ

ποικιλίᾳ] τῇ κυλίᾳ (655m 659) ποικλήσι 655c marg ποιήσει 260
   (149 471 606)

στροφῆς] διαστροφῆς 260 (149 471 606) τροφῆς 629 (769)

γλώσσης] γλωσης 769

πονηροῦ] ܪܘܐܒܝ ܬܢܪ

ὥσπερ...αὐτοῦ] ܪܠܒܐ ܪܬܐ ܬܘܐܒܐ

λαῷ] ἄλῳ 260 (149 471) ἄλλῳ 606

ἀνάπτον] ἀνάπτων 336

καλλονὴν] καλονὴν (655 659) καλάμην 260 (149 471 606)

12. Of Solomon: about the Discourse of those
who Manipulate the Law[187]

1. O Lord, save my life from the wicked man[188] who twists the law,
    from twisting and slandering language
    that speaks lies and deceits.
2. The discourse[189] of this wicked man takes many twists and turns.[190]
    It is like a fire burning among a people,
        scorching their beauty.[191]

---

[187] Gk: παρανόμων, "circumvent" or "twist the law."

[188] Gk: ἀνδρὸς: "the male."

[189] Gk: "The words of the tongue...." These next verses are obscure in both Greek
    and in Syriac, and have presented difficulties for ancient scribes and later
    translators.

[190] Other MSS add: "...for doing perversity."

[191] Other MSS read: "...are as a fire on a threshing floor (that) burns up straw."

3. ἡ παροικία αὐτοῦ ἐμπλῆσαι οἴκους ἐν γλώσσῃ ψευδεῖ·
   ἐκκόψαι δένδρα εὐφροσύνης φλογιζούσης παρανόμους·
   συνχέαι οἴκους παρανόμους
   ἐν πολέμῳ χείλεσιν ψιθύροις.

4. Μακρύναι ὁ θεὸς ἀπὸ ἀκάκων χείλη παρανόμων
      ἐν ἀπορίᾳ·
   καὶ σκορπισθείησαν ὀστᾶ ψιθύρων
      ἀπὸ φοβουμένων κύριον·
   ἐν πυρὶ φλογὸς γλῶσσα ψίθυρος ἀπόλοιτο ἀπὸ ὁσίων.

---

3. ἐμπλήσαι] ἐμπλῆσαι 629(769) 336 {ἐμπλήσαι Ra=vG=Hilg}
   γλώσσῃ] ܪܠܫܢܐ
   ψευδεῖ] ψευδῆ 336
   φλογιζούσης] ܪܡܘܩܕ
   παρανόμους[1]] παρανόμου 260 (149 471 606) 336
      ܪܥܘܠܐ ܒܝܬ
   συνχέαι] συνχὲμ (655 659) συγχέαι 260 (149 471 606) 629
    (769) 336
   οἴκους παρανόμους] παρανόμους οἴκους 260 (149 471 606)
   Παρανόμους[2]] παρανομου 769*
   χείλεσιν] χείλεσι 260 (149 471 606) 336 ιχίλεσι 769
   ψιθύροις] ψιθύρων 336
4. ἀκάκων] κακῶν 606
   σκορπισθείησαν] σκορπισθείη 260 (149 471 606) 629 (769) 336
   ἀπόλοιτο] ἀπώλοιτο 336
   ὁσίων] + ܕܫܡܝܢ

3. His visit fills homes[192] with lying speech;
   as a flickering flame has its own attraction to people;[193]
   he sets homes at war with his slanderous language.[194]

4. May God keep the lips of these criminals
   from distressing the innocent.
   May the bones of the slanderers be scattered
   far from those who fear the Lord.
   May the slanderous tongues be destroyed in flaming fire
   far from the devout.

---

[192] Gk: "may his visit fill homes...."

[193] Gk: "he cuts down their trees of friendliness."

[194] Gk: "he mixes together homes to fight by slanderous lips."

5. φυλάξαι κύριος ψυχὴν ἡσύχιον μισοῦσαν ἀδίκους·
   καὶ κατευθύναι κύριος ἄνδρα ποιοῦντα εἰρήνην
     ἐν οἴκῳ.
6. τοῦ κυρίου ἡ σωτηρία ἐπὶ Ἰσραὴλ
   παῖδα αὐτοῦ εἰς τὸν αἰῶνα·
   καὶ ἀπόλοιντο οἱ ἁμαρτωλοὶ
    ἀπὸ προσώπου κυρίου ἅπαξ·
   καὶ ὅσιοι κυρίου κληρονομί σαισαν ἐπαγγελίας κυρίου.

---

5. φυλάξαι . . . κατευθύναι] συνχέαι οἴκους καὶ φυλάξαι 253 (659)
   συνχέαι οἴκους καὶ φυλάξας (655*)

   ψυχὴν ...κύριος²] om 253 (655 659)

   ἡσύχιον] ܪܩܝܬܐ

   ἄνδρα ποιοῦντα] ἀνδρὸς ποιοῦντος 253 (655 659)

   οἴκῳ] + ܒܝܬܐ

6. ἐπὶ] ἐστὶ 769

   παῖδα] παίδων 336

   οἱ] ἡ (655 659)

   ἁμαρτωλοὶ] ἁμαρτλοὶ 471

   καὶ²] + οἱ 769 336

   ὅσιοι] ὅσοι (655 659)

   κληρονομίσαισαν] = ܢܐܪܬܘܢ κληρονομήσασαν (655 659)
     κληρονομήσαι 260 (149m) κληρονομήσαι ἐν 471 769 336
     κληρονομήσαιεν (606)

   ἐπαγγελίας] ἐπαγγελείας 253 (655 659) 336 ἠπαγγελίας 769

   κυρίου] om 253 (655 659)

5. May the Lord protect the quiet person who hates injustice,
        and may the Lord guide the person who lives quietly at home.[195]
6. May the salvation of the Lord be upon Israel
        his child forever and ever.
    May the sinners be destroyed once and for all
        from before the Lord.
    May the Lord's devout inherit
        the Lord's promises.

---

[195] Gk: "...who makes peace at home."

13. Τῷ Σαλωμών ψαλμός· παράκλησις τῶν δικαίων

1. Δεξιὰ κυρίου ἐσκέπασέν με·
   δεξιὰ κυρίου ἐφείσατο ἡμῶν·
2. ὁ βραχίων κυρίου ἔσωσεν ἡμᾶς
   ἀπὸ ῥομφαίας διαπορευομένης·
   ἀπὸ λιμοῦ καὶ θανάτου ἁμαρτωλῶν.
3. θηρία ἐπεδράμοσαν αὐτοῖς πονηρά·
   ἐν τοῖς ὀδοῦσιν αὐτῶν ἐτίλλοσαν σάρκας αὐτῶν
   καὶ ἐν ταῖς μύλαις ἔθλων ὀστᾶ αὐτῶν·
4. καὶ ἐκ τούτων ἁπάντων ἐρρύσατο ἡμᾶς κύριος.

13= ΙΓ] τρίτος και δέκατος 336
   Σαλωμών] σαλομων (655 659) 260 (149 606) 629 336

   ψαλμός] om 629 (769)

   τῶν] τῷ (655 659)

   δικαίων] δίκαιῳ (655 659)

1. ἐσκέπασέν] ἐσκέπασέ 659 260 (149 471 606) 629 (769) 336
   ἐσκέπασέν με] ܕܝܘܣ

2. ῥομφαίας διαπορευομένης] 769c (obliterated) [N.B: The original scribe left
   two partial lines. Part of a now lost text was added at end of these lines by a later
   hand, using a finer pen and a purple ink (Pantone #19-3632 "Petunia."). Added
   text was painted over with a brush, in the same purple ink.] αίας διαπορ]
   +769c ῥομφαία (655 659)

   λιμοῦ] λοιμου (655 659)

   καὶ θανάτου ἁμαρτωλῶν] 769 (obliterated)

3. ἐπεδράμοσαν] ἐπέδραμον 260 (149 471 606) 629? (769) 336
   ἐπήδράμουσαν (655 659)

   ἐτίλλοσαν] ἐπιλλοσαν 659 ἔτιλλον 260 (149 471 606) 769 336
   ἔτειλον 629 ἔτιλλσν 336

   μύλαις]+ αὐτων 260 (149 471 606) ܪܚܘܝ

   ἔθλων] ܥܨ ܣܡ

   ὀστᾶ] pr τά 336

4. κύριος] pr ὁ 629 336

13. A Psalm of Solomon: Encouragement to the Righteous

1. The right hand of the Lord covered me,[196]
     the right hand of the Lord spared us:
2. the arm[197] of the Lord saved us[198] from a piercing sword, [199]
     from famine and death[200] at the hands of sinners.
3. Wild animals attacked them viciously,
     They ripped at their flesh with their teeth
     and with their jaws[201] they crushed their bones:
4. And from all of these the Lord delivered us.

---

[196] Syr: "us."

[197] Gk: "...upper arm."

[198] Syr: "me."

[199] Gk: "a large broad sword." See Genesis 3. 24; Luke 2. 35; Revelation 6.8.

[200] Again, Rev 6.8.

[201] Gk: "molars."

5. Εταράχθη ὁ ἀσεβὴς διὰ παραπτώματα αὐτοῦ·
   μήποτε συμπαραληφθῇ μετὰ τῶν ἁμαρτωλῶν·
6. ὅτι δεινὴ ἡ καταστροφὴ τοῦ ἁμαρτωλοῦ·
   καὶ οὐχ ἅψεται δικαίου οὐδέν ἐκ πάντων τούτων.
7. ὅτι οὐχ ὁμοία ἡ παιδεία τῶν δικαίων ἐν ἀγνοίᾳ
   καὶ ἡ καταστροφὴ τῶν ἁμαρτωλῶν.
8. ἐν περιστολῇ παιδεύεται δίκαιος·
   ἵνα μὴ ἐπιχαρῇ ὁ ἁμαρτωλὸς τῷ δικαίῳ·
9. ὅτι νουθετήσει δίκαιον ὡς υἱὸν ἀγαπήσεως·
   καὶ ἡ παιδεία αὐτοῦ ὡς πρωτοτόκου.

---

5. ἀσεβὴς] {εὐσεβὴς Wellhausen=Ra=vG}

   παραπτώματα] τὰ παραπτώματα 260 (149 471 606) 629 336
   τα παραπτώματ 769

   συμπαραληφθῇ] ܬܫܬܒܩ

6. δεινὴ] δινῆ 253 (655 659)

   ἡ] om 260 (149 471 606) 629 (769) 336

   δικαίου] pr του 629 (769)

   οὐδέν] om 629 (769) ~ ἐκ πάντων τούτων οὐδέν 260 (149 471
   606) 336

   ἐκ πάντων τούτων (...) 629

7. ὅτι...ἁμαρτωλῶν] om 629 (769)

   παιδεία] παιδία (655 659)

   τῶν ἁμαρτωλῶν] τοῦ ἁμαρτωλου 253 (655 659)

8. ἐν περιστολῇ] ܪܕܝܢ.ܢܡܝ

   τῷ δικαίῳ] ܠܗ

9. παιδεία] παιδία (655 659)

   πρωτοτόκου] προτοτόκου 253 (655 659) πρωτουτόκου 629 (769)

5. The ungodly[202] were terrified[203] by their mistakes,
   lest they be swept along with the sinners:
6. because the destruction of the sinner is terrible,
   but none of all these things will touch the righteous.
7. Because the discipline of the righteous for things done in ignorance is not the
   same as the destruction of the sinners.
8. The righteous are disciplined quietly,
   so that the sinner might not rejoice over the righteous.
9. Because God[204] will admonish the righteous as a beloved son,[205]
   and his discipline is as for a first-born.

---

[202] Gk: "the non-worshiper."

[203] Gk: "shaken."

[204] Gk: "he."

[205] In the social economy of the ANE, a son is especially loved, a 'first-born' even
more so, and a 'beloved,' first-born the most cherished.

10. ὅτι φείσεται κύριος τῶν ὁσίων αὐτοῦ·
   καὶ τὰ παραπτώματα αὐτῶν ἐξαλείψει ἐν παιδείᾳ.
11. ἡ γὰρ ζωὴ τῶν δικαίων εἰς τὸν αἰῶνα·
   ἁμαρτωλοὶ δὲ ἀρθήσονται εἰς ἀπώλειαν·
   καὶ οὐχ εὑρεθήσεται μνημόσυνον αὐτῶν ἔτι·
12. ἐπὶ δὲ τοὺς ὁσίους τὸ ἔλεος κυρίου·
   καὶ ἐπὶ τοὺς φοβουμένους αὐτὸν τὸ ἔλεος αὐτοῦ.

---

10. φείσεται] φήσεται 659
   κύριος] ܟܐܢܐ
11. οὐχ] οὐκ 253 (659)
   12. αὐτὸν] om 253 (655 659) ܠܗ

10. Because the Lord will spare his devout,
> and he will wipe away their mistakes with discipline.

11. For the life of the righteous goes on forever,
> but sinners will be taken away to destruction,
> and no memory of them will ever be found again.

12. May the Lord's mercy be upon the devout,
> and may his mercy[206] be to those who fear him.

---

[206] Syr: "...he will treasure...."

14.Ὕμνος τῷ Σαλωμών

1. Πιστὸς κύριος τοῖς ἀγαπῶσιν αὐτὸν ἐν ἀληθείᾳ·
   τοῖς ὑπομένουσιν παιδείαν αὐτοῦ·
2. τοῖς πορευομένοις ἐν δικαιοσύνῃ
   προσταγμάτων αὐτοῦ·
   ἐν νόμῳ ᾧ ἐνετείλατο ἡμῖν εἰς ζωὴν ἡμῶν.
3. ὅσιοι κυρίου ζήσονται ἐν αὐτῷ εἰς τὸν αἰῶνα·
   ὁ παράδεισος τοῦ κυρίου· τὰ ξύλα τῆς ζωῆς·
   ὅσιοι αὐτοῦ.

14=ΙΔ

Σαλωμών] σαλομών 659 260 (149 606) 629 336 + ψαλμὸς 336

[NB: In the margin of MS 629, on folio 305r (307r in the new numbering)
14.1-4 is duplicated in a different but apparently contemporary hand. The leaf
is torn so that the new text is fragmentary from v. 2b.]

1. ὑπομένουσιν] ὑπομένουσι 260 (149 471 606) 629 (769) 336
   παιδείαν] παιδίαν (655 659)

2. πορευομένοις] + ἐν ἀκακίᾳ καὶ 336
   ᾧ] om 253 (655 659) ὡς 260 (149 471 606) ὃν 336
   ἐν νόμῳ ᾧ ἐνετείλατο] ܒܢ ܟܘܤ
   ἡμῖν] ἡμειν 655

3. ὅσιοι] ὁσιοει 655
   ζήσονται] ξουσονται 629
   τοῦ] om 260 (149 471 606) 629 (769)
   κυρίου²] θεου (655m 659m both c in marg)
   αὐτοῦ] αὐτά (655 659)

14. A Hymn of Solomon

1. The Lord is faithful to those who truly love him,
    to those awaiting his discipline,
2. to those living[207] in the righteousness of his commands,
    in the Torah that he commanded us for aour lives.[208]
3. The Lord's devout will live by it forever;
    his devout are the Lord's Paradise, the trees of life[209]

---

[207] Gk: "walking."

[208] Gk: "life." Syr: "He has given us the law for our life."

[209] See Prov 3.18; 11.30; 13.12; 15.4. Also Ps 1.3.

4. ἡ φυτεία αὐτῶν ἐρριζωμένη εἰς τὸν αἰῶνα·
    οὐκ ἐκτιλήσονται πάσας τὰς ἡμέρας τοῦ οὐρανοῦ·
5. ὅτι ἡ μερὶς καὶ κληρονομία τοῦ θεοῦ ἐστιν Ἰσραήλ.

6. Καὶ οὐχ οὕτως οἱ ἁμαρτωλοὶ καὶ παράνομοι·
    οἳ ἠγάπησαν ἡμέραν ἐν μετοχῇ ἁμαρτίας αὐτῶν·
7. ἐν μικρότητι σαπρίας ἡ ἐπιθυμία αὐτῶν·
    καὶ οὐκ ἐμνήσθησαν τοῦ θεοῦ.

---

4. φυτεία] φυτία (655 659)

  ἐρριζωμένη] ἐρριζομένη 253 (655 659) ἐρ ριζομένη 655 659
  ܪܝܙ

  ἐκτιλήσονται] ἐκτειλήσονται 253 (655m 659) ἐκτιλλήσονται 336

5. μερὶς] μερὶ (655 659)

  κληρονομία] pr ἡ 655 659 260 (149 471 606) 336
  θεου] ܐܠܗܐ
  Ἰσραὴλ] pr ὁ 260 (149 471 606)

6. ἁμαρτωλοὶ] ἁμαρτωλοί 655 659

  μετοχῇ] ܫܘܬܦܘ

7. σαπρίας] ܣܪܝܘ

  ἡ] ἐν 260 (149 471 606)

  τοῦ θεοῦ] αὐτοῦ 629 τοῦ 769

4. Their plant is rooted forever;[210]
   they will not be pulled up as long as heaven shall last,[211]
5. because God has reserved Israel for himself.[212]

6. But it is not so with sinners and criminals,
   who love the time enjoying their sins. [213]
7. Their enjoyment is brief and quickly decays,[214]
   and they do not remember God.

---

[210] See Mt 15.13; Ephesians 3.17-18.

[211] Gk: "...all the days of Heaven." See Sir 40.16.

[212] Gk: "the portion and inheritance of God."

[213] Gk: "who loved throughout the day in sharing of their sins."

[214] Gk: "meager." See Job 2.9c.

8. ὅτι ὁδοὶ ἀνθρώπων γνωσταὶ ἐνώπιον αὐτοῦ διὰ παντός·
    καὶ ταμεῖα καρδίας ἐπίσταται πρὸ τοῦ γενέσθαι.

9. διὰ τοῦτο ἡ κληρονομία αὐτῶν ᾅδης
    καὶ σκότος καὶ ἀπώλεια·
    καὶ οὐχ εὑρεθήσονται ἐν ἡμέρᾳ ἐλέους δικαίων·

10. οἱ δὲ ὅσιοι κυρίου κληρονομήσουσιν ζωὴν ἐν εὐφροσύνῃ.

---

8. ὁδοὶ] ὁδός (655 659)

    γνωσταὶ] ܟܠ

    ταμεῖα] ταμιεῖα 260 (149 606) 629 336 τὰ ταμιεῖα 629 (769)

    πρὸ] πρόο 769m

    γενέσθαι] γενέσαι 769?

9. σκότος] σκότως 659

    οὐχ] οὐκ (655 659)

    ἐλέους] ἐλέου 260 (149 471 606) 629 (769) 336

10. κληρονομήσουσιν] κληρονομήσουσι 260 (149 471 606) 629

8. Because he always knows how people live,[215]
 and he knows the secrets of the heart before they happen.[216]
9. Therefore there is reserved for them[217] the world of the dead,[218]
 darkness and destruction,
 and they will not be remembered[219]
 on the day of mercy for the righteous,
10. but a happy life is reserved[220] for the Lord's devout.

---

[215] Gk: "Because human ways are evident to him in every way."

[216] Gk: "the secret rooms of the heart." See Gen 43.30, Matt 6.6.

[217] Gk: "their inheritance."

[218] Or: "Hades," or "the grave."

[219] Gk: "found."

[220] Gk: "an inheritance."

15. Ψαλμὸς τῷ Σαλωμὼν μετὰ ᾠδῆς

1. Ἐν τῷ θλίβεσθαί με ἐπεκαλεσάμην τὸ ὄνομα κυρίου·
   εἰς βοήθειαν ἤλπισα τοῦ θεοῦ Ἰακώβ καὶ ἐσώθην·
   ὅτι ἐλπὶς καὶ καταφυγὴ τῶν πτωχῶν σύ· ὁ θεός.
2. τίς γὰρ ἰσχύει· ὁ θεός·
   εἰ μὴ ἐξομολογήσασθαί σοι ἐν ἀληθείᾳ;
   καὶ τί δυνατὸς ἄνθρωπος·
   εἰ μὴ ἐξομολογήσασθαι τῷ ὀνόματί σου;
3. ψαλμὸν καινὸν μετὰ ᾠδῆς ἐν εὐφροσύνη καρδίας·
   καρπὸν χειλέων ἐν ὀργάνῳ ἡρμοσμένῳ γλώσσης·
   ἀπαρχὴν χειλέων ἀπὸ καρδίας ὁσίας καὶ δικαίας·

15=ΙΕ

τῷ] *om* 629 (769)

Σαλωμών] σαλομών (655 659) 260 (149) 606) 629 σολομών 336

μετὰ] μετ' 260 (149 471 606) 336

μετὰ ᾠδῆς]*om* 629 (769)

1. τῷ] του (659)

εἰς] +τὴν 336

ἤλπισα] *om* 659 ἐσώθην 253 (655 659c marg) ܠܘ ܝܐ

σύ] +εἶ 336

2. τίς] τί 336

ἰσχύει] ἰσχύσει 336

ὁ θεός, εἰ μὴ] *om* Syr

σοι] = ܠܝ *om* 336

τί] το (655m 659)

ἄνθρωπος] pr ὁ (655 659)

ἐξομολογήσασθαι²] ἐξομολογήσασσθαι 336 +τῇ ἀληθείᾳ 655m

3. καινὸν] καὶ αἰνον 260 (149 471 606) καὶ νὸν 629? (769)

μετά] μετ' 260 (149 471 606) 629 (769) 336

ἡρμοσμένῳ] ܗܕܘܡ

γλώσσης] γνωσσης (655 659) ܠܫܢ

ἀπαρχὴν] ἀπαρχὶν (655 659) ἀπαρχὴ 629 (769) ἀπαρχῆς 336

15 A Psalm of Solomon with Song[221]

1.   When I was oppressed[222] I called upon the Lord's name.
   for I expected help from Jacob's[223] God, and I was saved:
   because you, O God, are the help and refuge of the poor.
2.   For why does anyone have strength, O God,
   except to honestly confess you?[224]
   And why is a person gifted,
   except to worship your name?
3.   A new psalm[225] sung from a happy heart;
   the fruit of the lips matched with a well-tuned tongue;
   the first harvest of the lips from a holy and righteous heart.

---

[221] Or: "with a song," or, "with a joyful song!"

[222] An echo of PsSol 1.1

[223] Syr: "I called to the God of Jacob for my help."

[224] Or: "truly confess you," or: "truly acknowledge you."

[225] Or: "A psalm and a song."

4. ὁ ποιῶν ταῦτα οὐ σαλευθήσεται εἰς τὸν αἰῶνα
    ἀπὸ κακοῦ·
    φλὸξ πυρὸς καὶ ὀργὴ ἀδίκων οὐχ ἅψεται αὐτοῦ·
5. ὅταν ἐξέλθῃ ἐπὶ ἁμαρτωλοὺς ἀπὸ προσώπου κυρίου·
    ὀλεθρεῦσαι πᾶσαν ὑπόστασιν ἁμαρτωλῶν·
6. ὅτι τὸ σημεῖον τοῦ θεοῦ ἐπὶ δικαίους εἰς σωτηρίαν.
7. Λιμὸς καὶ ῥομφαία καὶ θάνατος ἀπὸ δικαίων μακράν·
    φεύξονται γὰρ ὡς διωκομένου λιμοῦ ἀπὸ ὁσίων·

---

4. τὸν] om 336

    αἰῶνα] +ΣΗ marg 336

    ὀργὴ] om 629 (769*) c in marg

    οὐχ] οὐκ 253 (655 659)

5. ἐπὶ] εφ' 253 (655 659)

    κυρίου] ܟ̈ܪܝܐ

    ὀλεθρεῦσαι] ὀλωθρεῦσαι (655c 659) ὀλοθρεῦσαι 260 (149 471
      606) 629 (769) 336 ܠܡܘܒܕ

    ὑπόστασιν] ܩܘܡܬܗܘܢ

    ἁμαρτωλῶν] ἁμαρτωεᾶν 629

6. τοῦ θεοῦ] ܐܠܗܐ

7. ῥομφαία] ܚܪܒܐ

    ἀπὸ δικαίων μακράν] ἀπὸ μακρὰν ἀπὸ δικαίων 260 (149 471
      606) 629 (769) 336 ܡܢ ܙܕ̈ܝܩܐ ܢܬܪܚܩܘܢ

    διωκομένου] διωκόμενοι 336

    λιμοῦ] ἀπὸ λιμοῦ 253 336 ἀπὸλιμου (655 659) ܟܦܢܐ
      {πολέμου Ra=vG}

    ὁσίων] θείων 629 (769) 336 ܙ̈ܢܝ

4. Those doing these things will never be distressed[226] by evil;
        the flame of fire and anger against the unrighteous
            will not touch them,
5. whenever it goes out from the Lord's presence
        to destroy every confidence of sinners.
6. Because God's mark[227] of salvation is on the righteous.[228]
7. Famine, sword, and death shall be far from the righteous,
        for they will flee from the devout and pestilence from the living.[229].

---

[226] See Wis 4.19; Sir 28.14; Luke 6.38; Luke 21.26; 1 Macc 9.13; Acts 4.31; Acts
        17.13; 2 Thes 2.2.

[227] See vs. 9, and Ps2.6.

[228] Gk: "...is on the righteous for their protection."

[229] Gk: "as those pursued by famine."

8. καταδιώξονται δὲ ἁμαρτωλοὺς καὶ καταλήμψονται·
　　καὶ οὐκ ἐκφεύξονται οἱ ποιοῦντες ἀνομίαν
　　　　τὸ κρίμα κυρίου·
9. ὡς ὑπὸ πολεμίων ἐμπείρων καταλημφθήσονται·
　　τὸ γὰρ σημεῖον τῆς ἀπωλείας ἐπὶ τοῦ μετώπου αὐτῶν.
10. Καὶ ἡ κληρονομία τῶν ἁμαρτωλῶν ἀπώλεια καὶ σκότος·
　　καὶ αἱ ἀνομίαι αὐτῶν διώξονται αὐτοὺς
　　　　ἕως ᾅδου κατωτάτου.
11. ἡ κληρονομία αὐτῶν οὐχ εὑρεθήσεται
　　τοῖς τέκνοις αὐτῶν·
　　αἱ γὰρ ἁμαρτίαι ἐξερημώσουσιν οἴκους ἁμαρτωλῶν.

---

8. καταδιώξονται] = ـܢܦܕܪ καταδιώξεται 260 (149 471 606) 629
　　(769) 336 + γὰρ ὡς 655 659m
　　δὲ] + ωκομένου 655m
　　καταλήμψοντι] = ـܢܘܪܕ καταλήψεται 260 (149 471 606) 629 (769)
　　336
　　ποιοῦντες] πιοῦντες 629? (769) 336
　　κυρίου] τοῦ θεοῦ 629 (769)

9. ὑπὸ] om Syr
　　καταλημφθήσονται] καταληφθήσονται 253e (655 659) 260 (149
　　　　471 606) 629 (769) 336 καταληφθήσηται 629 ـܪܝܐ ـܘܬܡܣܘ
　　ἀπωλείας] ἀπολείας 336
　　μετώπου] μετόπου 336 ـܢܘܬܡܐ

10. ἀπώλεια] ἀπολεία 253 (655 659)
　　αἱ] om 253 (655 659)
　　διώξονται αὐτοὺς] διώξον 629
　　κατωτάτου] κάτω 253 (655 659) 260 (149 471 606) 629 (769)

11. αὐτῶν] αὐτοῦ (655 659)
　　οὐχ] οὐκ (655 659)
　　οὐχ εὑρεθήσεται] previous text erased; correction to common reading.
　　αἱ] καί 336
　　ἁμαρτίαι] ἀνομίαι 260 (149 471 606) 629 (769) 336
　　ἐξερημώσουσιν] ἐξερημώσωσιν 253 ἐξερημώσιν (655m 659)

8. But they will pursue sinners and overtake them,
      and those acting lawlessly will not escape the Lord's judgment.
9. they will be seized as if by mercenaries,[230]
      for the sign of destruction is right between their eyes.[231]
10. For destruction and darkness is reserved for sinners
      and their lawlessness[232] will pursue them even down into hell.[233]
11. What is reserved for them will not be found in their children.
      For sin[234] will turn the homes of sinners into deserts[235]

---

[230] Gk: "an experienced enemy," "seasoned troops," "veteran soldiers."

[231] Gk: "on their forehead, between their eyes." See Rev 13.6; 14.1; 17.5.

[232] Other MSS read: "sins."

[233] Or: "the world of the dead," "the grave." Gk: "hades."

[234] Syr: "their lawless acts."

[235] Or: "totally destroy the homes of sinners." See Lev 26.31.

12. καὶ ἀπολοῦνται ἁμαρτωλοὶ ἐν ἡμέρᾳ κρίσεως κυρίου
    εἰς τὸν αἰῶνα·
    ὅτ' ἂν ἐπισκέπτηται ὁ θεὸς τὴν γῆν ἐν κρίματι αὐτοῦ·
13. οἱ δὲ φοβούμενοι τὸν κύριον ἐλεηθήσονται ἐν αὐτῇ·
    καὶ ζήσονται ἐν τῇ ἐλεημοσύνῃ τοῦ θεοῦ αὐτῶν·[6]
    καὶ ἁμαρτωλοὶ ἀπολοῦνται εἰς τὸν αἰῶνα χρόνον.

---

12. αμαρτωλοί] pr οἱ 260 (149 471 606)

  ὅτ' ἂν] οἵ ἂν (655 659) ὅταν 336

  ἐπισκέπτηται] ἐπεσκέπτηται (655 659)

  αὐτοῦ] + ἀποδοῦναι ἁμαρτωλοῖς ἐις τὸν αἰῶνα χρόνον 260 (149
    471 606)

13. ζήσονται] ζήσωνται (655 659)

  τοῦ θεοῦ αὐτῶν] ܡܠܟ

  καὶ ἁμαρτωλοὶ...χρόνον] om 260 (149 471 606)

  ἁμαρτωλοί] pr ἀπολοῦνται 336

  ἀπολοῦνται] pr οἱ 769

12. On the day of the Lord's judgment sinners will perish forever,
   when God examines[236] the earth at his judgment:[237]
13. but then,[238] those fearing the Lord will find mercy,
   and they will live on in their God's mercy,
   but sinners will perish for all time.

---

[236] Or: "watches over," "oversees," "visits...in judgment."

[237] Other MSS add: "to punish sinners forever," and omit vs. 13c: "but sinners shall perish for all time."

[238] Gk: "on it (Judgement Day)."

16. Ὕμνος Τῷ Σαλωμών· εἰς ἀντίληψιν ὁσίοις

1. Ἐν τῷ νυστάξαι ψυχήν μου ἀπὸ κυρίου
    παρὰ μικρὸν ὠλίσθησα·
    ἐν καταφορᾷ ὕπνου· τῷ μακρὰν ἀπὸ θεοῦ·
2. παρ' ὀλίγον ἐξεχύθη ἡ ψυχή μου εἰς θάνατον·
    σύνεγγυς πυλῶν ἅδου μετὰ ἁμαρτωλοῦ·
3. ἐν τῷ διενεχθῆναι ψυχήν μου ἀπὸ κυρίου θεοῦ Ἰσραήλ·
    εἰ μὴ ὁ κύριος ἀντελάβετό μου τῷ ἐλέει αὐτοῦ
    εἰς τὸν αἰῶνα.

16= ΙϚ

ὕμνος] ψαλμὸς 260 (149 606)

Σαλωμών] σαλομών 655 659 260 (149 606) 629 "Σα..."? partially erased 336

ὁσίοις] om 260 (149 606)

1. νυστάξαι] νηστάξαι (655 659) ܕܢܬܡܪ

ψυχήν] ψυχή (655 659)

ὠλίσθησα] ὠλίσεησα 655 ὠλίσθησαν 769 ὕπνωσα 336
    ܟܕܫܝܢ

ἐν²] om 629 (769)

καταφορᾷ] καταφθορᾷ 260 (149 471) 629 (769) 336

ἐν καταφορᾷ ὕπνου] ܟܠܘܡ ܟܕܡܟ

τῷ] τὸ 629? 336

ὕπνου τῷ] {ὑπνούντων Ra=vG}

μακρὰν] + γενέσθαι 336 ܕܠܘܝܟ

θεοῦ] ܟܝܘ

2. σύνεγγυς] σύηγγος (655m cor: σύνηγγοϛ 659m)

3. διενεχθῆναι] διανεχθῆναι (655 659) ܕܒܬܝܟ

ψυχήν] ψυχή (655 659)

κυρίου] om Syr

κύριος] θεὸς 336

μοῦ²] + εἰς σωτερίαν 336

16 A Hymn of Solomon: Protection for the Devout [239]

1. When I[240] was drowsy, I slowly drifted down, away from the Lord,
    as I fell asleep, far from God.
2. For a moment my life was drained,[241] I was almost dead.
    I was standing with the sinner, very near to the gates of hell.[242]
3. So I would have been carried away from the Lord [243] God of Israel,
    If the Lord had not taken hold of me with his eternal care.[244]

---

[239] Some MSS omit "for the devout."

[240] Gk: "my soul."

[241] Gk: "poured out my soul."

[242] Or: "...the gates to the world of the dead," "...the gates to hades."

[243] Syr omits: "Lord."

[244] Or: "everlasting mercy."

4. ἔνυξέν με ὡς κέντρον ἵππου ἐπὶ τὴν γρηγόρησιν αὐτοῦ·
   ὁ σωτὴρ καὶ ἀντιλήπτωρ μου ἐν παντὶ καιρῷ ἔσωσέν με.
5. Ἐξομολογήσομαί σοι· ὁ θεός·
      ὅτι ἀντελάβου μου εἰς σωτηρίαν·
   καὶ οὐκ ἐλογήσομαι μετὰ τῶν ἁμαρτωλῶν εἰς ἀπώλειαν.
6. μὴ ἀποστήσῃς τὸ ἔλεός σου ἀπ' ἐμοῦ· ὁ θεός·
   μηδὲ τὴν μνήμηνσου ἀπὸ καρδίας μου ἕως θανάτου.
7. Ἐπικράτησόν μου· ὁ θεός· ἀπὸ ἁμαρτίας πονηρᾶς
   καὶ ἀπὸ πάσης γυναικὸς πονηρᾶς
      σκανδαλιζούσης ἄφρονα.
8. καὶ μὴ ἀπατησάτω με κάλλος γυναικὸς παρανομούσης
   καὶ παντὸς ὑποκειμένου ἀπὸ ἁμαρτίας ἀνωφελοῦς.
9. Τὰ ἔργα τῶν χειρῶν μου κατεύθυνον ἐν τόπῳ σου·
      καὶ τὰ διαβήματά μου ἐν τῇ μνήμῃ σου διαφύλαξον.

---

4. ἔνυξέν] ἔνυξέ 260 (149 471 606) 629 ἔνυξέν...σωτηρίαν
   (vs 5) om 336
   ἐπὶ τὴν γρηγόρησιν αὐτοῦ] ܡܕܝܢܬܐ
   ὁ] ὡς 659
   ἔσωσέν] ἔσωσέ 260 (149 471 606) 629 ܐܪܝܡ

5. σοι] σι (655 659m)
   ἀντελάβου] ἀντελάβετό 253 (655 659)
   ἐλογήσομαι] ἐλογήσωμεν 655 659 ἐλογίσωμε 260 (149 471 606)
      629 ἐλογίσομαι 769 ἐλογίσομε 769c ἐλογήσομαι 336 [vG=
   ἐλογήσω με]

6. ἀποστήσῃς] ἀποστήσεις (655 659)
   μηδὲ] μὴ δὲ 253 260 (149) 769 ܐܠ ܘܠܐ
   μνήμην] + περι 253 (655 659)
   σου] του (655 659)
   μου] om 253 (655 659)

7. Ἐπικράτησόν μου] ܦܩܘܕܝ
   ὁ θεός] ܐܠܗܐ
   ἀπὸ...καὶ¹ (vs. 8)] om 336
   ἄφρονα] 655m

8. ὑποκειμένου] αποκειμενου (655 659)
   ἀνωφελοῦς] ἀνοφελοῦς 253 (655 659) 336
   παντὸς...ἀνωφελοῦς] ܠܘ ܣܢܝܐܬ ܐܝܬ

9. ἐν τόπῳ σου] ܘܒܐܬܪܟ

4. In his vigilance he jabbed me as with a horse spur;
     My savior and protector rescued me again.[245]

5. I will confess you, O God, because you took hold of me
          and saved me
          and I wasn't included[246] with sinners for destruction.

6. Don't take your mercy from me, O God,
     nor your memory from my mind[247] until death.

7. Restrain me,[248] O God, from intentional[249] sin,
     and from every wicked woman who traps the foolish.[250]

8. And do not let me be deceived either
          by a lawless[251] woman's beauty,
          nor by anyone under the control of useless sin.

9. Guide my actions before you.[252]
     Guard carefully my steps through remembering you.[253]

---

[245] Gk: "my savior and protector who rescued me in every crisis."

[246] Gk: "counted," "considered."

[247] Gk: "heart."

[248] Gk: "Overpower me," "rule over me."

[249] Gk: "worthless," "useless."

[250] Gk: the trip-stick in an animal snare, thus: "...from every evil woman who triggers the trap for the foolish."

[251] Gk: "lawbreaker," "Torah-violator," "criminal."

[252] Gk: "Make straight the works of my hands in your place."

[253] Gk: "guard carefully my steps in your memory."

10. τὴν γλῶσσάν μου καὶ τὰ χείλη μου
　　　ἐν λόγοις ἀληθείας περίστειλον·
　　　ὀργὴν καὶ θυμὸν ἄλογον μακρὰν ποίησον ἀπ' ἐμοῦ.
11. γογγυσμὸν καὶ ὀλιγοψυχίαν ἐν θλίψει μάκρυνον ἀπ' ἐμοῦ·
　　　ἐὰν ἁμαρτήσω ἐν τῷ σὲ παιδεύειν εἰς ἐπιστροφήν.
12. εὐδοκίᾳ δὲ μετὰ ἱλαρότητος στήρισον τὴν ψυχήν μου·
　　　ἐν τῷ ἐνισχῦσαί σε τὴν ψυχήν μου ἀρκέσει μοι
　　　　τὸ δοθέν.
13. ὅτι ἐὰν μὴ σὺ ἐνισχύσῃς·
　　　τίς ὑφέξεται παιδείαν ἐν πενίᾳ;
14. ἐν τῷ ἐλέγχεσθαι ψυχὴν ἐν χειρὶ σαπρίας αὐτοῦ·
　　　ἡ δοκιμασία σου ἐν σαρκὶ αὐτοῦ
　　　　καὶ ἐν θλίψει πενίας·

---

10. λόγοις] λόγης 655*

　　περίστειλον] περίστειλους 471

11. γογγυσμὸν...ἐμοῦ] om 769

　　ὀλιγοψυχίαν] ὀλιγωψυχίαν 336

　　ἐν²] ἐνου] 769 ?

　　παιδεύειν] πεμδεύειν 336 cor to: πευδεύειν

12. στήρισον] στήριξον 260 (149 471 606) στήρξον 769

　　ἐν...μου] om 659

　　ἐνισχῦσαι] ἰσχύσαι 606ʺ ἐνισχῦσια 'Γ=Pά

13. ἐνισχύσῃς] ἐνισχύσαις 253*

　　παιδείαν] πεδίαν 253 (655m 659m cor marg)
　　παιδείαν ἐν πενίᾳ ᵝἐν πενίᾳ ᵃπαιδείαν 149* [marked with 'β' and 'α' to
　　　show misplacement] 471 606)
　　The sequence of scribal alterations in MS 260 appears to be:
　　　πενίᾳ [ ] παιδείαν 260 (unknown original text)
　　　πενίᾳ eee παιδείαν 260 c¹ (erasure)
　　　ἐν πενίᾳ παιδείαν 260 c² (ἐν added above line)
　　　ᵝἐν πενίᾳ ᵃπαιδείαν 260 c³ (β and 'α' inserted to show misplacement.)

14. ἐλέγχεσθαι] ἐλέχεσθαι (655 659m)

　　ψυχὴν] om Syr

　　ἐν χειρὶ σαπρίας αὐτοῦ] om Syr

　　αὐτοῦ¹] αὐτῆς 260 (149 606 769)

　　σαρκὶ] σαρκὴ (655 659)

　　πενίας] πενείας 659

10. May I speak the truth;[254]
     Put fierce rage and anger far from me.
11. Put grumbling and discouragement in trouble far from me,
     if ever I sin while under your discipline intended to bring me back.

12. Support me[255] with approval and happiness;
          when you strengthen me.[256]
     Whatever you will give is good enough for me.
13. Because if ever you fail to give us strength
     who can endure discipline when they are poor?
14. When people[257] are tested because of their mortality,[258]
     you are examining them in their flesh, and in the burden of poverty:

---

[254] Gk: "Clothe my tongue and my lips, in words of truth."

[255] Gk: "my soul."

[256] Gk: "my soul."

[257] Gk: "soul," "life."

[258] Gk: "...by the hand of his corruption." See Job 7.5.

15. ἐν τῷ ὑπομεῖναι δίκαιον ἐν τούτοις·
    ἐλεηθήσεται ὑπὸ κυρίου.

15. The righteous survive all these things,
        by the Lord's mercy.[259]

---

[259] Gk: "he will receive mercy from the Lord."

17. Ψαλμὸς τῷ Σαλωμὼν μετὰ ᾠδῆς· τῷ βασιλεῖ.

1. Κύριε· σὺ αὐτὸς βασιλεὺς ἡμῶν εἰς τὸν αἰῶνα καὶ ἔτι·
   ὅτι ἐν σοί· ὁ θεός· καυχήσεται ἡ ψυχὴ ἡμῶν.
2. καὶ τίς ὁ χρόνος ζωῆς ἀνθρώπου ἐπὶ τῆς γῆς;
   κατὰ τὸν χρόνον αὐτοῦ καὶ ἡ ἐλπὶς αὐτοῦ ἐπ᾽ αὐτόν.
3. ἡμεῖς δὲ ἐλπιοῦμεν ἐπὶ τὸν θεὸν σωτῆρα ἡμῶν·
   ὅτι τὸ κράτος τοῦ θεοῦ ἡμῶν
     εἰς τὸν αἰῶνα μετ᾽ ἐλέους·
   καὶ ἡ βασιλεία τοῦ θεοῦ ἡμῶν εἰς τὸν αἰῶνα
     ἐπὶ τὰ ἔθνη ἐν κρίσει.

17=IZ

   ψαλμὸς] om 3004
   Σαλωμών] σαλομὼν 659 260 (149 606) 336
   μετὰ] μετ᾽ 260 (149 606) 769 336

1. αὐτὸς] om 253 (655 659)
   βασιλεὺς] + εἰς τὸν αἰῶνα ὁ θεος 336
   ἡμῶν¹] +καὶ 336
   ἔτι] ἔτη (655 659)
   θεός] +ἡμων 253 (655 659)

2. ὁ χρόνος] om Syr
   καὶ² MS 3004 begins here, with this word.
   ἡ ἐλπὶς αὐτοῦ ἐπ᾽ αὐτόν] ܡܢܗ

3. ἡμεῖς] ἡμᾶς (655 659)
   ἐλπιοῦμεν] ἐλπίζομεν 336
   τὸν θεὸν] ~θεὸν τὸν 260 (149 471 606) 336
   σωτῆρα] pr τὸν (606 769 3004)
   τοῦ¹] σοῦ 655 στοῦ 655c
   ἐλέους] ἐλέου 260 (149 471 606 3004) 769 336
   ἐν κρίσει] om 253 (655 659)

17. A Psalm of Solomon with Song: For the king

1. O Lord, you yourself are our king for ever and ever:
   because in you, O God, we[260] will take pride
2. How long is a person's allotted lifetime on earth?[261]
   as long as he lives, he can hope.[262]
3. But we hope in God our savior:
   because the strength and mercy of our God will last forever,[263]
   and the kingdom of our God will last forever
   in judgment over the Gentiles.[264]

---

[260] Gk: "our soul."

[261] Gk: "And how long is a person's lifetime on earth according to his time?"

[262] Gk: "according to his [life]span, [so] also [is] his hope.."

[263] Gk: " the strength of our God is forever with mercy."

[264] Some MSS omit: "in judgment."

4. Σύ· κύριε· ἡρετίσω τὸν Δαυὶδ βασιλέα ἐπὶ Ἰσραὴλ·
   καὶ σὺ ὤμοσας αὐτῷ
   περὶ τοῦ σπέρματος αὐτοῦ εἰς τὸν αἰῶνα·
   τοῦ μὴ ἐκλείπειν ἀπέναντί σου βασίλειον αὐτοῦ.
5. καὶ ἐν ταῖς ἁμαρτίαις ἡμῶν ἐπανέστησαν
   ἡμῖν ἁμαρτωλοί·
   ἐπέθεντο ἡμῖν καὶ ἔξωσαν ἡμᾶς
   οἷς οὐκ ἐπηγγείλω· μετὰ βίας ἀφείλαντο·
   καὶ οὐκ ἐδόξασαν τὸ ὄνομά σου τὸ ἔντιμον.
6. ἐν δόξῃ ἔθεντο βασίλειον ἀντὶ ὕψους αὐτῶν
   ἠρήμωσαν τὸν θρόνον Δαυὶδ
   ἐν ὑπερηφανίᾳ ἀλλάγματος.

---

4. ἡρετίσω] ἡρετήσω 253 (655 659)

   ἐπὶ] ἕν 769*

   καὶ] om 769*

   αὐτοῦ[1]] om 253 (655 659)

   εἰς τὸν αἰῶνα] om Syr

   ἐκλείπειν] ἐκλιπεὶν 471 769 336

   σου] τὸ 769

   βασίλειον] βασίλιον 659 [βασιλέιαν] c=Cerda 3004}. (This and other
   marginal corrections in a similar hand appear to be later harmonizations with de
   la Cerda, by a Fr. Junius. See Introduction, p. 25.)

5. ἡμῖν] ἡμῶν 336

   ἐπέθεντο] ὑπέθεντο 336

   ἔξωσαν] ἐξώσαντο 253 (655 659)

   οὐκ[1]] om 769

   ἐπηγγείλω] ἐπιγγείλω 253 336

   μετὰ] μετὰ μετὰ 655 [folio marker] καὶ μετὰ 336

   ἀφείλαντο] ἀφείλοντο 260 (149 471 606 3004) 769 336

   ἔντιμον] εἴτιμον 336

6. δόξῃ] δόξει 659

   ἠρήμωσαν] ἐρήμωσαν 3004* 336

   ὑπερηφανίᾳ] ὑπερυφανία 659

   ἀλλάγματος] = ܘܡܠܘܬܐ ἀλαλάγματος 260 (149 471 606 3004)

4. It was you, O Lord, who chose David as king over Israel,
        and you promised him that his descendants
            would continue forever,[265]
        that you would not abandon his royal house.[266]
5. But sinners revolted against us because of our sins:
        they attacked us and drove us out.
    Those to whom you promised nothing,[267]
        they violently stole from us,[268]
6. In their pride they flamboyantly[269] set up their own royal house.
        Their arrogant substitution desolated David's throne.
        and they did not glorify your honorable name.

---

[265] Syr omits: "forever."

[266] Gk: "that his royal house would not be cut off before you."

[267] Gk: "those to whom you did not make the promise."

[268] Gk: "took it away with violence."

[269] Gk: "with glory," "with pomp."

7. Καὶ σύ· ὁ θεός· καταβαλεῖς αὐτοὺς
    καὶ ἀρεῖς σπέρμα αὐτῶν ἀπὸ τῆς γῆς·
    ἐν τῷ ἐπαναστῆναι αὐτοῖς ἄνθρωπον
    ἀλλότριον γένους ἡμῶν.

8. κατὰ τὰ ἁμαρτήματα αὐτῶν ἀποδώσεις αὐτοῖς· ὁ θεός·
    εὑρεθῆναι αὐτοῖς κατὰ τὰ ἔργα αὐτῶν.

9. οὐκ ἐλεήσει αὐτοὺς ὁ θεός·
    ἐξηρεύνησε τὸ σπέρμα αὐτῶν
    καὶ οὐκ ἀφῆκεν αὐτῶν ἕνα.

---

7. ὁ θεός] *om* Syr

  σπέρμα] pr τὸ 260 (149 471 606) 629 (769) 336
  ἡμῶν] ἡριτῶν 3004m c=Cerda

8. εὑρεθῆναι] εὑρεθείη 260 (149 471 606 3004)

9. ‎ܘ݀ܟ¹] = ‎ܠܐ *om* 260 (149 471 606 3004) *pr* κατὰ τὰ ἔργα αὐτῶν
  260 (149 471 606 3004) 769 336

  ἐλεήσει] = ‎ܢܚܘܣ 16h1ᶜ ‎ܢܚܘܣܐ 16h1* {ἠλέησεν Ra=vG}
  ἐξηρεύνησε] ἐξερεύνησεν 253 (655 659) ‎ܒܨܐ
  ἀφῆκεν] ‎ܫܒܩ
  αὐτῶν²] αὐτούς 260 (149 471 606 3004)
  ἕνα] *om* 260 (149 471 606 3004)

7. But you, O God, will throw them down,
       and root up their descendants from the earth,
       for there will rise up against them a man[270] alien to our race.
8. You will repay them according to their sins O God;
       It will happen to them according to their deeds.[271]
9. God showed them no[272] mercy.
       He hunted down their descendants,
          and did not let even one of them escape.

---

[270] Gk: ἄνθρωπον

[271] Some MSS and Syr omit: "according to their deeds."

[272] Some MSS and Syr omit: "no."

10. πιστὸς ὁ κύριος ἐν πᾶσι τοῖς κρίμασιν αὐτοῦ·
    οἷς ποιεῖ ἐπὶ τὴν γῆν.
11. Ἠρήμωσεν ὁ ἄνομος τὴν γῆν ἡμῶν
    ἀπὸ ἐνοικούντων αὐτήν·
    ἠφάνισαν νέον καὶ πρεσβύτην καὶ τέκνα αὐτῶν ἅμα·
12. ἐν ὀργῇ κάλλους αὐτοῦ ἐξαπέστειλεν αὐτὰ ἕως
        ἐπὶ δυσμῶν·
    καὶ τοὺς ἄρχοντας τῆς γῆς εἰς ἐμπαιγμὸν
        καὶ οὐκ ἐφείσατο.
13. ἐν ἀλλοτριότητι ὁ ἐχθρὸς ἐποίησεν ὑπερηφανίαν·
    καὶ ἡ καρδία αὐτοῦ ἀλλοτρία ἀπὸ θεοῦ ἡμῶν.
14. καὶ πάντα ὅσα ἐποίησεν ἐν Ἰερουσαλήμ·
    καθὼς καὶ τὰ ἔθνη ἐν ταῖς πόλεσι τοὺς θεοὺς αὐτῶν.

---

10. κύριος] θεὸς 336
    ποιεῖ] ἐποίησεν 336
    ἐπὶ] om 655 659
11. Ἠρήμωσεὐ Ἠρήμωσεν ὁ ἄνομος τὴν γῆν < 659 ἐρήμωσεν 336
    ἄνομος] ἄνεμος 260 (149 471 606 3004) +ἐπὶ 253 (655)
    τέκνα] pr τὰ 3004 336
12. ἐν ὀργῇ κάλλους αὐτοῦ] ᴅᵉᵗᵉᵗ ᴋ́ᵉ̄ᴅᵃᵗᵉ
    αὐτοῦ] = ᴅᵉᵗᵉᵗ αὐτῶν 336
    ἕως] om (655 659)
    ἐμπαιγμὸν] ἐμπεγμόν 253 (655 659)
    καὶ²] om 3004, marg c=Cerda
    ἐφείσατο] ἐφήσατο (655 659)
13. ἐποίησεν] ἐποίησε 336 + ἐν 253 (655) 336
    ὑπερηφανίαν] ὑπερηφανία 253 336 ὑπεριφανία 655 659
    ἀλλοτρία] ἀποτρία 471
    Θεοῦ] π_ρ τοῦ 253 (655 659) 260 (149 471 606) 769
14. ἐποίησεν] + ὁ θεός (655 659)
    ἐν¹] om Syr
    τοὺς θεοὺς] τοῖς θεοῖς 260 (149 471 606 3004) 769 336
        {τοῦ σθένους Ra=vG}
    θεοὺς] om (655 659)

10.   The Lord is faithful in all his judgments
          that he does on earth.

11.   The lawless one[1] devastated our land,[2]
              so that it was uninhabitable;[3]
              he eliminated young and old and their children together.
12.   In his magnificent wrath[4] God[5] sent them away to the west,
          and he did not spare even the officials of the country from ridicule.
13.   As the enemy was a foreigner, and his heart was foreign to our God, so he acted
          arrogantly.
14.   So in Jerusalem[6] he engaged in all the practices
          that Gentiles do for their gods in their great cities.

---

[273] Some MSS read: "the storm."

[274] Gk: "turned our land into a desert."

[275] Gk: "no one inhabited it."

[276] Gk: "the passion/wrath of his beauty." "The fire of God's wrath." Syr: "the beauty
of his wrath." Unless this awkward phrase is a mistranslation from the original Heb.,
it appears to refer to God's "righteous indignation."

[277] Gk: "he."

[278] Syr: "and Jerusalem did."

15. Καὶ ἐπεκρατοῦσαν αὐτῶν· οἱ υἱοὶ τῆς διαθήκης
    ἐν μέσῳ ἐθνῶν συμμίκτων·
    οὐκ ἦν ὁ ποιῶν ἐν μέσῳ ἐν αὐτοῖς ἐν Ἰερουσαλὴμ
    ἔλεος καὶ ἀλήθειαν.
16. ἐφύγοσαν ἀπ᾽ αὐτῶν οἱ ἀγαπῶντες συναγωγὰς ὁσίων·
    ὡς στρουθία ἐξεπετάσθησαν ἀπὸ κοίτης αὐτῶν.
17. ἐπλανῶντο ἐν ἐρήμοις· σωθῆναι ψυχὰς αὐτῶν ἀπὸ κακοῦ·
    καὶ τίμιον ἐν ὀφθαλμοῖς παροικίας
    ψυχὴ σεσωσμένη ἐξ αὐτῶν.

---

15. ἐπεκρατοῦσαν] ἐπεκράτουν 260 (149 471 606 3004) 769
    ἀπεκράτουν 336

    αὐτῶν] αὐτὸν 655* αὐτοῦ 471

    οἱ] om 253 (655 659)

    ἐν μέσῳ ἐν αὐτοῖς ἐν] ~ ἐν αὐτοῖς ἐν μέσῳ 260 (149 471 606
    3004) 769 336 {ἐν αὐτοῖς ὁ ποιῶν ἐν Ra=vG}

    ἐν μέσῳ] om Syr

    ἐν⁴] om 260, 606, 336

16. ἔφυγοσαν] ἔφυγον 260 (149 471 606 3004) 769 336
    ἀπ᾽] ἀπὸ 769

    αὐτῶν¹] τούτων 769

    ὁσίων] om 769

    στρουθία] στρουθί (655 659) στρούθιοι 655c

    ἐξεπετάσθησαν] ἐξεπέτασαν 769m

17. σωθῆναι] ܠܡܬܢܨܘ

    ἐν ὀφθαλμοῖς παροικίας ψυχὴ]
    ܡܗܢ ܕܒܡܓܠܘܬܐ ܕܢܦܫܬܐ ܢܦܩܬ

    ψυχὴ] ψυχῆς (655 659)

    σεσωσμένη] ἔωσμένη (655 659)

    αὐτῶν²] + ἐφύγοσαν ἀπ᾽ αὐτῶν οἱ ἀγαπῶντες συναγωγὰς ὁσίων
    253
        655 659

15. And the people of the covenant living among the many nations
        adopted these things.
    No one among them in Jerusalem acted with mercy or truth.
16. Those who loved the synagogues of the devout[279] escaped from them
        as sparrows fly[280] from their nest.
17. They wandered in the wilderness to save their lives[281] from evil.
        The life of even one who was saved from them
        was precious in the eyes of the exiles.

---

[279] Or: "assemblies of the pious." Some MSS omit: "of the devout."

[280] Gk: "spread out (their wings)."

[281] Gk: "souls."

18. Εἰς πᾶσαν τὴν γῆν ἐγενήθη σκορπισμὸς αὐτῶν
    ὑπὸ ἀνόμων·

    Ὅτι ἀνέσχεν ὁ οὐρανὸς τοῦ στάξαι ὑετὸν ἐπὶ τὴν γῆν.
19. Πηγαὶ συνεσχέθησαν αἰώνιοι
    ἐξ ἀβύσσων ἀπὸ ὀρέων ὑψηλῶν·
    ὅτι οὐκ ἦν ἐν αὐτοῖς ποιῶν δικαιοσύνην καὶ κρίμα.
20. ἀπὸ ἄρχοντος αὐτῶν καὶ λαοῦ ἐλαχίστου
    ἐν πάσῃ ἁμαρτίᾳ.
    ὁ βασιλεὺς ἐν παρανομίᾳ
    καὶ ὁ κριτὴς ἐν ἀπειθείᾳ
    καὶ ὁ λαὸς ἐν ἁμαρτίᾳ.
21. Ἴδε, κύριε· καὶ ἀνάστησον αὐτοῖς
    τὸν βασιλέα αὐτῶν· υἱὸν Δαυίδ·
    εἰς τὸν καιρόν· ὃν ἴδες σύ· ὁ θεός·
    τοῦ βασιλεῦσαι ἐπὶ Ἰσραὴλ παιδά σου·

---

18. σκορπισμὸς] pr ὁ 260 (149 471 606 3004) 769 336

    ἀνέσχεν] ἐνέσχεν 336

    τοῦ] τοὺς (655 659)

    τὴν γῆν] τῆς γῆς 336

19. πηγαὶ] αἱ πηγαὶ 3004

    συνεσχέθησαν] συνεχέθησαν (655 659)

20. αυτῶν] αὐτοῦ 336

    λαοῦ] ܟܢܫܐ

    ἁμαρτίᾳ] +ΣΗ (superimposed twice) in marg 336 + εἰς τὸν καιρόν, ὃν
      ἴδες σύ, ὁ θεός, τοῦ βασιλεῦσαι ἐπὶ Ἰσραὴλ παιδά σου·
      (transposed from vs.21)

    κριτὴς] κριθεις (655 659)

    ἀπειθείᾳ] ܒܚܛܝܬܐ

21. αὐτῶν] αὐτον 769

    υἱὸν Δαυίδ] υἱῷ Δαβίδ 253 (655 659)

    εἰς τὸν καιρόν...Ἰσραὴλ παιδά σου] ~ to vs. 20 336

    ἴδες] οἶδες 260 (149 οἶδας 606 471 3004) εἶδες 769 336
      {εἵλου Ra=vG}

    βασιλεῦσαι] βασιλεύσας (655 659)

    ἐπὶ] om 769

18.   They were scattered over the whole earth by the lawless ones.

     The heavens withheld rain from falling on the earth.
19.   Springs were stopped,
     From the perennial sources far underground
     To those in the high mountains.
     For there was no one among them who practiced
       righteousness or justice:
20.   From their leader to the commonest of the people
       they committed every kind of sin:
          the king broke the law,
          the judges disobeyed,
          the people sinned.
21.   Look,[282] O Lord, and raise up for them their king,
       a son of David, to rule over your servant Israel
       in the time that you know, O God.

---

[282] Other MSS read: "Know this...."

22. καὶ ὑπόζωσον αὐτὸν ἰσχύν
        τοῦ θραῦσαι ἄρχοντας ἀδίκους·
    καθάρισον Ἰερουσαλὴμ ἀπὸ ἐθνῶν
        καταπατούντων ἐν ἀπωλείᾳ
23. ἐν σοφίᾳ· ἐν δικαιοσύνῃ
        ἐξῶσαι ἁμαρτωλοὺς ἀπὸ κληρονομίας·
    ἐκτρῖψαι ὑπερηφανίαν ἁμαρτωλοῦ· ὡς σκεύη κεραμέως·
24. ἐν ῥάβδῳ σιδηρᾷ συντρῖψαι πᾶσαν ὑπόστασιν αὐτῶν·
        ὀλοθρεῦσαι ἔθνη παράνομα ἐν λόγῳ στόματος αὐτοῦ·
25. ἐν ἀπειλῇ αὐτοῦ φυγεῖν ἔθνη ἀπὸ προσώπου αὐτοῦ·
        καὶ ἐλέγξαι ἁμαρτωλοὺς ἐν λόγῳ καρδίας αὐτῶν.

---

22. ἰχὺν] ἰσχὴν 655
    καθάρισον] ܡܕܟܐ {καθαρίσαι Ra=vG}
    ἐθνῶν] ἐθνόν 659*
    καταπατούντων] 655m καὶ ἀπατούντων 3004 * marg c=Cerda
    ἀπωλείᾳ] ἀπωλείας (655m 659)
23. ἐν σοφίᾳ] om Syr
    ἐν δικαιοσύνῃ] om Syr {δικαιοσύνης Ra}
    ἐξῶσαι] ἔζωσαν (655m 659) ἔξοσον 769 336
    ἐκτρῖψαι] ἐκτρῖψας (655m 659m)
    ὑπερηφανίαν] ὑπερυφανίαν 655
    ἁμαρτωλοῦ] om Syr
    ἁμαρτωλοῦ] ἁμαρτωλοὺς 260 (149 606 3004) ἁμαρτωλῶν 336
    ὡς] ὥ 655 769 ἐν 336
24. συντρῖψαι] συντρῖψον 336
    ὀλοθρεῦσαι] ὀλεθρεῦσαι {Ra}
    αὐτοῦ] ἐν ἀπελλῇ αὐτοῦ φυγεῖν ἔθνη ἀπὸ προσώπου αὐτοῦ
        3004 marg addition c=Cerda
25. ἐν ἀπειλῃ αὐτοῦ φυγεῖν ἔθνη ἀπὸ προσώπου αὐτοῦ] om (471 606
        3004)
    ἐν ἀπειλῇ αὐτοῦ] ܒܠܘܚܡܗ

22.   Undergird him with the strength to destroy the unrighteous rulers,
          to purge Jerusalem from the Gentiles
              who trample her down to destruction;
23.   In wisdom and in righteousness[283]
          to drive out the sinners from the inheritance,
          to smash the arrogance of sinners like a potter's jar;
24.   to demolish all their resources[284] with an iron rod;
          to destroy the lawbreaking Gentiles with the word of his mouth;
25.   to scatter the Gentiles from his presence at his threat;
          to condemn sinners by their own consciences.[285]

---

[283] Syr omits: "in wisdom and in righteousness."

[284] Gk: "substance," "foundation," "confidence."

[285] Gk: "by the thoughts of their own hearts."

26. Καὶ συνάξει λαὸν ἅγιον οὗ ἀφηγήσεται ἐν δικαιοσύνῃ·
    καὶ κρινεῖ φυλὰς λαοῦ
    ἡγιασμένου ὑπὸ κυρίου θεοῦ αὐτοῦ·
27. καὶ οὐκ ἀφήσει ἀδικίαν ἐν μέσῳ αὐτῶν αὐλισθῆναι ἔτι·
    καὶ οὐ κατοικήσει πᾶς ἄνθρωπος
        μετ᾽ αὐτῶν εἰδὼς κακίαν·
    γνώσεται γὰρ αὐτοὺς
        ὅτι πάντες υἱοὶ θεοῦ εἰσιν αὐτῶν.
28. καὶ καταμερίσει αὐτοὺς ἐν ταῖς φυλαῖς αὐτῶν
        ἐπὶ τῆς γῆς·
    καὶ πάροικος καὶ ἀλλογενὴς οὐ παροικήσειαὐτοῖς ἔτι·
29. κρινεῖ λαοὺς καὶ ἔθνη ἐν σοφίᾳ δικαιοσύνης αὐτοῦ.

                                                    διάψαλμα

---

26. ἀφηγήσεται] ܝܬܡܪܚ
    ἡγιασμένου] *om* (655 659)
27. ἔτι] = ܣܐܕ *om* 260 (149 471 606 3004)
    πάντες] πάντας (655 659)
    εἰσιν αὐτῶν] αὐτῶν εἰσι 260 (149 471? 606 3004) 769 αὐτῶν
        εἰσιν 769 336
    αὐτῶν²] αὐτὸν 655*m
28. αὐτῶν] αὐτον 655*
    τῆς] *om* 336
    ἀλλογενὴς] ἀλλογενὲς 655 659
    παροικήσει] + ἐν 769
    αὐτοῖς ἔτι (vs 29) κρινεῖ] ܟ̈ܐܢ ܠܕܝܢ . ܘܥܡܡܐ
29. διάψαλμα] 3004* interlinear; *om* 471, Syr; διάψαλμ 655m 659m, in red
    606.

26. He will gather a holy people[286]
        whom he will lead in righteousness;[287]
    and he will judge the tribes of the people
        who have been made holy by the Lord his God.[288]
27. He will not tolerate unrighteousness to dwell[289] among them again,
        and no person who knows evil will live with them.
    For he will know them, because they are all
        children of their[290] God.
28. He will distribute them upon the land according to their tribes.
        The stranger and the foreigner will no longer live with them.[291]
29. He will judge peoples and nations in the wisdom of his justice.

                                                        Pause

---

[286] One Syr MS reads: "a righteous people."

[287] Syr: "...who will glorify themselves."

[288] Or: "the Lord their God."

[289] Gk: "sojourn," "spend the night."

[290] Syr omits: "their."

[291] Syr: "will live near them."

30. Καὶ ἕξει λαοὺς ἐθνῶν δουλεύειν αὐτῷ
        ὑπὸ τὸν ζυγὸν αὐτοῦ·
    καὶ τὸν κύριον δοξάσει ἐν ἐπισήμῳ πάσης τῆς γῆς·
    καὶ καθαριεῖ Ἰερουσαλὴμ ἐν ἁγιασμῷ ὡς
        καὶ τὸ ἀπ' ἀρχῆς·
31. ἔρχεσθαι ἔθνη ἀπ' ἄκρου τῆς γῆς
        ἰδεῖν τὴν δόξαν αὐτοῦ·
    φέροντες δῶρα τοὺς ἐξησθενηκότας υἱοὺς αὐτῆς·
    καὶ ἰδεῖν τὴν δόξαν κυρίου ἣν ἐδόξασεν αὐτὴν ὁ θεός.

---

29. διάψαλμα] 3004* interlinear; *om* 471, Syr; διάψαλμ 655m 659m, in red
    606.
30. ἕξει] ἕξ ἕξει (655 659)
    λαοὺς ἐθνῶν] ܟܢܫܐ ܡܢ ܥܡܡܐ
    ὑπὸ] κύπὸ 655
    τὸν¹] *om* 260 (149 606 3004) 769 336
    καὶ³] *om* (655 659)
    καθαριεῖ] κιθαριεῖ (655 659) καθαρίσει 260 (149 471 606 3004)
        336
    τὸ] τῷ 3004* marg c=Cerda
31. ἔρχεσθαι] ἔρχεσθε 769 336
    φέροντες] φέρωντες 659
    ἐξησθενηκότας] ἐξοσθενηκότας (655* 659)
    τοὺς ἐξησθενηκότας υἱοὺς αὐτῆς,] ܠܒܢܝܗ ܕܐܬܟܪܗܘ ܡܢܗ
    ἰδεῖν] ἰδεν 769
    ἣν] εἶν (655 659)
    αὐτὴν] αὐτῆς 659*

30. He will have Gentile peoples[292] serving him under his yoke,
        and he will glorify the Lord publically in the whole world.
     He will pronounce Jerusalem clean,
        consecrating it as it was in the beginning.
31. He will have nations come[293] from the ends of the earth
        to see his glory,
     giving back[294] her scattered children[295]
        and to see the glory of the Lord
            with which God has glorified her.

---

[292] Gk: "peoples of the nations."

[293] Other MSS read: "come nations...."

[294] Gk: "bearing as gifts."

[295] So Syriac. Gk: "her frail children" See Kuhn, *Die älteste Textgestalt* 72-73.

32. καὶ αὐτὸς βασιλεὺς δίκαιος διδακτὸς
        ὑπὸ θεοῦ ἐπ' αὐτούς·
     καὶ οὐκ ἔστιν ἀδικία ἐν ταῖς ἡμέραις αὐτοῦ
        ἐν μέσῳ αὐτῶν·
     ὅτι πάντες ἅγιοι καὶ βασιλεὺς αὐτῶν χριστὸς κύριος.
33. οὐ γὰρ ἐλπιεῖ ἐπὶ ἵππον καὶ ἀναβάτην καὶ τόξον·
     οὐδὲ πληθυνεῖ αὐτῷ χρυσίον οὐδὲ ἀργύριον
        εἰς πόλεμον·
     καὶ πολλοῖς οὐ συνάξει ἐλπίδας εἰς ἡμέραν πολέμου.

34. Κύριος αὐτὸς βασιλεὺς αὐτοῦ·
        ἐλπὶς τοῦ δυνατοῦ ἐλπίδι θεοῦ·
     Καὶ ἐλεήσει πάντα τὰ ἔθνη ἐνώπιον αὐτοῦ ἐν φόβῳ.

---

32. δίκαιος] + καὶ 606
    ἐπ'] ὑπ' 3004* marg c=Cerda
    ἀδικία] ἡ ἀδικία (655 659)
    αὐτῶν] αὐτὸν (655* 659*)
    ὅτι...κυρίος] om 336
    κύριος] =mss=vG, {κυρίου Ra}
33. ἐπὶ] ἐφ' 336
    οὐδὲ¹] οὐδὲν 655m
    πληθυνεῖ] πληθυνῶ (655 659)
    οὐδὲ²] καὶ 260 (149 471 606 3004) 769 336
    πολλοῖς οὐ συνάξει ἐλπίδας] ܪܟܠ ܠܐ ܪܟܐܘ ܐܠ
    ἐλπίδας] ἐλπίδα 3004
    εἰς] ἐς (655 659)
34. αὐτοῦ¹] om Syr
    τοῦ] αὐτοῦ 253 (655 659)
    ἐλπὶς τοῦ δυνατοῦ ἐλπίδι θεοῦ]
       ܗܠܐܪܐ ܡܙܘ ܠܐ ܡܠܘܐ ܡܙܘ

32. He will be a righteous king over them, taught by God,
      there will be no unrighteousness among them during his reign,[296]
    because everyone will be holy,
      and their king will be the Lord Messiah.
33. For he will not depend on cavalry and archers;[297]
      Nor will he need to finance a war;[298]
      He will not place his hope on making war.[299]

34. The Lord himself is his king,
      the hope of the one who hopes[300] in God.
    He will be merciful to all the Gentiles
      that fearfully stand before him.

---

[296] Gk: "in his days."

[297] Gk: "horse and rider and bow."

[298] Gk: "accumulate gold and silver for war."

[299] Gk: "a day of war."

[300] Gk: "hope."

35. πατάξει γὰρ γῆν τῷ λόγῳ τοῦ στόματος αὐτοῦ εἰς αἰῶνα·
    εὐλογήσει λαὸν κυρίου ἐν σοφίᾳ μετ' εὐφροσύνης·
36. καὶ αὐτὸς καθαρὸς ἀπὸ ἁμαρτίας·
        τοῦ ἄρχειν λαοῦ μεγάλου·
    ἐλέγξαι ἄρχοντας καὶ ἐξᾶραι ἁμαρτωλοὺς
        ἐν ἰσχύι λόγου.
37. καὶ οὐκ ἀσθενήσει ἐν ταῖς ἡμέραις αὐτοῦ ἐπὶ θεῷ αὐτοῦ
    ὅτι ὁ θεὸς κατειργάσατο αὐτὸν
        δυνατὸν ἐν πνεύματι ἁγίῳ
    καὶ σοφὸν ἐν βουλῇ συνέσεως
        μετὰ ἰσχύος καὶ δικαιοσύνης.
38. καὶ εὐλογία κυρίου μετ' αὐτοῦ ἐν ἰσχύι·
    καὶ οὐκ ἀσθενήσει.

---

35. πατάξει] κατάξει 253 (655 659) 336
    γῆν] 655m
    εἰς] + τὸν 336
36. ἀπὸ] ἐπ' (655 659)
    λαοῦ μεγάλου] λαούς μεγάλους 253 (655 659)
    ἰσχύι] ἰσχύει 253 (655 659) om Syr
37. ἀσθενήσει] ἀνθενήσει 659* ܬܚܫܠ
    κατειργάσατο] κατηργάσατο 655 (659 769)
    δυνατὸν] om 336 δύναμιν 769
    συνέσεως] συνέσως (655* 659*)
    μετὰ] μετ' 260 (149 471 606 3004)
    δικαιοσύνης] δικαιοσύνην 253 (655*)
38. καὶ'] om 659
    ἰσχύι] ἰσχύει 253 (655 659)

35. He will strike the earth with the word of his mouth forever;
    He will bless the Lord's people with wisdom and happiness.
36. And he himself will be free from sin,
       in order to rule such a great people.
    He will expose officials and drive out sinners
       by the strength of his word.
37. And he will not weaken[301] during his reign,[302] relying upon his God,
       because God will make him powerful by a holy spirit;
       and wise in intelligent counsel, with strength and righteousness.

38. And the blessing of the Lord will be with him in strength,
       and it will not weaken;

---

[301] Or "stumble." See Ward, *A Philological Analysis,* p. 265.

[302] Gk: "in his days."

39. Ἡ ἐλπὶς αὐτοῦ ἐπὶ κύριον·
    καὶ τίς δύναται πρὸς αὐτόν;
40. Ἰσχυρὸς ἐν ἔργοις αὐτοῦ καὶ κραταιὸς ἐν φόβῳ θεοῦ·
    ποιμαίνων τὸ ποίμνιον κυρίου
        ἐν πίστει καὶ δικαιοσύνῃ·
    καὶ οὐκ ἀφήσει ἀσθενῆσαι ἐν αὐτοῖς
        ἐν τῇ νομῇ αὐτῶν.
41. ἐν ἰσότητι πάντας αὐτοὺς ἄξει·
    καὶ οὐκ ἔσται ἐν αὐτοῖς ὑπερηφανία
        τοῦ καταδυναστευθῆναι ἐν αὐτοῖς.
42. Αὕτη ἡ εὐπρέπεια τοῦ βασιλέως Ἰσραήλ, ἣν ἔγνω ὁ θεός·
    ἀναστῆσαι αὐτὸν ἐπ᾽ οἶκον Ἰσραήλ, παιδεῦσαι αὐτόν.

---

39. Ἡ] om 606
    δύναται] ܡܩܡ

40. καὶ[1]] om (655 659)
    φόβῳ] φόβον (655 659)
    ποιμαίνων] ποιμένων (655 659)
    δικαιοσύνῃ] δικαιοσύνην (655m 659)
    ἀφήσει] ἀφῆσαι 336
    αὐτῶν] αὐτον (655 659) αὐτῷ 769

41. ἰσότητι] ὁσιότητι 260 (149 471 606 769* marg)
    ܟܐܘܝܘܬܐ
    ἄξει] ἥξει 655* 659* αὔξει 606 ܢܕܒܪ
    ὑπερηφανία] ὑπερυφανία (655m 659) ὑπερηφανέια 3004
    καταδυναστευθῆναι] καταδυναστευθῦναι 655
    αὐτοῖς[2]] αὐτῷ 3004* (Hann believes this to be a correction by the original
        scribe; Baars says it is a later correction)

39. His hope will be in the Lord.
       Then who can be stronger than he?[303]
40. He will be mighty in his actions and strong in the fear of God,
       faithfully and righteously shepherding the Lord's sheep,[304]
       he will not let any of them stumble[305] in their pasture.
41. He will lead them all impartially,[306]
       And there will be no arrogance among them,
          that any of them should be oppressed..
42. This is the magnificence of the king of Israel[307]
       that God acknowledged,
     to raise him over the House of Israel to discipline it.

---

[303] Syr: "for who will stand against him."

[304] Gk: "flock." ("Sheep" to preserve the alliteration in Greek.)

[304] Gk: "become weak."

[306] Gk: "in equality."

[307] One MS reads: "king of Jerusalem."

43. Τὰ ῥήματα αὐτοῦ πεπυρωμένα
        ὑπὲρ χρυσίον τὸ πρῶτον τίμιον·
     ἐν συναγωγαῖς διακρινεῖ λαοῦ φυλὰς ἡγιασμένου·
     οἱ λόγοι αὐτοῦ ὡς λόγοι ἁγίων ἐν
        μέσῳ λαῶν ἡγιασμένων.
44. μακάριοι οἱ γενόμενοι ἐν ταῖς ἡμέραις ἐκείναις·
        ἰδεῖν τὰ ἀγαθὰ Ἰσραὴλ
        ἐν συναγωγῇ φυλῶν· ἃ ποιήσει ὁ θεός.
45. ταχύναι ὁ θεὸς ἐπὶ Ἰσραὴλ τὸ ἔλεος αὐτοῦ·
        ῥύσεται ἡμᾶς ἀπὸ ἀκαθαρσίας ἐχθρῶν βεβήλων.
46. κύριος αὐτὸς βασιλεὺς ἡμῶν εἰς τὸν αἰῶνα καὶ ἔτι.

---

43. τὸ πρῶτον τίμιον] τίμιον τὸ πρῶτον 260 (149 471 606 3004) 769
        336

     τὸ πρῶτον] *om* Syr

     συναγωγαῖς] συναγωγάς 655*m

     διακρινεῖ] διακρίνει 655 m διακρινεῖς 3004* c=Cerda

     λαοῦ] λαούς 260 (149 471 606 3004) 769 336

     ἡγιασμένου] ἡγιασμένων 260 (149 471 606 3004)

     αὐτοῦ²] αὐτῶν 253 (655 659)

     ὡς] *om* 336

44. γενόμενοι] γινόμενοι 260 (149 471 606 3004) 769 336
        Ἰσραὴλ] Ἱερουσαλήμ 336
        ἃ] *om* 253 (655 659) 769 336
        ποιήσει] ποιῆσαι 253 (655 659) 769 336

45. ταχύναι] ταχύνη 253 (655 659)
        ῥύσεται] ῥῦσαι 769 {ῥύσαιτο Ra=vG}
        ἀκαθαρσίας] ἀκαρθασίας 769
        ἐχθρῶν] ܒܥܠܕ

46. βασιλεύς] βασιλεὸς (655 659)

43.   His words will be purer[308] than the finest gold.
      In the assemblies he will judge the tribes of a sanctified people.
      His words will be as the words of the holy ones,
         among sanctified peoples.

44.   Happy are the people born in those days
      who will see the good fortune of Israel [309]
      that God will cause in the gathering of the tribes.

45.   May God hasten his mercy to Israel;
      May he shield us from the contamination of defiled enemies;

46.   The Lord himself is our king forevermore.

---

[308] Gk: "proven true," "refined." See Ps 18.30.

[309] One MS reads: "Jerusalem."

18. Ψαλμὸς τῷ Σαλωμών · ἔτι τοῦ Χριστοῦ Κυρίου

1. Κύριε· τὸ ἔλεός σου ἐπὶ τὰ ἔργα τῶν χειρῶν σου
    εἰς τὸν αἰῶνα·
  ἡ χρηστότης σου μετὰ δόματος πλουσίου ἐπὶ Ἰσραήλ·
2. οἱ ὀφθαλμοί σου ἐπιβλέποντες ἐπ᾽ αὐτά·
    καὶ οὐχ ὑστερήσει ἐξ αὐτῶν·
    τὰ ὦτά σου ἐπακούει εἰς δέησιν πτωχοῦ ἐν ἐλπίδι.
3. τὰ κρίματά σου ἐπὶ πᾶσαν τὴν γῆν μετὰ ἐλέους·
    καὶ ἡ ἀγάπη σου ἐπὶ σπέρμα Ἀβραάμ· υἱοῦ Ἰσραήλ.

18=ΙΗ] incl. 3004

  Ψαλμὸς] om (655 659)

  τῷ] τοῦ (655 659)

  Σαλωμών] σαλομών 260 (149 606 3004) 336 + ΙΗ 3004

  ἔτι] ἐπὶ 260 (149) 769

  ἔτι τοῦ Χριστοῦ Κυρίου] om 3004

 1. ἡ] om 336

  μετὰ] ἐπι 253 (655 659)

  δόματος] δήματος 659

 2. ἐπιβλέποντες] ἐπιβλέπουσιν 769

  οὐχ] οὐκ (655 659)

  οὐχ ὑστερήσει] ܪܚܩܬ ܡܝܢ ܕܠ

  ἐξ] ἐς (655 659)

  αὐτῶν] αὐτὸν (655* 659*)

  τὰ] τῶ 769

  ἐπακούει] ἐπακούσει 260 (149 606 3004) 769 336

  δέησιν] om Syr

 3. μετὰ] μετ᾽ 260 (149 471 606 3004)

  ἡ] om 253

  ἀγάπη] marked on word and in margin with dot triangles, but not a variant
    from any known manuscript.

  σπέρμα] σπέρματα (655 659)

  Ἀβραάμ, υἱοῦ Ἰσραήλ] ܡܗܪܒܐܕ ܡܝܒ ܠܐܝܣܪܐܝܠܕ

  υἱοῦ] {υἱοὺς=Ra=vg=Fab}

18 A Psalm of Solomon. About the Lord's Messiah [1]

1. O Lord, your mercy is upon the works of your hands forever,
    your kindness to Israel with a lavish gift.
2. Your eyes are watching over them
    and none of them will be lacking[311]
    Your ears listen to the hopeful prayer of the poor.
3. Your compassionate judgements are over the whole world,
    and your love is for the descendants of Abraham, an Israelite.[3]

---

[310] Some MSS read: "still."

[311] Syr: "there is nothing hidden from them."

[312] Gk: "...of Abraham, of a son of Israel." This awkward (and anachronistic) syntax has prompted several conjectures, including: (1) emend to "Israelites;" (2) emend to "the Israelite;" (3) transpose 'Abraham' and 'Israel' with the Syriac to read: "...the descendants of Israel, the son of Abraham;" 4) emend to "sons," i.e: "...the descendants of Abraham, the sons of Israel."

4. ἡ παιδεία σου ἐφ᾽ ἡμᾶς ὡς υἱὸν πρωτότοκον μονογενῆ
   ἀποστρέψαι ψυχὴν εὐήκοον ἀπὸ ἀμαθίας ἐν ἀγνοίᾳ
5. Καθαρίσαι ὁ θεὸς Ἰσραὴλ εἰς ἡμέραν ἐλέους ἐν εὐλογίᾳ·
   εἰς ἡμέραν ἐκλογῆς ἐν ἀνάξει χριστοῦ αὐτοῦ.
6. Μακάριοι οἱ γενόμενοι ἐν ταῖς ἡμέραις ἐκείναις·
   ἰδεῖν τὰ ἀγαθὰ κυρίου ἃ ποιήσει γενεᾷ τῇ ἐρχομένῃ
7. ὑπὸ ῥάβδον παιδείας χριστοῦ κυρίου
      ἐν φόβῳ θεοῦ αὐτοῦ·
      ἐν σοφίᾳ πνεύματος
      καὶ δικαιοσύνης καὶ ἰσχύος·

---

4. παιδεία] παιδία 253 (655 659)

   πρωτότοκον] πρωτότοκου 769

   μονογενῆ] μονογενοῦς 769

   εὐήκοον] ὑπήκοον 260 (149 471 606 3004)

   ἀμαθίας] ἀμαθείας 336 [ἀνάχει c=Cerda 3004]
   ἀγνοίᾳ] MS 336 ends PssSol here, followed by Sirach 33.1-13
      See Wright & Hann, "A New Fragment."

5. καθαρίσαι] vss. 5 to end *om* 336 καθαρίσῃ 253 (655m 659)

   ὁ θεὸς] *om* Syr

   ἐλέους] ἐλέος 655 659 ἐλέου 260 (149 471 606 3004) 769 ἐλέου ἐν
   εὐλογίᾳ 149

   ἀνάξει] underlined with marg c=Cerda: αἰνέσει 3004 with note: "Cerda
      interpre haher, Regno:"

6. γενόμενοι] γινόμενοι 260 (149 471 606 3004) 769

      ταῖς] *om* 253 (655 659)

7. ὑπὸ] ἀπὸ 3004* c above

   παιδείας] ἀπαιδίας (655 659)

4. Your discipline for us is as for a firstborn son, an only child,[313]
    to dissuade the perceptive person[314] from unintentional sins.[315]
5. May God cleanse Israel for the blessed day of mercy,
    the appointed day for the appearance of his Messiah.
6. Happy are those living in those days,
    to see the good things of the Lord,
    that he will do for the coming generation;

7. That will be under the rod of discipline of the Lord's Messiah,
    in the fear of his God, in the wisdom of the spirit,
    and in righteousness and strength.

---

[313] See 4 Ezra 6.58.

[314] Gk: "one who hears (and listens and obeys)."

[315] Gk: "from ignorance in incomprehension."

8. κατευθῦναι ἄνδρα ἐν ἔργοις δικαιοσύνης φόβῳ θεοῦ.
   καταστῆσαι πάντας αὐτοὺς ἐνώπιον κυρίου.
9. γενεὰ ἀγαθὴ ἐν φόβῳ θεοῦ ἐν ἡμέραις ἐλέους.

διάψαλμα.

10. Μέγας ἡμῶν ὁ θεὸς καὶ ἔνδοξος· ἐν ὑψίστοις κατοικῶν·
    ὁ διατάξας ἐν πορείᾳ φωστῆρας
       εἰς καιροὺς ὡρῶν ἀφ᾽ ἡμερῶν εἰς ἡμέρας·
    καὶ οὐ παρέβησαν ἀπὸ ὁδοῦ ἧς ἐνετείλω αὐτοῖς.
11. ἐν φόβῳ θεοῦ ἡ ὁδὸς αὐτῶν καθ᾽ ἑκάστην ἡμέραν·
    ἀφ᾽ἧς ἡμέρας ἔκτισεν αὐτοὺς ὁ θεὸς καὶ ἕως αἰῶνος.
12. καὶ οὐκ ἐπλανήθησαν ἀφ᾽ ἧς ἡμέρας ἔκτισεν αὐτούς·
    ἀπὸ γενεῶν ἀρχαίων
    οὐκ ἀπέστησαν ὁδῶν αὐτῶν·
       εἰ μὴ ὁ θεὸς ἐνετείλατο αὐτοῖς
    ἐν ἐπιταγῇ δούλων αὐτοῦ.   τέλος σὺν θεῷ

---

8. ἄνδρα] ἄνδρας 253 (655 659)
   ἐνώπιον] ἐν φόβῳ 260 (149 471 606 3004)

9. ἐλέους] ἐλέου 260 (149 471 606 3004) 769

   διάψαλμα] om 471 διάψαλμ 253 (655m 659) 260 (149) διάψ 769. 3004
      in left margin. NB: in red ink in MS 149 & 606.
   +ψαλμὸς τῷ σαλομών ΙΘ 3004 (marks this MS's division to form
      psalm 19).

10. ἡμῶν ὁ θεὸς] ~ ὁ θεὸς ἡμῶν 260 (149 471 606 3004) 769
    πορείᾳ] πορία 253 (655 659) κυρεία 3004 marg c=Cerda.
    φωστῆρας] ἡμέρας 3004

11. ὁδὸς] ὁδὼς 655*
    αὐτῶν] αὐτὸ 655c
    ἀφ᾽ ἧς] ἀφιῆς 655*

12. ὁδῶν] ἀπὸ ὁδοῦ 260 (149 471 606 3004) 769
    αὐτῶν] om 3004 * in marg.
    αὐτοῦ]+ψαλμοὶ σολόμωντος ΙΗ 3004 769
    + Ψαλμοὶ σολομῶντος ΙΗ ἔχουσιν ἔπη Α 149 260
    +ψαλμοὶ σολομῶντος δεκαοκτω ἔχουσιν ἔπη τριάκοντα 606 in red.
    +ψαλμοὶ στίχ ψν 655 659
    +ψαλμοὶ σαλομῶντος ιή
    +ἔχουσιν ὁ ἔπη ἀ 3004
    +σολομῶντος ψαλμοὶ στίχ ψν 253

8.   to direct people to righteous actions, in the fear of God,
        to confirm them all in the presence of the Lord.[1]
9.   This will be a good generation living in the fear of God,
        in the days of mercy.   *Pause*

10.   Our God is great and glorious living in the highest heavens,
        who arranged the sun and moon into orbits
            to mark the times of the hours from day to day.[2]
        And they have not deviated from their course,
            that he appointed for them.
11.   Their course each day is in the fear of God,
        from the day God created them and until forever.

12.   And they have not wandered from the day he created them,
        from ancient generations.
        They have not veered off their course
        except when God directed them by the command of his servants.[3]

(The end, thank God!)

---

[316] Other MSS read: "in the fear of the Lord."

[317] Gk: "for times of the hours from days to days."

[318] See Josh 10.12,13; Isa 38.8. This harmonistic but intrusive ending may well
have been added by a subsequent scribe.

ANNOTATED LIST OF EDITIONS AND TRANSLATIONS OF THE TEXT OF THE PSALMS
OF SOLOMON

(Full citations may be found in "Bibliography of the Greek Text of the Psalms of Solomon," p. 215)

Editions of the Greek Text

de la Cerda, Johannes Ludovici. *Adversaria Sacra* 1626, reprinted MS 149 (incorrectly claimed to be the "Augsburg MS;" accompanied by a Latin translation; numerous errors).

Nieremberg, Johannes Eusebius (Juan Eusebio). *De origine Sacrae Scripturae* 1641 (Pss Sol 1, 18, and part of 17 with a Latin translation and brief preface).

Janeski, G. *Dissertatio historico-critica de Psalterto Salomonis,* 1687 (text of PssSol 1 and 11 with the Latin translation of de la Cerda).

Neumann, S. G. 1687 (Edited a text in Wittenberg mentioned by Migne and Fabricius).

Fabricius, Johannes Albertus. *"Psalterium SALOMONIS cum Io. Ludovici de la Cerda"* 1713 [2d ed. 1722] (Reproduced de la Cerda's Greek text and Latin translation; corrected some of de la Cerda's misprints; only some errors in the first edition were corrected in the second, that itself included new mistakes).

Hilgenfeld, Adolph. "Die Psalmen Salomo's und die Himmelfahrt des Moses, griechisch hergestellt und erklärt" 1868 (based on de la Cerda's text).

—. *Messias Iudaeorum,* 1869 (based on de la Cerda's text supplemented by readings from Haupt's collation of MS 149 (sic); additional readings from Fabricius and some conjectures of Paul de Lagarde; he argued that Greek, not Hebrew, was the original language of the PssSol).

Fritzsche, Otto. *Libri Apocryphi Veteris Testamenti–Graece* 1871 (included readings from de la Cerda, Fabricius, Hilgenfeld, and Haupt; attempted to improve upon the Greek text by frequent conjectural emendations).

Geiger, Eduard. *Der Psalter Salomo's, herausgegeben und erklärt.* 1871 (based on de la Cerda's text and Haupt's collation; attempted to explain difficulties in the Greek manuscripts by allusion to an assumed Hebrew original).

Hilgenfeld, Adolph. *Die Psalmen Salomo's* 1871 (edition with translation and critical notes issued as a refutation of E. Geiger's proposed Hebrew original).

Ryle, Herbert Edward and Montague Rhodes James. *YALMOI SOLMONTOS: The Psalms of the Pharisees* 1891 (Sources: MSS 149 260, 471, and 606. This was the first edition to use more than one manuscript. They believed in the existence of the "Augsburg" manuscript and repeatedly make comparisons between readings of MS 149 and MS "A" [actually de la Cerda's text]. Some conjectures were based upon a presumptive Hebrew archetype. Their copy of MS 471 was in places defective.).

Swete, H. B. *"The Psalms of Solomon."* 1894 (Sources: MSS 149, 260, 471, 606, and 253. First to use MS 253. Added three conjectural emendations.).

Gebhardt, Oscar von.*YALMOI SOLOMONTOS: Die Psalmen Salmo's.* 1895 (sources: MSS 149, 253, 260, 336, 471, 606, 629, and 769; recognized the virtual identity of MSS 149 and 260; concluded that MS 253 has preserved the greatest proportion of early readings). This text is the source of many later editions, including Rahlfs'.

Swete, H. B. *The Psalms of Solomon.* 1899 (added the new MSS included by von Gebhardt: MSS 336, 629, and 769; somewhat dependent upon von Gebhardt).

Ecker, Jacob. *Porta Sion. Lexikon zum lateinischen Psalter (Psalterium Gallicanum) unter genauer Vergleichung der Septuaginta und des hebräischen Textes mit einer Einleigung über die hebr.=griech.=latein-- Psalmen und dem Anhang der apokryphe Psalter Salomons* 1903 (used MSS 149, 253, 260, 336, 471, 606, 629, and 769; somewhat dependent upon von Gebhardt).

Lindblom, (Christian) Johannes B. *Senjudiskt Fromhetslif Enligt Salomos Psaltare.* 1909 (Used von Gebhardt's text).

Viteau, J. *Les Psaumes de Salomon.* 1911 (includes significant variants from a Syriac edition by Francois Martin).

Rahlfs, Alfred. *Septuaginta Id est Vetus Testinentum.* 1935 (source text was von Gebhardt).

Kuhn, Karl Georg. *Die älteste Textgestalt der Psalmen Salomos.* 1937 (Greek and Syriac texts of PssSol 13–17).

Baars, W. *A New Fragment of the Greek Version of the Psalms of Solomon.* 1961 (collation of a newly discovered MS 3004 containing PssSol 17:2-18:12).

Wright, Robert B. *The Psalms of Solomon. A Provisional Collation of the Greek Text.* 1974 (privately circulated and included with Joseph Trafton, *The Syriac Version of the Psalms of Solomon: A Critical*

Evaluation (SBLSCS 11; Atlanta, GA: Scholars Press/Society of Biblical Literature, 1985).

Agouridou, Sabba (Agouridou, Sabba). "Yalmoi Swntolomo" (Sisagwgika—Keimeno kai Scolia)." *Theologia* 49 (1978) 703–751 (reproduces von Gebhardt's text with only minor alterations).

Atkinson, Kenneth. *An Intertextual Study of the Psalms of Solomon Pseudepigrapha.* (Lewiston, NY: The Edwin Mellen Press 2001). (Greek text largely based on MS 253 that is similar to von Gebhart, but which includes some conjectural emendations.)

Wright, Robert B. *The Psalms of Solomon: A Critical Greek Edition of the Greek Text.* 2007 (this edition).

[NB: For a complete list of partial texts and translations through the nineteenth century, see J. Viteau, *Les Psaumes de Salomon,* 245–251.]

Editions of the Syriac Text:

Harris, J(ames) Rendel. *The Odes and Psalms of Solomon.* 1909 (2d ed. 1911) (based upon a single Syriac MS).

Harris, J(ames) Rendel and Alphonse Mingana. *The Odes and Psalms of Solomon.* 1916 (2d ed. 1920) (based on three Syriac MSS).

Kuhn, Karl Georg. *Die älteste Textgestalt der Psalmen Salomos.* 1937 (Greek and Syriac text of PssSol 13–17).

Baars, W. "Psalms of Solomon." 1972 (based on the four known Syriac MSS).

TRANSLATIONS:
Dutch:
Goeij, M. de. "Psalmen van Salomo." 1980 (text of PssSol translated from Gray's English translation).

English:
Whiston, William. *A Collection of Authentick Records.* 1727. The first English translation of the PssSol.

Pick, Bernhard. *The Psalter of Solomon.* 1883 (The first widely available English translation. The text is dependent upon Hilgenfeld, E. Geiger, and Wellhausen; the translation suffers from an imprecise knowledge of English and from numerous transcriptional errors).

Ryle, Herbert Edward and Montague Rhodes James. *YALMOI SOLMONTOS: The Psalms of the Pharisees.* 1891.

Harris, J(ames) Rendel. *The Odes and Psalms of Solomon.* 1909 [2d. ed. 1911].

Gray, George Buchanan. "The Psalms of Solomon." 1912 (the standard English edition for seventy-five years).

Harris, J(ames) Rendel and Alphonse Mingana. *The Odes and Psalms of Solomon.* 1916 [2d ed. 1920].

Klausner, Joseph. *The Messianic Idea in Israel.* 1955 (selections from PssSol 8, 17, 18).

Glatzer, N. N. "Thou Art Our King: From the Psalms of Solomon." 1963 (translation of PsSol 17 from an unknown source).

Bonsirven, Joseph. *Palestinian Judaism in the Time of Jesus Christ.* 1964 (English translations of several selections from PssSol 11 and 17 from the French edition; there are two different translations of PssSol 17.32–47).

Moeller, Henry R. *The Legacy of Zion.* 1977 (selections from PssSol, various psalms).

Davenport, Gene L. *Ideal Figures in Ancient Judaism.* 1980. (Discussion and translation of PssSol 17: 21–46).

Brock, Sebastian P. *The Psalms of Solomon,* in *The Apocryphal Old Testament.* ed. H. F. D. Sparks, 649–682 (Oxford: Clarendon, 1984).

Wright, Robert B. "The Psalms of Solomon." 1985 (translation and notes with accompanying introduction), *OTP.*

De Jonge, Marinus. *The Psalms of Solomon.* 1985 (introduction and translation of PssSol 1, 3, 8, 17, 18).

Atkinson, Kenneth. An Intertextual Study of the Psalms of Solomon Pseudepigrapha. (Lewiston. NY: The Edwin Mellen Press. 2001). (Emphasizes the intertextual allusions in the PssSol.)

—. *I Cried to the Lord: A Study of the Psalms of Solomon's Historical Background and Social Setting.* (Leiden: Brill. 2003). (A more literal English translation than the author's previous book. Contains numerous detailed textual discussions based on Wright's critical apparatus as well as on the Syriac manuscripts.)

—. "The Psalms of Solomon: An English Translation of the Greek Text." In The New English Translation of the Septuagint. A. Pietersma and B.G. Wright, eds. (Oxford, England: Oxford University Press, forthcoming). Available at: http://ccat.sas.upenn.edu/nets/edition/.

Wright, Robert B., *The Psalms of Solomon: A Critical Edition of the Greek Text,* Continuum Press, 2007.

(This edition).

French:

Bonsirven, Joseph. "Les Psaumes de Salomon" in: *La Bible Apocryphe en marge de l'Ancien Testament.* 1953, 157-170 [= "Die Psalmen Salomos," in: *Die Apokryphe Bibel am Rande des Alten Testaments.*1959. 153-166]

Migne, M. "Psautier de Salomon, 1856 (described by Viteau as "médiocre").

Nöldeke, Theodor. Alttestamentliche Literatur, 1869 (translation by H. Derenbourg and J. Soury).

Jacquier, E. *Le Psaumes de Salomon,* 1893.

Peyrollaz, A. Le Psautier de Salomon, 1899 (translated from von Gebhardt's text).

Viteau, J. *Les Psaumes de Salomon,* 1911.

La Grange, M.-J. "La Renaissance du Messianisme Personnel Davidique," 1931 (translation of PssSol 17).

Prigent, Pierre. *Psaumes de Salomon* in André Dupont-Sommer and Marc Philonenco, La Bible: Écrits Intertestamentares.

German:

Neumann, S. G. 1687 (possible allusion to a translation by Neumann in Migne's *Dictionaire des Apocryphes ou Collection de tous les Livres Apocryphes relatifs à l'Ancient et au Nouveau Testament* (Paris: Barrière d'Enfer. 1856) I col. 940. (A apparently based on de la Cerda's text).

Anonym us. 1716 (reported by Viteau to have been described by Fabricius as a translation appearing in Leipzig. Also noticed by E. Geiger; apparently based on de la Cerda's text).

Berlenburgische Bibel. *Die Heilige Schrift Altes und Neues Testaments: {nach dem Grund-Text aufs neue übersehen und übersetzet}; nebst einiger Erklärung des buchstäblichen Sinnes, wie auch der fürnehmsten Fürbildern und Weissagungen von Christo und seinem Reich und zugleich {einigen Lehren, die auf den Zustand der Kir}* Berlenburg : [J. F. Haug], 1742. .(Attributed by some to Fabricius; apparently based on de la Cerda's text).

Anonym us. *Auswahl der besten apocryphischen Schriften, welche noch ausser der biblischen vorhanden sind.* 1776. First Collection. Corburg: Sammlung. (Reprint of the *Berlenburgische Bibel,* with corrections).

Akibon, Richard (pen-name of Ludwig Noack). *Achtzehn Psalmen Salomo's...in's Deutsche übertragen.* 1850 (apparently based on de la Cerda's text).

Aechte apokryphische Bücher der heiligen Schrift, welche noch ausser der Bibel vorhanden sind. Tübingen 1852. Translation with an introduction. Viteau reports that the editor "...croit fermement que les Psaumes de Salomon sont un livre inspirè."(p. 242).

Nöldeke, Theodor, Die alttestamentliche Literatur, Leipzig : Quandt & Handel, 1868.

Hilgenfeld, Adolph. *Die Psalmen Salomo's, deutsch übersetzt und aufs Neue untersucht.* 1871 (translation and critical notes issued as a refutation of E. Geiger's proposed Hebrew original).

Wellhausen, Julius. *Die Pharisäer und die Sadducäer.* 1874 (reprint 1924) (included several conjectural emendations based upon his theory of a Hebrew original).

Winter, J. and August Wünsche. *Geschichte der jüdisch-hellenistischen und talmudischen Literatur.* 1894 (translation of PssSol 1, 9, and 17 based on de la Cerda, Fabricius, and Hilgenfeld).

Zöckler, Otto. "Die pseudepigraphische Lyrik: Der Psalter Salomos." 1891.

Kittel, Rudolf. "Die Psalmen Salomos." 1900 (somewhat dependent upon von Gebhardt).

Perles, Felix. *Zur Erklärung der Psalmen Salomos.* 1902 (brief study that compares some verses in the back-translations of Delitzsch and Frankenberg; somewhat dependent upon Gebhardt).

Ecker, Jacob. *Porta Sion.* 1903 (extensive notes with many comparative translations).

Reißler, Paul. *Psalmen Salomos.* 1928.

Kuhn, Karl Georg. *Die älteste Textgestalt der Psalmen Salomos.* 1937 (argued that Syriac is a direct translation from Hebrew; translation of PssSol 13–17).

Holm-Nielsen, Svend. *Poetische Schriften.* 1977.

ANNOTATED LIST OF EDITIONS AND TRANSLATIONS

Greek:

Agouridou, Sabba (Agouridou, Sabba). "Yalmoi Solomwnto" (Sisagwgika—Keimeno kai Scolia)" (Not strictly a "translation," but an edition of the Greek text with a commentary and notes in modern Greek; based on von Gebhardt. Gray, and Viteau).

Hebrew:

Wellhausen, Julius (apparently written, but not published; ca. 1874).

Frankenberg, W. *Die Datierung der Psalmen Salomos*. 1896.

Kamenetzky, Abraham Shaloam. *Eine hebräische ubersetzung der PsS* . 1904.

Stein, M. "The Psalms of Solomon." 1959 (translation of the Greek text into modern Hebrew).

Delitzsch, Frantz. "Rückübersetzung der Psaumes Salomon ins Hebräische" (unpublished manuscript number 01503 in the Universitätsbibliothek Leipzig. ca. 1860).

Latin:

de la Cerda, Johannes Ludovici. *Adversaria Sacra*. 1623 (occasionally the Latin translation does not match the Greek text).

Nieremberg, Johannes Eusebius. *De origine Sacrae Scripturae*. 1641 (text and translation of PssSol 1, 18, and part of 17).

Janeski, G. "Dissertatio historico-critica de Psalterio Salomonis." 1687 (text of PssSol 1 and 11 with Latin translation of de la Cerda).

Fabricius, Johannes Albertus. *Codex Pseudepigraphus Veteris Testamenti*. 1713, and 2nd ed., 1722 (reproduced de la Cerda's Greek and Latin texts with corrections; second edition, while correcting mistakes in the first edition, allowed additional errors).

Portuguese:

Revista Bíiblica Brasileira 17 (2000) 5-29. (Translation, introduction, and footnotes.A Portuguese translation of "Psalms of Solomon" from Hedley F. Sparks. *The Apocryphal Old Testament* (1984) The translation included the introduction and footnotes.)

Russian:

Smirnoff, A. "Psalmy Solomona ö prilozenijem od Solomona." 1896 (based on von Gebhardt's edition).

Spanish:

Sáent, Antonio Piñero. "Salmos de Salomón" in Alejandro Diez Macho, Maria Angeles Navarro, Alfonso de la Fuente, and Antonio Piñero Sáent. *Apocrtfos del Antiguo Testamento*, 1982.

Swedish:

Lindblom, (Christian) Johannes B. *Senjudiskt Fromhetslif Englit Salomos Psaltare*. 1909 (translation dependent upon von Gebhardt).

BIBLIOGRAPHY OF THE GREEK TEXT OF THE PSALMS OF SOLOMON

Agouridou, Sabba, "YALMOI SOLOMWNTOS (SISAGWGIKPA – KEIMENO KAI SCOLIA)," *Theologia* 49, pp. 703–751 (Athens, Greece: Epistemonikon Periodikon Ekdidomenon kata Trimenon, 1978)

Aechte apokryphische Bücher der heiligen Schrift, welche noch ausser der Bibel vorhanden sind (Tübingen, 1852).

Alpe, P. Andreas de, "La redenzione nei Salmi di Salomone," La Redenzione Conferenze Bibliche tetute nell'Anno Giubilare 1933 al Pont. Instituto Biblico, ed. P. A. Vaccari, IV Settimana Biblica, pp. 301-320 (Rome, 1934).

—, "Christologia in Psalmis Salomonis," *VD* 11, Fasc. 2–4 (1931) pp. 56–59, 84–88, 110–120.

Akibon, Richard (pen–name of Ludwig Noack), *Achtzehn Psalmen Salomon's welch sich in unserer Bibel nicht finden: aus einer gehaimgehaltenen Schrist in's Deutsche übertragen und mit Anmerkungen begleitet* (Kassell: J.C.J. Raabe, 1850).

Auswahl der besten apocryphischen Schriften, welche noch ausser der biblischen vorhanden sind First Collection ed.(Coburg: Sammlung, 1776).

Anastasius Sinaita, "Indiculus liborum ca nonicorum et apocryphorum, quem Anastasii Niceni Quaestionibus subiectum in publica Oxoniensis Academiae bibliotheca invenimus, ubi didacai; tw'n ajpostovlwn et didaskaliva Klhvmento" ut distincta opera recensentur et in scriptorum apocryphorum censu pariter reponuntur" in Jean-Baptiste Cotelier, *S. Patrum, qui temporibus apostolicis florenrunt*, I, p. 196 (Antwerp: Io. Clericus, 1700; and 2nd ed. (Amsterdam: Wetstenios, 1724).

Athanasius, "Synopsis Sanctae Scripturae," in J.-P. Migne, *Patrologiae cursus completus , series graeca*, 28, col 432 (Paris: Migne, 1857–1966).

Atkinson, Kenneth, "Towards a Redating of the Psalms of Solomon: Implications for Understanding the *Sitz im Leben* of an Unknown Jewish Sect," *JSP*, Vol. 17 (1998): 95-112.

—, *An Intertextual Study of the Psalms of Solomon* (Lewiston, NY: The Edwin Mellen Press, 2001).

—, *I Cried to the Lord: A Study of the Psalms of Solomon's Historical Background and Social Setting* (Leiden: Brill, 2003).

Baars, W., "A New Fragment of the Greek Version of the Psalms of Solomon," *VT* 11 (1961) pp. 441–444.

— , "Psalms of Solomon,"*The Old Testament in Syriac According to the Peshitta Version*, edited by the Peshitta Institute, Part IV Fasc. 6 (Leiden: E. J. Brill, 1972).

Balsamon, Th. and Johanes Zonaras, "Canones synodi Laodicenea," in J.-P. Migne, *Patrologiae cursus completus, series graeca* (161 vols) (Paris: Migne, 1857–1966).

Bancalari, Francesco, "Index codicum graecorum bibliothacae Casanatensis,"*Studi Italiani di Filologia Classica*, ed. F. le Monnier, II pp. 161–207 (Florence: Sansoni, 1894).

Beer, G., "Salmono-Psalmen," *PRE* 2, Row 1 (1920) 2001-2003.

Begrich, Joachim, "Der Text der Psalmen Salomos," *ZNW* 38 (1939) pp. 131–164.

Bentzen, Aage, *King and Messiah*, Ed. G. W. Anderson (Oxford: Basil Blackwell, 1970).

Berlenburgische Bibel, *Die Heilige Schrift Altes und Neues Testaments: {nach dem Grund-Text aufs neue übersehen und übersetzet}; nebst einiger Erklärung des buchstäblichen Sinnes, wie auch der fürnehmsten Fürbildern und Weissagungen von Christo und seinem Reich und zugleich {einigen Lehren, die auf den Zustand der Kir}*, Berlenburg, (dt.) Section VIII 271–279 (Berlenburg:: J. F. Haug. 1742 (Attributed by some to Fabricius; apparently based on de la Cerda's text).

Beverage, W., *Synodicum sive Pandectae Canonum* (Oxford: n.p., 1672).

Bibliothecae Apostolicae Vaticanae Codces manuscripti Recensiti, Codices Vaticani Graeci Tomus II Codices 330-603, Recdnsivit Robertus Devreesse (Rome: Bibliotheca Vaticana, 1937).

Brelje, Larry, Albert Buelow, George Nickelsburg, "A Word Index of the Greek Text of the Psalms of Solomon," unpublished student report (St. Louis, MO: Concordia Seminary, May 1961).

Brock, Sebastian P., "The Psalms of Solomon," *The Apocryphal Old Testament*, Ed. H. F. D. Sparks pp. 649–682 (Oxford: Clarendon, 1984).

—, Professor of Syriac Studies, Oxford University, Personal correspondence, January 8, 2002.

Bruun, Christian Walther, *Aarsberetningen og meddelelser fra det Store Kongelige Bibliothek Udgivne*, Annual of Communication of the Great Royal Library of Copenhagen, 2nd ed.(Copenhagen: Gyldendalske, 1877).

Burke, David G., *The Poetry of Baruch, A Reconstruction and Analysis of the Original Hebrew Text of Baruch 3:9–5:9*, *SBLSCS* 10 (Chico, California: Scholars Press/Society of Biblical Literature, 1982).

Caquot, André, "Les Hasmonéens, les Romains et Hérode: observations sur *Ps Sal* 17," *Hellenica et Judaica*, Ed. A. Caquot, M. Hadas-Lebel, and J. Riaud, Leuven (Paris: Éditions Peeters,, 1986).

Cerda, Johannes Ludovici de la, *Adversaria Sacra. Opus varium ac veluti fax ad lucem quam multorum locorum utriusque Testamenti Patrumque et Scriptorum quorum cumque: Christianæ antiquitatis et sacorum rutuum pancarpia; polotoris denique litteraturæ thesaurus multiplex. Accessit eodem auctore Psalterii Salomonis ex graeco MS codice pervetusto latina versio et ad Tertulliani librum de Pallio Commentarius auctior. Produnt omnia nunc primum. Cum privelegio* (Lyon: Ludovici Prost Haeredis Roville, 1626).

Collins, John J., "The kingdom of God in the Apocrypha and Pseudepigrapha: Dan, Sib Or, Enoch, Testament of Moses, Pss Sol, T 12 Patr, Targum Jonathan", *Kingdom of God in 20th-century interpretation*, pp. 81-95 (Peabody, Mass: Hendrickson, 1987).

— , *The Scepter and the Star: The Mesiahs of the Dead Sea Scrolls and Other Ancient Literature*, The Anchor Bible Reference Library (New York: Doubleday, 1995).

Cotelier, Jean–Baptiste, S. Patrum, qui temporibus apostolicis floruerunt (Antwerp: Io. Clericus 1700; and 2nd ed. Amsterdam: Wetstenios, 1724)

Delcor, Mathias, "Psaumes de Salomon," *Dictionnaire de la Bible, Sup*, fasc. 48, cols. 239–242 (Paris: Letouzey et Ané, 1973).

Denis, Albert-Marie, "Les Psaumes de Salomon" in A.M Denis and M. de Jonge eds. *Introduction aux Pseudépigraphes grecs d'Ancien Testament, SVTP*, I pp. 60–69 (Leiden: Brill, 1970).

Ecker, Jakob, *Porta Sion: Lexikon zum lateinischen Psalter (Psalterium Gallicanum): unter genauer Vergleichung der Septuaginta und des hebräischen Textes: mit einer Einleitung über die hebr.-griech.-latein. Psalmen und dem Anhang der apokryphe Psalter Salomons* (Trier/Treves: Paulinus-Druckerie, 1903).

Eissfeldt, Otto, *Einleitung in das Alte Testament, unter Einschluss der Apokryphen und Pseudepigraphen sowie der apokryphen–und pseudepigraphenartigen Qumran–Schriften; Entstehungsgeschichte des Alten Testaments* (Tübingen: Mohr, 1956), *The Old Testament: An Introduction*, Tr. by P.R. Ackryod (New York: Harper and Row, 1965).

Epp, Eldon Jay, "The Claremont Profile Method for Grouping New Testament Minuscule Manuscripts," in Boyd L. Daniels and M. Jack Suggs, *Studies in the History and Text of the New Testament, SD 29* ed. Jacob Geerlings pp. 27–38 (Salt Lake City: University of Utah Press, 1967).

— , "The Claremont Profile Method for Grouping New Testament Minuscule Manuscripts," in Eldon Jay Epp and Gordon D. Fee, *Studies in the Theory and Method of New Testament Textual Criticism, SD 45* ed. Irving Alan Sparks pp. 211–220 (Grand Rapids: Eerdmans, 1993).

Ewald, Heinrich H., *Die jüngsten Propheten des alten Bundes*, I-IV (Göttingen: Vandenhoeck & Ruprecht, 1868).

Fabricius, Johannes Albertus, "Psalterium SALOMONIS cum Io. Ludovici de la Cerda notis & brevibus castigationibus editoris," *Codex Pseudepigraphus Veteris Testamenti, Collectus Castigatus, Testimoniisque, Censuris & Animadversionibus illustratus* (Hamburg and Leipzig: Christiani Liebezeit, First ed, 1713, second ed, 1722).

Flusser, David, "Psalms, Hymns, and Prayers," *Jewish Writings of the Second Temple Period: Apocrypha, Pseudepigrapha, Qumran Sectarian Writings, Philo, Josephus*, pp. 551–577, *CRINT II* (1984).

Фонкич, Б. Л., Ф. Б. Поляков (Fonkich, B. L., F. B. Polyakof), *Греческие Рукописи Синодальной Библиотеки (Grecheskye Rukopisi Sinodal'noy Biblyoteki)* (Moscow: Sinodal'naya Biblyoteka, 1993).

Frankenberg, Wilhelm, *Die Datierung der Psalmen Salomos, ein Beitrag zur jüdischen Geschichte, BZAW no. I* (Giessen: J. Ricke, 1896).

Fritzsche, Otto Fridolinus, *Libri Apocryphi Veteris Testamenti-Graece, recensuit et cum commentario critico, accedunt libri veteris testamenti pseudepigraphi selecti* (Leipzig: Brockhaus, 1871).

Gebhardt, Oscar Leopold von, *YALMOI SOLOMWNTOS: Die Psalmen Salomo's zum ersten Male mit Benutzung der Athoshandschriften und des Codex Casanatensis*, Texte und Untersuchungen zur Geschichte der altchristlichen Literatur, vol. XIII, pt. 2 (Leipzig: J. C. Hinrichs, 1895).

Geiger, P. Edward Ephraem, *Der Psalter Salomo's, herausgegeben und erklärt* (Augsburg: J. Wolff, 1871).

Girbal, Jules, *Essai sur les Psaumes de Salomon* (Toulouse: A. Chauvin et Fils, 1887).

Goeij, M. de, "Psalmen van Salomo," *De Pseudepigrafen* (Kampen: J. H. Kok, 1980).

Graux, Charles Henri, "Nouvelles Recherches sur la Stichométrie," *Revue de Philologie, de Littérature et d'Histoire anciennes* new series II pp. 97–143 (Paris: F. Klincksieck, 1878)

— , Review *Aarsberetningen og Meddelelser fra det Store Kongelige Bibliothek Udgivne*, by Christian Walthe Bruunr (Annual of Communication of the Great Royal Library of Copenhagen) 2nd ed. Copenhagen: Gyldendalske 1877; pt. III, *Revue Critique* 2 (1877) pp. 291–293.

Gray, George Buchanan, "The Psalms of Solomon," *APOT*, ed. R. A. Charles II pp. 625–652 (Oxford: Clarendon, 1912).

Hadjidakis, E. Personal correspondence as Director of the Benaki Museum (Athens: June 28, 1973).

Hann, Robert R., *The Manuscript History of the Psalms of Solomon*, SBLSCS, no. 13 (Chico, CA: Scholars

Press, 1982).

—, "Christos Kyrios in PsSOL 17.32: 'The Lord's Anointed' Reconsidered," *NTS* (1985) 31, pp. 620-627.

Harris, J(ames) Rendel, "Notes on the Sinaitic and Vatican Codices," *Johns Hopkins University Circular* no. 29 March 1884.

— , *The Odes and Psalms of Solomon: Now First Published from the Syriac Version* (Cambridge (England) Cambridge University Press, 1909).

— , *The Odes and Psalms of Solomon: Published from the Syriac Version* (Cambridge (England) Cambridge University Press 2nd ed., 1911).

— , and Alphonse Mingana, *The Odes and Psalms of Solomon, re-edited for the Governors of the John Rylands Library Vol. I The Text with Facsimile Reproductions* (Manchester: University Press; London; New York: Longmans, Green & Co., 1916), Vol. II *Translation with Introduction and Notes* (Manchester: Manchester University Press; London/New York: Longmans, Green & Co., 1920).

— , *The Odes and Psalms of Solomon Vol. II The Translation with Introduction and Notes* (Manchester: University Press; London/New York: Longmans, Green & Co., 1920).

Hartom, A. S., *Ketuvim aharonim /meturgamim u-meforashim al yede,* Sefarim ha-hitsoniyim (Tel Aviv: Yavneh, 1962).

— , *Mizmori shelmah,* Sefarim ha-hitsoniyim (Tel Aviv: Yavneh, 1962).

Hausrath, Adolf, *Neutestamentliche Geschichte* (Heidelberg: Bassermann, 1873).

— , *A History of the New Testament Times: the time of the apostles,* Tr. L. Huxley, 4 vols. (London: Williams and Norgate, 1895).

Hilgenfeld, Adolf Bernhard Christoph Christian, "Prologomena; Psalmi Salomonis " in *Messias Judaeorum, libris eorum paulo ante et paulo post Christum natum conscriptis illustratus* (Leipzig: Reisland 1869).

— , "Die Psalmen Salomo's, deutsch übersetzt und aufs Neue untersucht," *ZWT* 14 (1871) pp. 383–418.

— "Die Psalmen Salomo's und die Himmelfahrt des Moses, griechisch hergestellt und erklärt," *ZWT* 11 (1868) pp. 133–168.

Holm-Nielsen, Svend, "Erwägungen zu dem Verhältnis zwischen den Hodajot und den Psalmen Salomos " *Bibel und Qumran Wissenschaft,* pp. 112–131, ed. S. Wagner (Berlin: Evangelische Haupt–Bibelgesellschaft, 1968).

—, "Die Psalmen Salomos," *Poetische Schriften, Jüdische Schriften aus hellenistisch–römischer Zeit,* vol. IV part 2 pp. 51–112, ed. W. G. Kümmel, et al, tr. Folkert Krieger from Danish (Gütersloh: Mohn, 1977).

— , "Erwägungen zu dem Verhältnis zwischen den Hodajot und den Psalmen Salomos," *Bibel und Qumran,* ed. S. Wagner (Berlin: Evangelische Haupt-Bibel gesellschaft, 1968).

— , "Salmos Salmer " in: *De Gammeltestamentlige Pseudepigrafer,* ed. E. Hammershaimb, et al, Vol. 5(Copenhagen: 1970) 548-595.

Jacquier, E., "Les Psaumes de Salomon," *L' Université catholique* XII pp. 94–131, 251–275 (Lyon: n. p., 1893).

Janenski, G., "Dissertatio historico-critica de Psalterio Salomonis, præside Neumann publicæ disquistionis," *Primitae Dissertationum Academicarum* VIII pp. 274ff, ed, J. G. Neumannus (Wittenberg: Neumann, 1687).

Jansen, H(erman) Ludin, Die spätjüdische Psalmendichtung: ihr Entstehungskreis und ihr 'Sitz im Leben': eine literaturgeschichtlich-soziologische Untersuchung (Oslo: Norske Videnskap-Akademie, 1937).

Jaubert, Annie, "La notion d'alliance dans le judaisme aux abords de l'ère chrétienne," *Patristica Sorboniensia* 6 (Paris: Editions du Seuil, 1963).

Jonge, Marinus de, De Toekomstverwachting in de Psalmen van Salomo (Leiden: E. J. Brill, 1965).

— , "Psalms of Solomon," *Outside the Old Testament,* Cambridge Commentaries on Writings of the Jewish and Christian World 200 BC to AD 200, pp. 159–177 (Cambridge (England): Cambridge University Press, 1985).

— , "The Expectation of the Future in the Psalms of Solomon," *Neotestamentica* 23.1 (1989) pp. 93–117.

— , "The Expectation of the Future in the Psalms of Solomon," Jewish Eschatology, Early Christology and the Testaments of the Twelve Patriarchs: Collected Essays of Marinus de Jonge (Leiden: E. J. Brill, 1991).

Kamenetzky, Abraham Shaloam, *Eine hebräische Übersetzung der PsS mit Einleitung und Anmerkungen in neuhebräischer Sprache* (Krakaw: n.p., 1904).

Kaufmann, Yehezkel The Messianic Idea: The Real and the Hidden Son-of-David. *Jewish Bible Quarterly* (1994, 22(3)141-150 (The idea of the King Messiah being redeemer first appeared in the **Psalms of Solomon** and became the official view in Judaism.)

Kautzsch, Emil Freiedrich, *Die Apocryphen und Pseudepigraphen des Alten Testaments* (Tübingen: J. C. B. Mohr, 1900)

Keim, (Karl) Theodor, *Geschichte Jesu von Nazara in ihrer Verkettung mit dem Gesamtleben seines Volkes* (Zurich: Orell, Fussli, 1867).

Kittel, Rudolf, "Die Psalmen Salomos," *Die Apokryphen und Pseudepigraphen des Alten Testaments* ed. Emil Kautzsch II pp. 127–148 (Tübingen: J. C. B. Mohr, 1900; reprinted 1962).

Kuhn, Karl Georg, *Die älteste Textgestalt der Psalmen Salomos insbesondere auf Grund der syrischen Übersetzung neu untersucht*, Beiträge zur Wissenschaft vom Alten und Neuen Testament, vol. 21, part 4 (Stuttgart: Kohlhammer, 1937).

La Grange, M.-J., "La Renaissance du Messianisme Personnel Davidique," *Le Judaïsme avant Jésus-Christ* (Paris: Librairie Lecoffre, 1931).

Lactantius, *Divinae institutiones,* ed. Helmut Hross (Munich: Kösel-Verlag, 1963).

Lambeck, Peter, *Petri Labecci Hamburgensis Commentariorum de augustissima Bibliotheca caesarea vindobonensi liber primus–octavus* (Vienna: Thomae Nob. De Trattnern, 1766-1782).

Lindblom, (Christian) Johannes B., *Senjudiskt fromhetslif enligt Salomos psaltare*, Akademisk Afhandling (Uppsala: Almqvist & Wiksells, 1909).

Loretz, Oswald, *Gottes Thron in Tempel und Himmel nach Psalm 11 : von der altorientalischen zur biblischen Tempeltheologie* (Kevelaer, Germany : Butzon & Bercker, 1995).

Lüdtke, W., *Beiträge zu slavischen Apokryphen, ZAW* 31 (1911).

Mackeprang, Mourita, Victor Madsen, and Carl S. Peterson, *Greek and Latin Illminated Manuscripts of the X to the XIII Century in Danish Collections* (Copenhagen: A. Marcus, 1921).

Martin, François, *Psaumes de Salomon : introduction, texte grec et traduction / par J. Viteau: avec les principales variantes de la version syriaque par François Martin,* Documents pour l'étude de la Bible (Paris: Letouzey et Ané, 1911).

McGovern, Joseph, "The Status of MS A of the Psalms of Solomon: A Re-Examination of Von Gebhardt's Thesis," (Philadelphia: Temple University, Department of Religion, unpublished research report, 1989).

Meurs, Johannes van, *Operum*, Vol. XI cols. 249, 250–251, 253, ed. Ioannis Lami (Florence: Regis Magni Etruiea Ductis Typis, 1763).

Meyier, K. A. de, *Codices Manuscripti VI Codices Vossiani Graeci et Miscellanei* (Leiden: Bibliotheek der Rijksuniversiteit, 1955).

Migne, M, "Psautier de Salomon." *Dictionnaire des Apocryphes, ou Collection de tous les Livres Apocryphes relatifs à l'Ancien et au Nouveau Testament*, pp. 939–956, (Paris: Barrière d'Enfer, 1856).

Miller, Julian H., "The Psalms of Solomon," Handwritten, unpublished master's thesis (New York: Hebrew Union College, 1906).

Müller, Ulrich B., "Messias und Menschensohn in jüdischen Apokalypsen und in der Offenbarung des Johannes," SNT 6 (1972).

Neumann, S. G. (An allusion to a translation into German, apparently based on de la Cerda's text, in M. Migne *Dictionaire des Apocryphes* p. 940 (1687).

Nickelsburg, George William Elmer, Jewish Literature between the Bible and the Mishnah: A Historical and Literary Introduction, (Philadelphia: Fortress, 1981).

Nieremberg, Johannes Eusebius, *De origine Sacrae Scripturae*, XII pp. 336–339 (Lyon: Sumptibus Petri Prost, 1641).

Noack, Ludwig (see under Richard Akibon, his pen–name).

Oehler, Gustav Friedrich, "Messias," *RE*, ed. J. J. Herzog, G. F. Plitt, and A. Hauck cols. 641–656 (Leipzig: Hinrichs, 1881).

O'Dell, Jerry, "The Religious Background of the Psalms of Solomon Re-Evaluated in the Light of the Qumran Texts " *Revue de Qumran* 3, 2 May (1961), pp. 241–257.

Pérez, Aranda G., "Apócrifos del Antiguo Testamento," in G. Aranda Pérez, F. García Martínez, M. Pérez Fernández, *Literatura judía. intertestamentaria, Introduccón al estudio de la Biblia 9*, 387-391(Estella, 1996).

Perles, Felix, *Zur Erklärung der Psalmen Salomos*, Sonderabzug aus der orientalistischen Literatur-Zeitung no. 5 (Berlin: Wolf Peiser, 1902).

Pesch, Wilhelm, "Die Abhängigkeit des 11. Salmonischen Psalms vom letzten Kapitel des Buches Baruch," ZAW 67 (1955) pp. 251–263.

Peyrollaz, A., "Le Psautier de Salomon," *RTP* XXXII pp. 493–511 (Lausanne: G. Bridel, 1899).

Pick, Bernhard, "The Psalter of Solomon " *Presbyterian Review*, 1883, pp. 775–813.

Prigent, P., "Psaumes de Salomon," in André Dupont-Sommer and Marc Philonenco, *La Bible: Écrits Intertestamentares,* pp. 945–952 (Paris: Gallimard, 1987).

Rahlfs, Alfred, Verzeichnis der griechischen Handschriften des Alten Testaments (Göttingen: K. Gesellschaft der Wissenschaften, 1914).

— , *Septuaginta Id est Vetus Testmentum graece iuxta LXX interpretes* 2 vols. (Stuttgart: Württembergische Bibelanstalt, 1962).

Reißler, Paul, "Psalmen Salomos," *Altjüdisches Schriftum außerhalb der Bibel* pp. 881–902, 1323–1324 (Augsburg: 1928).

Richard, Marcel, Personal letter as Chief of the Greek Section of the Institut de Recherche et d'Histoire des Textes of the Centre National de Recherche Scientifique, May 17, 1972.

Rosen, Debra and Alison Salvesen, "A Note on the Qumran Temple Scroll 56:15–18 and Psalm of Solomon 17:33 " *JJS* 38 (1987), pp. 99–101.

Ryle, Herbert Edward and Montague Rhodes James, *Yalmoi Solomontos: The Psalms of the Pharisees, Commonly Called the Psalms of Solomon* (Cambridge, England: Cambridge University Press, 1891).

Schartau, Bjarne, *Codices Graeci Haunienses: Ein deskripiver Katalog des griechischen Handscriftenbesandes der Königlichen Bibliothek Kopenhagen* (Copenhagen: Museum Tusculanum, 1994).

Schmidt, Carl, *Pistis Sophia,* tr. Violet MacDermot (Leiden: E. J. Brill, 1978).

Schüpphaus, Joachim, *Die Psalmen Salomos: ein Zeugnis Jerusalemer Theologie und Frömmigkeit in der Mitte des vorchristlichen Jahrhunderts,* ALGHJ 7 (Leiden: E. J. Brill, 1977.

Sáent, Antonio Piñero, "Salmos de Salomón" in Alejandro Diez Macho, Maria Angeles Navarro, Alfonso de la Fuente, and Antonio Piñero Sáent, *Apocrifos del Antiguo Testamento* (Madrid: Ediciones Cristiandad, 1982–1987, III [1982] pp. 11–57).

Smirnoff, A., "Psalmy Solomona ö prizozenijem od Solomona," (The Psalms of Solomon, with an Appendix Containing the Odes of Solomon), *Pravoslavnyj sobesjednik* (Kazan, Tatarstan: "The Ecclesiastical/Church Academy ," 1896).

Sommervogel, Carlos, *Bibliothèque de la Compagnie de Jésus* Nouvelle Edition vols. II, VII, and XII (Brussels: Oscar Scheppens, 1891–1896).

Spink, Deborah J., "A City-Lament Genre in the Psalms of Solomon," (Philadelphia: Temple University Ph.D. dissertation, 2001).

Suski, Andrzej, "Wprowadzenie do psalmów Salomona, " *Studia Theologica Varsaviensia,* vol. 17, No. 1 (1979), pp. 187–244.

Swete, Henry Barclay, "The Psalms of Solomon," *The Old Testament in Greek According to the Septuagint* Greek text: III pp. xvi–xvii 765–787, 874, "Introduction " IV pp. 225, 282–283. First ed (Cambridge, England: Cambridge University Press, 1894).

—, *The Psalms of Solomon with the Greek Fragments of the Book of Enoch* (Cambridge, England: Cambridge University Press, 1899.

Trafton, Joseph L., "The Psalms of Solomon in Recent Research, "*JSP* 12 (April 1994) pp. 3–19.

__, "Solomon, Psalms of," *The Anchor Bible Dictionary,* ed. David Noel Freedman, VI, pp. 115–117 (New York: Doubleday, 1992).

—, "The Psalms of Solomon: New Light from the Syriac Version?" *JBL* 105 (June, 1986), pp. 227–237.

__, *The Syriac Version of the Psalms of Solomon: A Critical Evaluation, ABLSCS* no. 11, (Atlanta, GA: Scholars Press/Society of Biblical Literature, 1985).

Tromp, Johannes, "The Sinners and the Lawless in Psalm of Solomon 17," *NovT* 35 (1993), pp. 344–361.

VanderKam, James C., "Psalms of Solomon" in *An Introduction to Early Judaism,* p. 129ff. (Grand Rapids: William B. Eerdmans, 2001).

Viteau, J, *Les Psaumes de Salomon: Introduction, texte grec et traduction, avec les principales variantes de la version Syriaque par François Martin,* Documents pour l'étude de la Bible (Paris: Letouzey et Ané, 1911).

Ward, Grant, *A Philological Analysis of the Greek and Syriac Texts of the Psalms of Solomon* (Philadelphia: Temple University Department of Religion doctoral dissertation, 1995).

Werline, Rodney A., "The Psalms of Solomon and the Ideology of Rule," Society of Biblical Literature Seminar Papers Series No. 39 774-795 (Atlanta, Ga: Society of Biblical Literature, 2000).

Whiston, William, "The Psaltery (The Psalms and Odes) of Solomon, XVIII in Number," *A Collection of Authentick Records Belonging to the Old and New Testaments* I pp. 117–161 (London: "Printed for the Author, and are to be Sold by the Booksellers of London and Westminster, "1727).

Winckler, Hugo, "Jason und die Zeit der Psalmen Salomos," *Altorientalische Forschungen* Nr. 2, pp. 556–564 (Leipzig: Eduard Pfeiffer, 1901) .

Winninge, Mikael, *Sinners and the Righteous: A Comparative Study of the Psalms of Solomon and Paul's Letters* (Stockholm: Almqvist & Wiksell, 1995).

Winter, J. and August Wünsche, *Geschichte der jüdisch-hellenistischen und talmudischen Literatur*, Die jüdische Literatur seit Abschluß des Kanons I, pp. 687–696 (Trèves: Mayer, 1894.

Wright, Robert B. "Solomon, Psalms of," *Eerdmans Dictionary of the Bible*, ed. by David Noel Freedman (Grand Rapids: William B. Eerdmans, 2000).

—, Review *The Syriac verson of the Pslams of Solomon: A Critical Edition* by Joseph Trafton, in *JBL*, v. 107, p. 131-134, March 1988.

—, "The Psalms of Solomon" *The Old Testament Pseudepigrapha,* ed. James H. Charlesworth, 639–670 (Garden City, NY: Doubleday, 1985).

—, and Robert R. Hann, "A New Fragment of the Greek Text of Sirach" *JBL* 94, 1 (1975), pp. 111–112.

__, "The Spiritualization of Sacrifice in the Prophets and in the Psalter," S.T.M. thesis, Hartford Seminary Foundation, 1964.

__, "Sacrifice in the Intertestamental Literature," Ph.D. dissertation, Hartford Seminary Foundation, 1966.

ADDITIONAL BIBLIOGRAPHY OF THE PSSSOL

Abel, Felix-Marie, "Le Siege de Jerusalem par Pompee" *RB* 54 (1947), pp. 243-255.

Aberbach, Moses, "The Historical Allusions of Chapters IV, XI, and XIII of the Psalms of Solomon" *JQR* 41 (April 1951), pp. 379-396.

Ackroyd, P. R., *The Problem of the Maccabean Psalms, with Special Reference to the Psalms of Solomon*, Dissertation, Cambridge (England) University, 1947.

Adler, Ada, Catalogue supplémentaire des manuscrits grecs de la Bibliothèque Royale de Copenhagen: N. P. 1916.

—, Den græske Litteraturs Skæbne i Oldtid og Middelalder, Klikforvideresgning.(Copenhagen: V. Pio, 1920).

Atkinson, Kenneth, "Herod the Great, Sosius, and the Siege of Jerusalem (37 B.C.E.) in Psalm of Solomon 17" *NovT* 38 (1996): pp. 313-322.

—, "Toward a Redating of the Psalms of Solomon: Implications for Understanding the *Sitz im Leben* of an Unknown Jewish Sect," *JSOP* 17 (1998), 95-112.

—, "On the Herodian Origin of Militant Davidic Messianism at Qumran: New Light from Psalm of Solomon 17," *JBL* 118 (1999), 435-460.

—, "On the use of Scripture in the Development of Militant Davidic Messianism at Qumran: New Light from *Psalm of Solomon* 17" in Craig A. Evans ed., The Interpretation of Scripture in Early Judaism and Christianity (*Studies in Scripture in Early Judaism and Christianity* VII, 106-123 (Sheffield, England: Sheffield Academic Press Ltd. 2000).

—, *An Intertextual Study of the Psalms of Solomon Pseudepigrapha* (Lewiston, NY: The Edwin Mellen Press, 2001).

—, "Theodicy in the Psalms of Solomon" in *Handbook of Theodicy in the World of the Bible*, A. Laato and J.C. de Moor eds. (Leiden: E. J. Brill, 2003).

—, 4QMMT and Psalms of Solomon 8: Two Anti-Sadducean Documents?" *The Qumran Chronicle 11* (2003).

Backer, Augustin de, Bibliotheque de la Compagnie de Jesus (Brussels: Schepens; Paris: Picard, 1890-1919).

Bengel, Ernest Gottlieb von, *D. Ernesti Theoph. De Bengeli, Opuscula Academica*, ed. Jo. Godofr. Presse (Hamburg: Apud Fridericum Perthes, 1834).

—, *Opuscula Academica* (Hamburg: Fridericum perthes, 1834).

Bentzen, Aage, *Introduction to the Old Testament 2ⁿᵈ ed.2* vols. Tr of: *Inledning til det Gamle Testament* (Copenhagen: G. E. C. Gad, 1952).

—, *King and Messiah,* tr by author from: *Messias–Moses Redividus– Menschensohn* (Oxford: Basil Blackwell, 1970).

Blackburn, Rollin J., *Hebrew Poetic Devices in the Greek Text of the Psalms of Solomon,* Philadelphia: Temple University, Department of Religion, Ph.D. dissertation, 1998.

Bonsirven, J. Joseph, *Palestinian Judaism in the Time of Jesus Christ*, tr. William Wolf (New York: Holt, Rinehart and Winston, 1964).

—, "Les Psaumes de Salomon" in: *La Bible Apocryphe en marge de l'Ancien Testament* 1953 157-170 [= "Die Psalmen Salomos " in: Die Apokryphe Bibel am Rande des Alten Testaments (Zürich: Daniel-Rops 1959, 153-166)].

Boor, Karl (Carolus) de, *Nicephori Archiepiscopi Constantinopolitani Opuscula Historica*, in *Bibliotheca Scriptorum Graecorum et Romanorum Teubneriana* (Leipzig: Teubner, 1880).

Braun, Herbert, "Salomo-Psalmen," In Die Religion in Geschichte und Gegenwart, ed. by H.F. Campenhausen et al, Vol 5: 1342-1343 (Tübingen: J. C. B. Mohr, 1961).

Bretschneider, K. G., *Die historisch-dogmatische Auslegung des Neuen Testaments* (Leipzig: J.A. Barth, 1806).

Brierre-Narbonne, J., *Exégèse apocryphique des prophéties messianiques* (Paris: P. Geuthner, 1936).

Buchler, Adolf, *Types of Jewish-Palestinian Piety from 70 BCE to 70 CE: The Ancient Pious Men*, III: "Psalms of Solomon, Criticism, Interpretation...." (London: Oxford, 1922).

Campenhausen, Hans F. et a.l, ed. *Die Religion in Geschichte und Gegenwart*: 1342-1343 (Tübingen: J. C. B. Mohr, 1961).

Carriere, Augustus, *De Psalterio Salomonis disquisitionem historico-criticam / Scripsit ampl. ordini theologorum Argentoratensium proposuit et pro licentia summos in theologia honores rite capessendi die mensis Junii H.L.O.S.* publ. tueri conabitur. Argentorati (Straßburg: Heitz,1870).

Cassius Dio Cocceianus, *Dio's Roman History*, 9 vols. (London : W. Heinemann 1914-1927).

Causse, Antonin, Les *"pauvres" d'Israel (prophetes, psalmistes, messianistes)*, Fasc. 3 of *Etudes d'histoire et de philosophie religieuses, publiees par la Faculte de theologie protestante de l'Universite de Strasbourg*), (Strasbourg: Librairie Istra, 1922).

Ceillier, R., *Histoire Générale des Auteurs Sacrés et Ecclésiasgtiques* (Paris: Luis Vivès, 1858).

Chambers, E.K. . *William Shakespeare: A Study of the Facts and Problems.* Oxford University Press, 1988.

Charles, Robert Henry, *A Critical History of the Doctrine of a Future Life, in Israel, in Judaism, and in Christianity,* 2nd ed. (London: Adam and Charles Black, 1913).

__, *Commentary on the Pseudepigrapha of the Old Testament* (ed. Robert Henry Charles;Bellingham,

WA: Logos Research Systems, Inc., 2004).

Choi, Phuichun Richard, "Abraham our father: Paul's voice in the covenantal debate of the Second Temple period," dissertation: Fuller Theological Seminary, School of Theology, 1997.

Coakley, J. F., "A Catalogue of the Syriac Manuscripts in the John Rylands Library," *Bulletin of the John Rylands Library 75* (1993) 105–207.

Cosaert, Carl P. *The Use of* hagios *for the Sanctuary in the Old Testament Pseudepigrapha, Philo, and Josephus.* (Andrews University Seminary Studies, 2004).

Credner, Karl August, *Zur Geschichte des Kanons* (Halle: Waisenhauses, 1847).

Deane, William John, *Pseudepigrapha; an account of certain apocryphal sacred writings of the Jews and early Christians,* (Edinburgh: T. & T. Clark, 1891).

Delitzsch, Franz Julius, *Biblischer Commentar über den Psalter* (Leipzig, 1860).

—, "Rückübersetzung der Psaumes Salomon ins Hebräische" (unpublished manuscript number 01503 in the Universitätsbibliothek Leipzig, ca. 1860).

— , *Biblical Commentary on the Psalms,* tr from 2nd ed by Francis Bolton, 3 vols. (Edinburgh: T. & T. Clark, 1871).

Dillmann, August, "Pseudepigraphen des A. T.," *Herzog Real-Encyklopädie für protestantische Theologie und Kirche,* 3rd ed. ed. by Johann Jakob Herzog and Gustav Leopold Plitt, pp. 341-367 (Hamburg: R. Besser, 1905).

Dimant, Devorah, "A Cultic Term in the Psalms of Solomon in the Light of the Septuagint " *Textus* 9 (1981) pp. 28–51.

Dio's Roman History, with an English translation by Earnest Cary on the basis of the version of Herbert Baldwin Foster, Vol. IV (Cambridge, MA: Harvard University Press, 1954).

DiTommasco, L., *A Bibliography of Pseudepigrapha Research 1850–1999* (JSPSup, 39; Sheffield: Sheffield Academic Press 2001). [This bibliography, in fact, includes works from 2000.]

Dupont-Sommer, Andre, *The Essene Writings from Qumran,* tr. G. Vermes (London: Blackwell, 1961).

Eiseman, Leatrice and Lawrence Herbert *The Pantone Book of Color* (New York: Harry N. Abrams, 1990).

Efron, Joshua, "Holy War and Visions of Redemption " in *Studies on the Hasmonean Period, SJLA* 39 pp. 219-286, ed. Jacob Neusner (Leiden: Brill, 1987).

— , "The Psalms of Solomon, The Hasmonean Decline and Christianity " *Studies on the Hasmonean Period, SJLA* 39 pp. 219–286, ed. Jacob Neusner (Leiden: Brill, 1987).

Embry, Brad. *The Psalms of Solomon and the New Testament: Intertextuality and the Need for a Re-Evaluation. (JSOT 2002, 13(2), 99-136).*

Evans, Craig A., *Noncanonical Writings and New Testament Interpretation,*

Peabody, MA: Hendrickson, 1992.

Ewald, Georg Heinrich August von, *The History of Israel* 2nd ed. 1880, orig. pub. as *Geschichte des*

Volkes Israel, Göttingen: Dieterich 1852, tr. J. Estlin Carpenter (London: Longmans, Green, 1876-1886).

Fisher, Thomas Wilson, "The dragon/serpent in Revelation: The rhetoric of an apocalyptic motif," dissertation: the Southern Baptist Theological Seminary 2000

Fitzmyer, Joseph A. and Daniel J. Harrington, *A Manual of Palestinian Aramaic Texts* (Rome: Biblical Institute Press, 1978).

Flemming, J., *Ein jüdisch-christliches Psalmbuch aus dem ersten Jahrhundert. Aus dem Syrischen üubersetzt, bearbeitet un hg. V. A. Von Harnack* (Leipzig: J.C. Hinrichs, 1910).

Franklyn, P. N., "The Cultic and Pious Climax of Eschatology in the Psalms of Solomon," *JSJ* XVIII (June 1987) pp. 1-17.

Friedlander, Mory, *Geschichte der Judischen Apologetik* (Amsterdam: Philo, 1973).

Fujita, Shozo, "The Temple Theology of the Qumran Sect and the Book of Ezekiel-- their relation to Jewish Literature of the Last Two Centuries B. C" (Princeton: Princeton Theological Seminary Doctoral Dissertation, 1970).

—, "The Metaphor of Plant in Jewish Literature of the Intertestamental Period " *JSJ* VII,1(1976) 30-33.

Gamillscheg, Ernst, *Repertorium der Griechischen Kopisten 800–1600*, Vol 3. Österreische Akadaemie der Wissenschanten (Vienna: Verlag der Österreichischen Akademie der Wissenschaften, 1997).

Geiger, Abraham, "Aus Brifen," *Jüdische Zeitschrift für Wissenschaft und Leben*, VI, 1868 (Published 1862-1875: Breslau : H. Skutsch)

Glatzer, Nahum Norbert, "Thou Art Our King: From the Psalms of Solomon," *Faith and Knowledge; the Jew in the Medieval World*, vol. 2 of *The Judaic Tradition*, pp. 68–72 (Boston: Beacon Press, 1963).

Graetz, Heinrich, *Geschichte der Judäer von den ältesten Zeiten bis auf die Gegenwart: ous den Quellen neu bearbeitet*, 12 vols. 2nd ed. (Leipzig: O. Leiner, 1853-1876).

Graux, Charles Henri *Notices sommaires des MSS. grecs de la Grande Bibliothèque Royal de Copenhague* (Paris: Imprimerie Nationale, 1879).

Gry, Léon, *Le Messie des Psaumes de Salomon*, NS VII (Louvain: Muséon, 1906).

Hann, Robert R., "The Communtity of the Pious: The Social Setting of the Psalms of Solomon " *SR* 17 2 (1988) pp. 169-189.

Harrington, Daniel J. "Research on the Jewish Pseudepigrapha During the 1970s." CBQ, (1980 42(2) 147-159)

Hausrath, Adolf, *Die Zeit Jesu* (Heidelberg: Bassermann, 1873).

— , *The Time of Jesus*, tr from 2nd German edition by Charles T. Poynting and Philip Quenzer, 2 vols,(London: Williams and Norgate, 1878-1880).

Huet, (aka: Huetius) Pierre Daniel, *Demonstratio Evangelica ad Serenissimum delphinum* 4th ed. (Leipzig: J. Thomam Fritsch, 1694).

Hitzig, Ferdinand, *Geschichte des Volkes Israel von Anbeginn bis zur Eroberung Masada's im Jahre 72 nach Christus* (Leipzig: S. Hirzel, 1869).

Huebsch, Robert William, "The Understanding and Significance of the 'Remnant' in Qumran Literature: Including a Discussion of the Use of this Concept in the Hebrew Bible, the Apocrypha and the Pseudepigrap Mcmaster University (Canada), 1981.

Hultgård, Anders, "Figures messianiques d'Orient comme sauveurs universels dans le monde greco-rom : (Ps/Sol 17:21,46; Apoc of Baruch 72:2b-4; pp749-752)" *Soteriologia dei culti orientali nell'Imperio*

Romano pp. 734-748 (Leiden : E. J. Brill 1982).

Hunger, Herbert and Otto Kresten, *Katalog der griechischen Handschriften der Österreichischen National Bibliothek Teil 3/1: Codices Theolog. 1-100* (Vienna: Brüder Hollinek, 1976).

Jongkind, D., "Psalms of Solomon: Introductory Notes," in "Justification and Variegated Nomism " Cambridge (England) University Seminar for NT PhD students, M.N.A. Bockmuehl and P.M. Head, professors in charge, 2001-2002. Online at: http://www.tyndale.cam.ac.uk/Tyndale/staff/Head/PssSol.htm (Last accessed 11/2003)

Josephus, Flavius, *Antiquities; The Jewish War, Books I–III,* Vol. II, Loeb Classical Library, tr. H. St. J. Thackeray (Cambridge (England), MA: Harvard University Press, 1927, 1928).

Kahana, Abraham Al, *Ha–Sefarim ha–hitsonim* (Tel Aviv: Masadah, 1959).

Klausner, Joseph, *The Messianic Idea in Israel, from Its Beginning to the Completion of the Mishnah,* tr. W.F. Stinespring (New York: Macmillan, 1955).

Lampe, Geoffrey William Hugo, *A Patristic Greek Lexicon* (Oxford: Clarendon Press, 1961-68) Includes references to Psalms of Solomon.

Lane, William L, "Paul's Legacy from Pharisaism: Light from the Psalms of Solomon," *Concordia Journal* 8 (1982) pp. 130-138.

Langen, Joseph, *Das Judenthum in Palästina zur Zeit Christi: ein Betrag zur Offerbarungs– und Religions–Geschichte als Einleitung in die Theologie des N. T.* (Freibourg im Breisgau: Herder, 1866).

Laperrousaz, E. M., "Hérode le Grand est-il «l'ennemi (qui) a agi en étranger» des Psaumes de Salomon?"in *Politique et religion dans le judaïsme ancien et médiéval,* ed. D. Tollet, pp. 29-32 (Paris: Decsclee, 1989).

Lehnardt, Andreas, "Die Psalmen Salomos," Bibliographe zu den Jüdischen Schriften aus hellenistisch-römischer Zeit, in Hermann Lichtenberger, *Jüdischen Schriften aus hellenistisch-römischer Zeit Band VI Supplementa,* XVI 501 S (Gütrsloher:Gutersloher Verlagshaus, 1999).

Le Moyne, Jean, *Les sadducéens* (Paris: Lecoffre, 1972).

Leszynsky, Rudolf, *Pharisaer und Sadduzaer,* in *Volkschriften uber die judische Religion,* 1,2 (Frankfurt a. M.: J. Kauffmann, 1912).

Liver, Jacob, *Toldot bet David mi-hurban mamlekhet Yehudah ve-ad le-ahar hurban ha-Bayit ha-Sheni,*<in Hebrew>*(The House of David from the Fall of the Kingdom of Judah until the Destruction of the Second Temple of Jerusalem),* (Jerusalem: Magnes and Hebrew University, 1959).

Mack, Burton, "Wisdom Makes a Difference: Alternatives to 'Messianic' Configurations ," *Judaisms and Their Messiahs at the Turn of the Christian Era,* in *Judaisms and their messiahs at the turn of the Christian era,* pp. 15-48, ed. by Jacob Neusner, William Scott Green, Ernest S. Frerichs (Cambridge (England): Cambridge University Press, 1987).

Manson, T(homas) W(alter), The Servant-Messiah: A Study of the Public Ministry of Jesus, (Cambridge (England): Cambridge University Press, 1953).

Martin, Raymond A., *Syntactical Evidence of Semitic Sources in Greek Documents, SBLSCS* no. 3 (Cambridge, MA: Society of Biblical Literature 1974).

Massaux, E., *La Venue du Messie; messianisme et eschatologie* in *Recherches bibliques 6* (Paris: Desclee de Brouwer, 1962).

Mathews, Shailer, "Psalms of the Pharisees," *A History of New Testament Times in Palestine ,* 96–98 (New York: MacMillan, 1918).

McReynolds, Paul R., "The Claremont Profile Method and the Grouping of Byzantine New Testament

Manuscripts," Claremont Graduate School Ph.D. Dissertation, 1968.

Metzger, Bruce M., *The Text of the New Testament* (New York & London: Oxford University Press, 1964, repr. 1992).

—, "The Critic Correcting the Author," *Philologus*, 99 (1955), pp. 295-303).

Moeller, Henry R., *The Legacy of Zion: Intertestamental Texts Related to the New Testament* (Grand Rapids: Baker, 1977).

Moore, Carey A., "Toward the Dating of the Book of Baruch," *CBQ* 36 (July 1974) pp. 312-320.

Morawe, G., "Vergleich des Aufbaus der Danklieder und hymnischen Bekenntnislieder (1QH) von Qumran mit dem Aufbau der Psalmen im Alten Testament und im Spätjudentum," *RevQ* IV (1963), pp. 233–254.

Movers, Franz Karl C., "Apokryphen-Literatur," *Kirchen-Lexikon, oder Encyklopädie der katholischen Theologie und ihrer Hilfswissenschaften* 1/2 ed., ed. H. J. Wetzer and B. Welte pp. 334-355 (Freiburg im Breisgau: Herder, 1847-1882).

Mowinckel, Sigmund, *The Psalms in Israel's Worship*, Tr of: *Offersand og sangoffer*, by D. R. Ap-Thomas (New York: Abingdon, 1962).

Mukenge, André Kabasele, *L'unité du livre de Baruch, Etudes bibliques;* nouv, Sér. no38 (Paris: J. Gabalda 1998).

Nicephorus, S.. "Chronographis," *Patriarchæ Constantinopolitani Breuiarium Historicum*, pp. 286-414 (Paris: S. Chappelet, 1616).

Nickelsburg, G. W. E., "Resurrection–Unrelated to Persecution, Oppression, and Injustice" in *Resurrection, Immortality, Eternal Life in Intertestamental Judaism, HTS* XXII, 1972, pp. 131-43.

Perrin, Nicholas. "Messianism in the Narrative Frame of Ecclesiastes?" (RB 2001.108(1) 37-60).

Plöger, Otto, *Theokratie und Eschatologie, WMANT* (Neukirchen: Kreis Moers, 1959).

Pomykala, Kenneth E., *The Davidic Dynasty Tradition in Early Judaism: Its History and Significance for Messianism, SBLEJL* (Atlanta: Scholars Press, 1995).

Reumann, M. Jop. Georg., *Dissertationem Historico Criticam de Psalterio Salomonis* (Wittenberg: Christiani Fincelii).

Sacci, P., *Salmi di Salomone. Apocrifi dell' Antico Testamento*, ed. P. Sacci, Vol. 2, Cdr 2 (Torin: 1989).

Sailhamer, John, H., *The Traditional Technique of the Greek Septuagint for the Hebrew Verbs and Participles in Psalms 3–41* (New York: P. Lang 1991).

Sandys, John Edwin, *A History of Classical Scholarship*, vol. 2 (Cambridge, England: Cambridge University Press, 1908).

Schroter, Jens. "Gerechtigkeit und Barmherzigkeit: Das Gottesbild der Psalmen Salomos in seinem Verhaltnis zu Qumran und Paulus (Justice and Mercy: The Picture of God in the **Psalms of Solomon** and Its Relation to Qumran and Paul)" (electronic).

Schürer, Emil, *Neutestamentliche Geschichte*, (Leipzig: Hinrichs 1898-1901).

— , *A History of the Jewish People in the Time of Jesus Christ,* (Edinburgh: Clark, 1894).

Scott, Donald L., "The Role of Remembrance in The Psalms of Solomon." Chicago Theological Seminary Dissertation, 1995.

Seifrid, Mark Arthur, "Justification by faith: The origin and development of a central Pauline Theme," dissertation: Princeton Theological Seminary, 1990.

Smith, Barry Smith, "Psalms of Solomon," (An introduction on a college course web site, Barry D. Smith,

Atlantic Baptist University: http://www.abu.nb.ca/Courses/NTIntro/InTest/TestF3.htm.)., E-mail: barry.smith@abu.nb.ca.

Sparks, H. F. D. (Hedley Frederick Davis), The Old Testament in the Christian Church (London: S. C. M. Press, Ltd., 1944).

Stanley, Arthur Penrhyn, *The History of the Jewish Church*, (New York: Schribner, 1879).

Stade, Bernhard, *Geschichte des volkes Israel: Allgemeine geschichte in einzeldarstellungen* 1.6 (Berlin: G. Grote, 1887-1888).

Stein, Menachem, "The Psalms of Solomon," *The Outside Books* (in Hebrew) vol. II, ed. A. Kahana (Tel Aviv: Masada 1959).

Stemberger, Günter, tr: Allan W. Mahnke, *Jewish Contemporaries of Jesus: Pharisees, Sadducees, Essenes* (Minneapolis: Fortress Press 1995).

Stone, Michael E., "Reactions to Destructions of the Second Temple: Theology, Perception and Conversion." JSJ (1981, 12(2) 195-204)

Strijdom, Johannes Matthys, "An evaluation of John Dominic Crossan's construct of the historical Jesus: The Baptist as test case," dissertation, (Afrikaans text), University of Pretoria (South Africa), 1998.

Thompson, E. M. ed., *Facsimile of the Codex Alexandrinus*, 4 Vols. (London: British Library, 1879-1883).

Thomson, John Ebenezer Honeyman, *Books Which Influenced Our Lord and His Apostles: Being a Critical Review of Apocalyptic Jewish Literature* (Edinburgh: T. & T. Clark, 1891).

Torrey, C. C., *The Apocryphal Literature: a Brief Introduction* (New Haven: Yale University Press, 1945).

Winninge, Mikael. "Den intertestamentala litteraturen och Nya testamentet" (The Intertestamental Literature and the New Testament). (*Svensk Teologisk Kvartalskrift*, (1994, 70(4)176-183.

Yu, Young Ki, "The New Covenant: the Promise and its Fulfilment. An Inquiry into the Influence of the New Covenant Concept of Jer 31.31-34 on Later Religious Thought with Particular Reference to the Dead Sea Scrolls and the New Testament," University of Durham (United Kingdom), 1989.

A CD-ROM containing 350 high-resolution color images of all
the extant Greek and Syriac Manuscripts of the Psalms of
Solomon is available without cost, except for shipping and
handling. The CD is for faculty and students for research and
teaching purposes only. The images may not be sold or
reproduced, nor posted to a Web site, without permission of the
copyright owners.

Write to:

Dr. Robert B. Wright
Psalms of Solomon CD
Department of Religion
Temple University
619 Anderson Hall
Berks & 12th Street
Philadelphia, PA 19122 USA

Please include $15.00 USD for shipping and handling.